AS CRITICAL THINKING FOR AQA

AS Critical Thinking for AQA is the definitive textbook for students of the AQA Advanced Subsidiary Level syllabus. Structured very closely around the AQA specification, it covers the two units of the AS level in an exceptionally clear and student-friendly style.

The chapters are helpfully subdivided into short digestible passages, and include:

- learning objectives at the beginning of each chapter
- icons highlighting key terms, tips and links to other sections of the book
- student exercises, sometimes with a 'stretching activity' for more advanced learners
- exam-orientated questions
- summary checklist at the end of each chapter.

The book also features:

- a chapter on exam technique at the end of Units 1 and 2
- links to web-based resources
- glossary.

In line with the AQA specification there is a heavy emphasis on more imaginative forms of source material, for example music, film, artwork, historical documents, adverts, moral dilemmas and scientific debates, as a means of illustrating key points. A great deal of emphasis is also placed on 'live' or 'real' arguments. The book also includes examples of actual dialogues and real debates extracted from a wide variety of sources.

Oliver McAdoo is Head of Critical Thinking at Godalming College. He is part of the team that developed the new philosophy specification for AQA beginning in 2009. He has also created specimen assessment material for this new specification.

AS CR
THINK

Oliver McAd

R Routledge
Taylor & Francis Group
LONDON AND NEW YORK

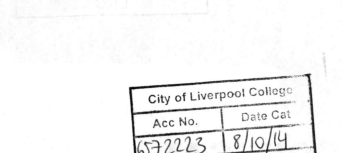
First published 2011
by Routledge
2 Park Square, Milton Park, Abingdon, Oxon, OX14 4RN

Simultaneously published in the USA and Canada
by Routledge
270 Madison Ave, New York, NY 10016

Routledge is an imprint of the Taylor & Francis Group, an informa business

© 2011 Oliver McAdoo

Typeset in Mixage by
Saxon Graphics Ltd, Derby
Printed and bound in Great Britain by
MPG Books Group. UK

British Library Cataloguing in Publication Data

A catalogue record for this book is available from the British Library

Library of Congress Cataloging in Publication Data

A catalog record for this book has been requested

ISBN: 978-0-415-55925-6 (pbk)

MIX
Paper from
responsible sources
FSC® C004839

Printed and bound in Great Britain by the MPG Books Group

CONTENTS

ACKNOWLEDGEMENTS

The author and publisher have attempted to contact all copyright holders. If any items are not fully credited, this will be corrected in future editions. The author and publisher wish to thank the following for permission to use copyright material:

The AQA for permission to use extracts from the specification, question papers and mark schemes. For the most up-to-date specification, please visit the AQA website at
http://web.aqa.org.uk/qual/gce/humanities/critical_thinking_materials.php

(Page 12) All images used under licence from Shutterstock.com http://www.shutterstock.com

(Pages 20–21) strange-mysteries.co.cc used with kind permission of Vinay Swastik

(Page 27) Peter Stanton, Letters to the Editor, *The Independent*, 31 March 1995. Used with permission of *The Independent* www.independent.co.uk

(Page 52) Extract from David Bain, Four philosophical questions to make your brain hurt. http://news.bbc.co.uk/1/hi/7739493.stm accessed 20 December 2010

(Page 32) Josie Appleton, Conceptual Art: What's the Idea? http://www.spiked-online.com/articles/00000006DFD9.htm accessed 20 December 2010. Used with permission of www.spiked-online.com

(Page 52) FOODSAFE Excellence cartoon. Used with permission from BC FOODSAFE Secretariat, British Columbia foodsafe.ca

(Page 97) Question from OCR Advanced Subsidiary GCE Critical Thinking Unit 2 Question Paper, May 2006. Ref: F492/01, F492/02. Used with permission.

(Page 102) Extract from OCR Advanced Subsidiary GCE Critical Thinking Unit 2 Resource Booklet, May 2006. Ref: F492/01/RB, F492/02/RB. Used with permission.

(Page 108) Cartoon by Dan Piraro http://www.bizarro.com/ Used with permission

(Page 149) Palestine West Bank Bethlehem. Separation wall. Image ref: ACXH3N. Jenny Matthews / Alamy

(Page 149) Vincent van Gogh 1853 1890 Sunflowers Netherlands Dutch. Image ref: AM7ND6. Peter Horree / Alamy

(Page 151) 'Child use of antidepressants up four-fold' by Graeme Paton, 19 April 2008. © Telegraph Media Group Limited 2008. Used with permission.

(Page 161) Stephen Moore, Clear-Eyed Optimists; The world is getting better, though no one likes to hear it (2007). *The Wall Street Journal* (Dow Jones and Company, Inc). Permission granted by Copyright Clearance Center.

(Pages 222–3) Cathy Gordon, Conviction for robbery ruled unsafe (1999). *The Independent*. Used with permission www.independent.co.uk

(Pages 234–5) Used with kind permission of Ernesto, torrentfreak.com

(Page 238) Data from Recording Industry Association of America. Used with permission.

INTRODUCTION

ABOUT THE BOOK AND HOW TO USE IT

The aim of this book is to provide a comprehensive guide to the AQA Critical Thinking AS Level specification. The structure of the book mirrors precisely that of the specification itself and there are two chapters offering a step-by-step guide on how to tackle both units of the exam. Because there is no specific 'content' to be covered, this book draws on as wide a variety of resources as possible in order to equip the learner with the required set of thinking skills (more of this in this Introduction). It is hoped that not only will this make the material more engaging, but that it will also illuminate just how relevant and applicable these skills are to *all* areas of study, not just the exam itself. There are plenty of textbooks out there which claim to offer an 'easy' introduction to critical thinking. This is not one of them. Heeding Einstein's remark that 'things should be made as simple as possible, but not any simpler', a real effort has been made to avoid the kind of oversimplification that fails to do justice to the subtlety of the subject. Needless to say, those of you ready for a challenge will not be disappointed!

A final point worth mentioning is that there is no 'correct' way to work through this book. Whilst links flagging up where points overlap and material developed are made frequently throughout the text, each chapter has been written in such a way so as to avoid presupposing any knowledge of previous chapters. This was deliberate. There is no more a natural starting place for the acquisition of critical thinking skills than there is a natural starting point to a circle. What is important is that, as your studies progress, you learn how to apply these skills appropriately and fairly. Learning how to do this will be a matter of fine tuning and here there is no substitute for practice. For this reason, any serious student of critical thinking ought to keep abreast of current affairs, read newspapers, watch news bulletins and engage people in discussion as often as possible. You will be surprised at how quickly you

For the most up-to-date specification, visit the AQA website www.aqa.org.uk. For the link to this and all other websites mentioned in the book, visit www.routledge.com/textbooks/mcadoo

become adept at spotting errors in the reasoning of others – and hopefully your own too!

GUIDED TOUR

Alongside the explanations, examples and activities to be found in the book itself, there are a range of 'key features'. These will help develop your understanding of the material covered and offer advice on how to apply it to the exam. These include:

- 'Learning objectives' – to give you a clear idea of what will be covered in each chapter and what you should be able to do/understand/demonstrate as a result of working your way through it.

- 'Exercises' – to help prepare you for the exam.

- 'Stretching activities' – to challenge the braver student!

- 'Summary checklists' – which can be used to monitor your progress.

- 'Summary questions' – to get you to focus on and express in your own words what has just been covered. It would be a good idea to keep an ongoing record of your responses to these; once complete, they will give you a valuable overview of the course.

- 'Links to other chapters' – flagging up where points overlap and material is developed.

- 'Tips' and pitfalls to avoid.

- 'Weblinks' and suggestions for further reading – to give you an idea of where you might go to find out more about a particular topic. These will include links to assessment material (i.e. past papers and mark schemes) which you can use to prepare yourself for the exam.

Glossary

Key terms are explained when they are first introduced, and there is a glossary providing definitions of the most important ones, so that wherever you start to read from, you can always look up the words you don't understand. Words that appear in the glossary are in **bold** in the text.

Companion website and further resources

You can find further resources, including more activities, weblinks, exam practice and further reading, on the companion website www.routledge.com/ textbooks/mcadoo. Wherever you see the companion website logo in the margin, visit the site for all of the links you need. Here, you will also find links to some of the documents referred to in this book which, for copyright reasons, cannot be included here in full.

THE EXAMINATION

The book will include a chapter at the end of each unit dealing with each of the assessment criteria laid out in the specification (see below). Each of these chapters will build upon material covered in the preceding chapters so, upon completion, you will have developed a clear understanding of what you will be expected to do in the exam. These will include actual exam materials that can be used to hone your skills and develop your competence and a walkthrough guide showing you the kinds of responses that will be required for each section. There will also be links to past papers and mark schemes from previous examinations for you to work through independently. The examination itself will consist of two one-and-a-half-hour written papers (Units 1 and 2) and the criteria you will be examined on are as follows:

Assessment objectives

- AO1 Analyse critically the use of different kinds of reasoning in a wide range of contexts.

AO1 questions, broadly speaking, require you to identify the type of reasoning being employed and/or explain its function. You might, for example, be asked to 'identify an implicit assumption/flaw/weakness/point of agreement/disagreement' etc. or to 'explain how a piece of reasoning/example/argument/claim' etc. is being used. These questions will draw on your skills of analysis.

- AO2 Evaluate critically the use of different kinds of reasoning in a wide range of contexts.

AO2 questions require you to assess the strength of a particular piece of reasoning, often by getting you to evaluate whether or not the reasons or evidence provided support the conclusion they are intended to bring about. You might, for example, be asked to 'comment critically on/assess the extent to which/explain the weakness of' a particular piece of 'reasoning/claim/argument' etc. These questions will draw on your skills of *judgement*.

- AO3 Develop and communicate relevant and coherent arguments clearly and accurately in a concise and logical manner.

AO3 questions, for which the most amount of overall marks are available, require you to present or develop your *own* argument in relation to a specific theme or issue. You might, for example, be asked to 'write a reasoned argument' in support of a particular conclusion you have reached or 'construct a reasoned case for or against' a particular argument or position. These questions will draw on your skills of *reasoning* and *communication*.

Of course, in practice, these AOs will often overlap. The command 'comment critically on the use of the word ...' will require you to *identify* how the word functions (AO1) and also to *judge* whether its use is legitimate given the context in which it occurs (AO2). A question which asks you to 'explain and evaluate the author's reasoning' will draw on skills of both analysis (AO1) and evaluation (AO2). Mastering the command words which accompany the individual assessment objectives (AOs 1, 2 and 3 respectively) will place you at a considerable advantage in the exam as they reveal the type of response each question requires. It is important you have a clear understanding of these as you progress through the book.

All of the relevant documents relating to the exam (including past papers and mark schemes) can be accessed via the companion website. www.routledge.com/textbooks/mcadoo.

The assessment objectives (AOs) are what you will be examined on. The command words associated with them (identify, assess, develop etc.) will offer a clear indication of what each question requires you to do. It is important you become acquainted with them right from the start.

Each of the assessment objectives will be explored in greater detail in both of the end of unit exam chapters. The issue of developing your own argument (AO3) is taken up in greater detail in Chs 13 and 20.

Assessment weighting

A breakdown of the weighting of assessment (i.e. how many marks each assessment objective carries with it) runs as follows:

Assessment objectives	Unit weightings (%)		Overall weighting of AOs (%)
	Unit 1	Unit 2	
AO1	17	11.5	28.5
AO2	17	17	34
AO3	16	21.5	37.5
Overall weighting of units (%)	50	50	100

CRITICAL THINKING: WHAT IS IT AND WHY DO WE NEED IT?

> In the case of any person whose judgement is really deserving of confidence, how has it become so? Because he has kept his mind open to criticism of his opinions and conduct. Because it has been his practice to listen to all that could be said against him; to profit by as much of it as was just, and expound to himself, and upon occasion to others, the fallacy [error] of what was fallacious ... No wise man ever acquired his wisdom in any mode but this; nor is it in the nature of human intellect to become wise in any other manner. (John Stuart Mill, *On Liberty*, Chapter 2)

Much of the current emphasis on teaching focuses on showing students *what* to think. Critical Thinking aims to show students *how* to think. In this sense, critical thinking skills are so fundamental that they are now, to use the words of the renowned critical thinker Alec Fisher, 'widely seen as a basic competency, akin to reading and writing'. So what is it to think critically? At its most basic level Critical Thinking addresses the question 'what does thinking involve?' but perhaps a more important question is 'how do we go about improving it?' Thinking, of course, is not the only skill the subject looks to develop. A good critical thinker will be able to argue clearly and put their thoughts to paper. The ability to think clearly, argue constructively and structure one's thoughts precisely are skills that are highly valued in the classroom, as in life.

From the start, it is important to note that Critical Thinking has no particular subject matter as such (at least not in the way that, for example, History, Politics or Science has). The reasons for this are twofold. Firstly, Critical Thinking is a skills-based course. It looks to equip the thinker with a set of cognitive tools which can then be developed and applied to subjects both in and outside the classroom. Secondly, the core nature of these skills is such that they don't just lend themselves to the study of particular material, but rather to the study of material in general. This last point, often regarded as a potential disadvantage for the subject, is actually its greatest asset. The range and breadth of resources that can, and should, be used to develop one's reasoning skills are arguably broader than that of any other discipline. This is one of the key points of which this book seeks to take advantage. Music, film, art, historical documents, adverts, laws, cartoons, scientific debates, moral dilemmas, arguments that erupt during our daily lives and much more besides will all be used as sources for the development of these skills. This will involve borrowing material from such disciplines as Philosophy, Politics, History, Law, Psychology, Music and English Literature to illustrate their scope and wide-ranging application.

Before moving on, we should say a little bit more about the central component of the course – namely, *argument*. What an argument actually *is* is addressed in the first chapter of this book. Argument forms the basis of reasoning and thought. For the 'foundational' unit of this course (Unit 1) you will be expected to be able to identify (recognise), 'analyse' (break down into simpler components), 'evaluate' (judge the strengths and weaknesses of) and develop your own arguments within a wide variety of contexts. A simple way of explaining argument is to draw an analogy with the human body. The human body is not just a single unit, but, rather, a complex one which can be broken down into many separate parts. Each of these parts has a function: the heart pumps blood around the body; the eyes provide us with sight, and the ears, sound etc, and these individual functions combine to contribute to the body's functioning as a whole. An argument is like this, composed of separate parts, each with a specific role. Reasons are used to support a conclusion; evidence can be supplied in place of, or in support of, reasons; counter-arguments and examples are used to test whether or not a conclusion or hypothesis is sound; and so on. The question of whether or not an argument as a whole is sound will depend very much upon whether the individual parts out of which it is composed are sound. Thus, one of the principal skills you will need to develop as a critical thinker will be the ability to recognise when this is so. When parts of the body malfunction, it is important we know how to identify and remedy such problems and the same is true of arguments. There are a range of ways in which an argument can misfire: perhaps the reasons don't support the conclusion strongly enough; perhaps the evidence doesn't lend enough weight to what the reasons propose; perhaps the conclusion itself does not follow from the premises given, or, if it does, perhaps there are alternative conclusions that might be drawn with greater force. The essence of a good critical thinker is that they will know how to identify such problems when they arise and, perhaps more importantly, what to do about them when they do.

A final word of warning: if studied correctly, the skills you will acquire as your studies progress will be very powerful indeed. They will change the way you think and hopefully influence how you act. For anyone who has lost an argument without realising how, or been persuaded into accepting a position that they instinctively know to be incorrect without realising why, or simply been defeated in debate as a result of lacking the skills required to argue a position clearly and powerfully, will know, from their scars, something of the value of these skills! Many individuals that acquire them, however, do not use them for the purposes they are intended. In an ideal world, one might reasonably think the main function of argument to be a co-operative activity aimed at gaining insight into some issue. In real life, however, this ideal is only too often overridden by the common desire to win an argument, come what may. Having spent a lifetime developing the art of arguing, the ancient Greek philosopher Socrates noted:

> how difficult the parties find it to define exactly the subject
> which they have taken in hand and to come away from their
> discussion mutually enlightened; what usually happens is that,
> as soon as they disagree and one declares the other to be mistaken
> or obscure in what he says, they lose their temper and accuse one
> another of speaking from motives of personal spite and in an endeavour
> to score a victory rather than to investigate the question at issue. (Plato,
> *Gorgias* 457–8)

His own view is that, if you ever want to become really skilled at debate, then you must realise right from the start that there is a more important goal than the egotistical satisfaction of knocking down the arguments of others. That is: getting at the truth, even if it means admitting to getting it wrong:

> I am one of those people who are glad to have their own mistakes pointed out and glad to point out the mistakes of others, but who would just as soon have the first experience as the second. (Plato, *Gorgias* 458)

In practice, of course, this is never easy!

The aim of critical thinking, then, should be to get things right, not to win arguments. Of course, if you know that your position is strong, and you have the tools to argue it well, then winning an argument may well be the consequence of the gaining of such skills, but such a result will only ever be a consequence, never a goal. The only goal of critical thinking is objectivity, nothing else. One should always be prepared to abandon a position if new evidence comes to light that throws it into question. The philosopher Plato, having spent his entire life establishing an account of philosophical knowledge that allowed him to address the most fundamental questions about existence and reality, discarded this account towards the very end of his life when he discovered a fatal flaw to which he could find no answer. There are plenty of other examples of great thinkers who also did just this – put truth and objectivity before their own goals and aspirations. The possession of a set of skills in any discipline is no guarantee they will be used to good effect. The most skilled doctor, Plato argues, will also, as part of his medical studies, have gained knowledge of and access to the most effective poisons required to kill a person without trace. The greatest teacher, with all the tools of eloquence and persuasion at their disposal, will also, in the absence of moral constraint, be the greatest corruptor of youth. If we do not practise such skills with good intent, then our practice will do more harm than good. This is a point worth remembering.

UNIT 1   # FOUNDATION UNIT

1

Chapter 1: Reasoned argument

LEARNING OBJECTIVES ✔

By the end of this chapter you should:

✔ Understand the difference between an everyday argument and a reasoned argument.
✔ Have a basic understanding of the terms 'premise', 'inference', 'persuasion' and their roles.
✔ Understand what reasoning indicators are and how they help us to identify when reasoned argument is taking place.
✔ Be able to tell apart arguments from explanations.
✔ Understand what a dialogue is and be able to identify its key features – arguments, counter-arguments, examples, the use of critical questioning and refutation.
✔ Understand what an 'embedded' argument is and be able to 'extract' an embedded argument in order to treat it as an argument in its own right.

REASONED ARGUMENT

The most important skill you will need to use for critical thinking purposes will be the ability to recognise when reasoned argument is taking place, and, conversely, when it isn't. The first question we need to ask then is: what do we mean by 'reasoned argument'? In everyday life, an 'argument' often refers to a squabble or spat, usually won by the person with the loudest or most persistent voice, as the following tongue-in-cheek example should make clear:

Monty Python's argument clinic
Come in.
Ah, is this the right room for an argument?
I told you once.
No you haven't.
Yes I have ...
[this continues]
Oh, I'm sorry, just one moment. Is this a five-minute argument or the full half hour?

argument – A **persuasive** piece of reasoning formed of **reasons** (premises) and a **conclusion**.

reason – A reason (sometimes referred to as a **premise**) provides grounds for why we should accept (be persuaded of) the conclusion of an argument.

conclusion – The conclusion of an argument is the point an argument is trying to get us to accept.

The way critical thinkers understand the term, needless to say, is quite different from this! For critical thinking purposes, an **argument** is a piece of reasoning that attempts to persuade the thinker of something. In order to do this, it uses **reasons** (sometimes called 'premises' or 'grounds') which lead to a **conclusion.** The conclusion of an argument is what an argument is trying to get us to accept and the reasons provide us with grounds for why we should accept it. The following example, taken from Sir Arthur Conan Doyle's 'Hound of the Baskervilles', should make this clear:

Premise 1: Guard dogs bark at strangers.

Premise 2: On the night that Sir Charles was murdered, the guard dogs did not bark.

Conclusion: Sir Charles cannot have been murdered by a stranger.

This is an example of an argument insofar as the reasons provided in premises 1 and 2 provide persuasive grounds for accepting Holmes' conclusion that whoever murdered Sir Charles must have been known to him.

Arguments can be simple, where only *one* premise is used to persuade us of a conclusion:

Premise: John is a werewolf!

Conclusion: Therefore it is unsafe to go out with him on the night of a full moon!

Or more complex, where a number of premises are used:

Premise 1: Mars is a cold and inhospitable planet with temperatures dropping to minus 130° centigrade.

Premise 2: Despite several spacecraft having landed on the planet, there is no photographic evidence to suggest that it supports life.

Premise 3: Nor have we had any 'extraterrestrial' response to the radio signals we have been sending to this planet for many years now.

Premise 4: And even if life had the potential to form, the amount of meteor showers experienced by the planet would wipe it out in its first stages.

Conclusion: We can safely conclude that there is no such thing as life on Mars.

So long as a piece of reasoning provides us with at least one premise and a persuasive conclusion that follows from this, then it can be regarded as an argument.

It is important to remember, however, that not all pieces of reasoning attempt to persuade and, conversely, not all acts of persuasion involve reasoning. Because of this, the following example, relating to the aim of this book, is not a genuine argument and it is important that we understand why:

Critical Thinking aims to:

*   develop skills and encourage attitudes which complement other studies across the curriculum
*   prepare candidates for the academic and intellectual demands of higher education, as well as future employment and general living
*   introduce concepts, terms and techniques that will enable candidates to reflect more constructively on their own and others' reasoning. (AQA specification)

Here we have a set of possible reasons for why we *ought* to study critical thinking, but no conclusion persuading us that we *should* do so. As such, this example is not an argument. It is only once we supply this missing material – i.e. 'if you value these skills, then you should take a course in critical thinking' – that an argument is formed.

Turning this point on its head, look at the following examples:

Each of these examples tries to persuade us of something, i.e.:

* We *should* donate money to charity.
* We *need* to become more energy efficient.
* We *ought* to purchase a particular brand of a product.

But they lack reasons telling us *why* we should be persuaded. It is only once we supply at least one supporting reason for each conclusion that an argument is created. For example:

* Innocent children are dying of starvation, therefore …
* Increasing temperatures caused by the burning of fossil fuels are endangering the future of our planet, therefore …
* Brand X is better quality than any of its rivals, therefore …

If a piece of reasoning includes a persuasive inference and at least one premise/reason offering grounds for why you should be persuaded, then it is an argument. If either of these is lacking, it won't be.

The essential features of an argument then are: (1) it must have at least one premise (reason) and a conclusion and (2) its conclusion must be persuasive, and the reasons must provide us with grounds for being persuaded. If either of these elements is missing, the example is not an argument, at least not in the technical sense. The simplest way of deciding whether or not a piece of reasoning presents us with an argument then is to ask the questions: 'Is this trying to get me to accept something?' and 'Does it provide reasons for why I ought to accept it?' If the answer to both of these questions is 'yes', you are dealing with an argument. If 'no', then you are not. It's that simple!

If the questions are answered in the positive and you are happy that you are dealing with an argument, the next two questions you need to consider are, firstly: 'What, in plain English, is this trying to get me to accept?' and secondly: 'What reasons does it provide in order to do this?' The first question will allow you to identify the argument's conclusion, the second, the premises used to support it.

Applying these points to an example should make this clear:

Smoking clogs the arteries

and causes heart attacks   Reasons

and strokes.

Therefore you ought to give up smoking.   Conclusion

Taken as a whole, this example *is* persuasive and provides grounds for my being persuaded and can thus be regarded as an argument. It is trying to get me (the smoker) to stop smoking (conclusion) and the reasons it uses to do this are: (1) it clogs arteries and (2) it causes heart attacks and strokes. *Note* how the order could be reversed without affecting its overall effectiveness. Do not always expect the conclusion of an argument to come at the end of a piece of reasoning:

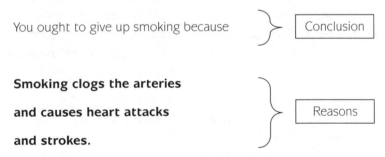

You ought to give up smoking because   Conclusion

Smoking clogs the arteries

and causes heart attacks   Reasons

and strokes.

Bearing in mind the above points, read through and respond to the following summary questions and then complete the following activities:

> To locate the conclusion of an argument, you will need to identify the point it is trying to get you to accept. To locate the reasons, you will need to identify the grounds it provides for why you should accept it.

Summary questions . . .

1. Summarise in your own words what critical thinkers understand by the term 'argument'.
2. How is the everyday sense of this word different from the way critical thinkers understand this term?

Exercises

1. Look at the following four examples and decide which are arguments and which non-arguments:

   (a) Twenty-eight children in the United States were killed by falling television sets between 1990 and 1997. That is four times as many people as were killed by great white shark attacks in the twentieth century ... This means that watching 'Jaws' on TV is more dangerous than swimming in the Pacific. ('The Statistical Shark', *The New York Times*, 6 September 2001)

   (b) Smoking causes fatal lung disease.

   (c) Carbon dioxide in the atmosphere is a 'greenhouse gas' – it traps some of the radiation that would otherwise be lost to space, and causes the Earth's atmosphere to be warmer than it would otherwise be. Man-made emissions of carbon dioxide have caused the amount in the atmosphere to increase by about 30% since pre-industrial times, and this is a major cause of global warming.

   (d) If God existed, he would not allow evil and suffering to take place. The world is filled with evil and suffering so God can't exist.

2. Break down the examples of actual arguments above into their reasons and conclusions. You might find the following template helpful for doing this:

   > Example_____is an argument because _____. The point it is trying to get us to accept is _____(conclusion) and the reason/s it uses to do this are _____.

3. Stretching activity: Convert the examples of non-argument above into examples of argument by supplying the missing material (either reasons or conclusions).

INFERENCE

The nature of inference

We all, whether realising it or not, draw **inferences** on a daily basis. We might infer, for example, that if a friend has been regularly unreliable in the past then we ought not to trust him or her in the future. If we know that downloading music illegally carries a heavy penalty, we might infer that such a practice is unwise. If we are aware that drinking tequila causes an unpleasant hangover the next morning, we can infer that such a drink is best avoided.

> **inference** – An inference is the move from the **premises** to the **conclusion** of an argument.

But what exactly is 'inference'? For critical thinking purposes, it is the move from a single premise, or set of premises, to a conclusion. It is what allows us to make a judgement on the basis of something else being true. For example, if the weather forecast has predicted showers and people outside are carrying umbrellas, the obvious inference to draw would be that people think it is going to rain. In order to draw an inference then, we need to ask ourselves the question: 'What follows from the facts or premises presented?' Think about the following joke:

> Sherlock Holmes and Dr Watson went on a camping trip. After a good meal and a bottle of wine, they were exhausted and went to sleep.
>
> Some hours later, Holmes awoke and nudged his faithful friend. 'Watson, look up at the sky and tell me what you see.' Watson replied, 'I see millions and millions of stars.'
>
> 'What does that tell you?'
>
> Watson pondered for a minute. 'Astronomically, it tells me that there are millions of galaxies and potentially billions of planets. Chronologically, I deduce that the time is approximately a quarter past three. Theologically, I can see that the Lord is all powerful and that we are small and insignificant. Meteorologically, I suspect that we will have a beautiful day tomorrow. What does it tell you?'
>
> Holmes was silent for a minute, then spoke.
>
> 'Watson, you idiot, someone has stolen our tent.'

Whilst all of Watson's 'deductions' might follow from the initial fact (the sight of millions of stars) here, Holmes directs our attention to the most straightforward one!

It is also important to note here, that simply being an inference does not in itself guarantee its validity. In order to test whether or not an inference is acceptable, we need to ask ourselves 'does this really follow from the premises provided?' Contrasting the following two examples should help make this clear:

1. George is terrified of dragons. Therefore, if he comes across one, he will be terrified (inference).

2. George is terrified of dragons. George is terrified; therefore he's just seen a dragon (inference).

You should be able to tell, just by thinking about them carefully, that only the first example contains an inference which follows from the premise. The inference in the second example, that 'George must have just seen a dragon' (because he is terrified) does not necessarily follow from the original premise because there may be other causes of his terror. Perhaps he is also afraid of needles, has a dental appointment, suffers from paranoia etc.

The role of inference

Inferences come in many forms. They can be right or wrong; plausible or implausible; valid (i.e. they follow from the premises of an argument) or invalid (they do not), but for the time being, these points need not concern us. This is an issue to which we will return in Chapter 6. What is important is that we understand the role of inference: what inferences allow us *to do*. This is fairly straightforward. If a piece of reasoning lacks an inference, as we saw with some of our earlier examples, then it is not an argument. This is because an inference is what gives an argument its persuasive form. For this reason, an example like the following:

> People who oppose a smoking ban are fond of talking about the rights of the individual. Of course, they mean the right of smokers to smoke, not the right of non-smokers to enjoy clean air. Smoking is a filthy habit which no one has the right to inflict on others. (AQA specification)

is *not* an argument as no inference is drawn (for example 'therefore, smoking should be banned in enclosed places') whereas:

The nature and role of inference is taken up again in greater detail in Ch. 6: 'Varying standards' and 'Evaluating arguments'.

If a piece of reasoning lacks an inference, it will not contain an argument.

Passive smoking is a serious health hazard. Non-smokers should not be subjected to the antisocial habits of a thoughtless minority. Therefore it is right to prohibit smoking in all enclosed public spaces. (AQA specification)

is an argument because the inference 'it is right to prohibit smoking in all enclosed public spaces' is drawn and supported by the premises 'passive smoking is a serious health hazard' and 'non-smokers should not be subjected to ...'.

Summary questions . . .

1. What do we mean by the term 'inference'?
2. What do inferences allow us to do?

Exercises

1. Identify the inference drawn in the following piece of reasoning:
    The death penalty should be adopted only if it deters murder. However, it could only do this if murderers understood the consequences of their actions before acting and, since this is not so, we must reject adopting the death penalty. (Internet Encyclopedia of Philosophy)

2. What inference can be drawn from the following examples?
    (a)
    *   All A's are B
    *   All B's are C
    *   Therefore _____.
    (b) The world functions like an incredibly complicated machine. All machines function as they do because they have been designed, therefore _____.

3. Draw one inference from each of the following three claims. You might find adding 'so' or 'therefore' after each example helps you to do this:
    (a) Computer games glorify violence.
    (b) Victims of knife crime are nearly always young males.
    (c) University graduates typically earn more money than those who have no degree.

REASONING INDICATORS

We have seen that the most straightforward method of identifying an argument is to ask 'Is this trying to get me to accept (i.e. persuade me of) something?' and 'Does it provide reasons for why I ought to accept it?' But this is not the only way. **Reasoning indicators** can act as a shortcut for identifying when reasoned argument is taking place. They can be organised into three groups which correspond to their respective roles. Understanding these roles can simplify the process of recognising and analysing (i.e. breaking down) arguments into their component parts. This is because they not only indicate *when* reasoned argument is taking place but also what *type* of reasoning is being used:

- Expressions such as 'as', 'since', 'because' etc. usually indicate that a reason will follow.
- Expressions such as 'however', 'conversely', 'alternatively' etc. usually indicate that a counter-example will follow.
- Expressions such as 'thus', 'hence', 'therefore', 'should', 'ought to', 'must' etc. usually indicate the arrival of conclusions or inferences.

If we were going to present the earlier example on smoking in a more formal fashion, like you may find in an exam, it might look like this:

- *Since* smoking clogs the arteries and
- *because* it causes heart attacks and strokes,
- you *should* quit.

Reasoning indicators can also be used as a highly effective tool for developing your own arguments.

The first kind of indicator will force you to provide reasons for a position; the second will force you to consider counter-examples, criticisms and possible objections, and the third kind will force you to reflect on what you have argued for so that you can put forward a position in the light of this (try asserting anything other than a relevant conclusion after a 'therefore, we should ...' and it will sound absurd!).

Before moving on, a final word of warning. Whilst reasoning indicators are often a good indication that reasoned argument is taking place, this will not always be the case. Some arguments might not use these indicators and, equally, some pieces of reasoning, as we shall see, which are not arguments will. Where this is true, we need to go back to our original questions: 'Is this trying to persuade me of something?' and 'Does it provide reasons for why I ought to be persuaded?' in order to establish this.

Summary questions . . .

1. What questions do we need to ask in order to establish whether or not reasoned argument is taking place?
2. How might the use of reasoning indicators simplify this task?

Exercises

1. Try to separate the following piece of reasoning into reasons, counter-examples and conclusion by identifying the reasoning indicators used:

    We will soon be able to genetically modify human genes. Because of this, couples with enough money will be able to create their own 'designer babies' where they will be able to choose not just the sex of their child, but also the level of its intelligence, attractiveness and physical ability. Some have argued, however, that this breakthrough will mean an end to disease as cells prone to various diseases can be identified and screened out. Nevertheless, such an example misses the point. Since the technology will be open to abuse, it will only be a matter of time before designer babies are a reality. This is a prime example of humans playing God and should be outlawed at all costs.

2. Choose *one* of the following conclusions below and using the following reasoning indicators:
    *   Because ...
    *   As a result of this ...
    *   So ...
    *   However ...
    *   Nevertheless ...
    *   Therefore ...

    create an argument that supports it. The conclusions are deliberately absurd/controversial because this activity gets you to focus on the role of these indicators rather than on the content of the argument.

(a)   Men are better drivers than women.

(b)   Vampires should pay for the blood they drink.

(c)   Red is superior to green.

(d)   Quangs are better than Quees.

3.   Stretching activity: Choose your own (serious) conclusion and use the same reasoning indicators to create an argument for it.

EXPLANATIONS AND ARGUMENTS

> If a piece of reasoning is persuasive, then it is not an explanation.

> **explanations** – These explain *why*, but do not persuade *that* something is the case. They are superficially similar to arguments but have no persuasive function.

> The issue of explanations is taken up in further detail in Ch. 3: 'Causal explanations' and in Ch. 18: 'Plausible explanations'.

Explanations are examples of reasoning that share a similar form to arguments, but perform a very different role. It is important that you know how to tell them apart. The main difference is that explanations draw no persuasive inference. They explain *why*, rather than persuade us *that*, something is the case. Like arguments, explanations are formed of two parts. Firstly, there is the part being explained (sometimes referred to as the *explicandum*), for example the fact that 'aspirin cures headaches'. Secondly, there is the explanation itself (sometimes referred to as the *explicans*), that is, 'because it lowers the amount of chemicals in the body that are responsible for producing pain'. Here, I am not trying to persuade you of anything; the fact that aspirin cures headaches is already taken for granted and so doesn't need arguing for. What I am doing is explaining *how* aspirin does this.

Here are some further examples:

- 'Tides are caused primarily by our moon's gravity. While the moon takes a whole month to orbit the earth, the earth turns on its axis once per day. So the earth moves through the tidal bulges of water produced by the moon's gravity.' (WikiAnswers.com)

- 'The most probable explanation, given the facts, was that the *Mary Celeste* hit a terrible patch of bad weather. As the ship bucked on the waves, some alcohol spilled from the cargo barrels, covering the hold floor. Coupled with this, the ship's movement caused the galley stove to become unstable. Fearing the ship was about to explode, Briggs ordered everybody into the lifeboat, and planned to follow behind the *Mary Celeste* attached to the ship's main halyard, a strong, thick rope. As the storm worsened, somehow the halyard snapped and the *Mary Celeste* sailed off. Briggs, his

family and crew were left stranded in a small boat in the middle of the Atlantic Ocean.' (www.strange-mysteries.co.cc, used with kind permission of Vinay Swastik)
- 'A clear cloudless day-time sky is blue because molecules in the air scatter blue light from the sun more than they scatter red light. When we look towards the sun at sunset, we see red and orange colours because the blue light has been scattered out and away from the line of sight.' (math.ucr.edu)
- 'What else is love but understanding and rejoicing in the fact that another person lives, acts and experiences otherwise than we do.' (Nietzsche)

The difference between arguments and explanations is most clearly shown through examples:

- Mark is bald because his father was bald.
- Androids can be distinguished from robots on account of their resembling humans.
- The Roman Empire collapsed as a result of expanding too quickly.

Whilst these examples use similar reasoning indicators to arguments – e.g. 'because', 'on account of' etc. – none of them draw an inference. Once again, asking the question 'is this piece of reasoning trying to persuade me of something?' should help you identify whether you are dealing with an argument or an explanation (explanations will be answered in the negative). If you are satisfied you are dealing with an explanation, asking the questions 'what is being explained?' and 'how is it being explained?' will allow you to identify its two parts. For example:

What is being explained?	How is it being explained?
Mark's baldness	On account of his father's baldness
The difference between androids and robots	Because only androids resemble human beings
The collapse of the Roman Empire	As a result of it expanding too quickly

Contrasting these examples with the following examples of arguments (where a persuasive inference has been added) should help you to understand this point:

- Mark is bald because his father is bald. Therefore, if baldness is hereditary, then if Mark has any male sons, we can expect them to go bald as well.

- 'Androids can be distinguished from robots on account of their resembling humans. If you really do want an electronic helper that reminds you of your late husband Mrs Jenkins, can I suggest that you opt for the more expensive, android model!'
- The Roman Empire collapsed as a result of it expanding too quickly. Future empires should take note and keep expansion to a minimum.

Summary questions . . .

1. What do we mean by the term 'explanation'?
2. How do explanations differ from arguments?

Exercises

1. Look at the following examples and decide (explaining your decision) which one is an argument and which an explanation:

   (a) 'Soils provide water and nutrients for plant growth and development. [This is because they contain] essential plant nutrients which include phosphorus, nitrogen, potassium and sulphur.' (www.lmpc.edu.au)

   (b) 'Callisto orbits Jupiter. Hence, *it is not a planet*, because something must orbit a star in order to be a planet.' (iep.com)

   (c) Oliver isn't in today, so he must be ill.

   (d) Oliver isn't in today, because he is ill.

2. Read through the following passage and *briefly* summarise (a) *what* is being explained and (b) *how* it is being explained:

   Flying Spaghetti Monsterism (FSM) is a modern religion which claims the world was created by an invisible monster formed out of pasta and meatballs. Using its 'noodly appendage' it plays around with carbon-dating tests trying to convince us that the planet is actually far older than it appears to be, and hence evolution, far from being a valid scientific theory, is actually the work of this 'FSM'!

3. Stretching activity: Offer your own brief explanation for each of the following points (there is no single 'correct' explanation):

(a) The rise in knife crime.

(b) Global warming.

(c) The popularity of *Hello* magazine.

DIALOGIC REASONING

So far, we have looked at fairly straightforward examples of arguments where the premises are clearly laid out and either followed or preceded by the conclusion they support. But arguments, as we encounter them in real life, are rarely this simple. This is where dialogic reasoning comes in. A dialogue is a debate held between two or more people. These might include discussions in the classroom, conversations with friends, internet blog-spots, courtroom cases and much more besides. Often dialogues are confrontational, as when politicians debate an issue in the House of Commons, or when couples engage in a slanging match on the Jerry Springer show. But they do not have to be. A good dialogue aims at reaching truth and resolving conflict. It addresses questions, responds to problems, clarifies concepts and ideally ends in mutual agreement or understanding between the debaters involved, or at least in an agreement to disagree. Key features of this type of reasoning include arguments and **counter-arguments**/examples (where the initial argument is challenged), **critical questioning** (used to reveal flaws or weaknesses in an opponent's position), **refutation** (where an argument is disproved) and **resolution** (where the debaters come to an agreement on the issue being discussed). For exam purposes, you will also need to be able to identify the issue being debated; explain where each debater stands in relation to this issue (for or against), and summarise the differences between the rival positions. The following brief example should give you a clearer idea of how this works:

Amy: Cannabis should be legalised. Smoking a joint has never done anyone any harm.

Guy: But what do you mean by harm here? It is a well-known fact that cannabis smoke causes lung cancer and leads to other respiratory diseases.

counter-argument – A counter-argument is put forward to challenge the premises or conclusion of an argument.

critical questioning – Used to challenge or reveal flaws or weaknesses in an opponent's reasoning.

refutation – To **refute** an argument by proving it wrong (using reasons and evidence).

resolution – Resolution occurs when two conflicting viewpoints come to a mutual agreement.

Amy: But so does cigarette smoke and cigarettes haven't been banned.

Guy: But cigarette smoke doesn't cause any dangerous psychological effects. My friend Neil, who was a heavy cannabis user, was recently diagnosed with schizophrenia and claims that it was a direct result of smoking that stuff.

Amy: But he was a heavy user, and I bet he used a stronger strain of the drug. I've never heard of anybody smoking the weaker variety and suffering such problems.

Guy: But now you've changed your initial argument. What you're really arguing for is that milder strains of cannabis should be legalised.

Amy: OK, I'd go along with that.

Here, the issue being debated is the legalisation of cannabis. Amy argues for this position, Guy against it. Amy's initial (weak) reason that 'smoking a joint has never done anyone any harm' is challenged by Guy's use of critical questioning: 'what do you mean by harm?' He offers the counter-example that 'smoking causes lung cancer and other forms of respiratory disease'. Amy offers the weak counter-example that cigarettes do too and they are still legal. Guy challenges this analogy by emphasising that cigarette smoke doesn't cause any 'dangerous psychological effects'. He backs this up with a further example: a friend who was recently diagnosed with schizophrenia as a direct result of heavy cannabis use. Amy counters this by appealing to (a) the friend being a 'heavy user' and (b) smoking the stronger, more dangerous strain of the drug. Guy accepts this but points out that Amy has now changed her initial argument to 'milder strains of cannabis should be legalised'. Amy accepts this and the debate is resolved.

Summary question . . .

1. What is meant by the term 'dialogue'? What are the important features of 'dialogic' reasoning?

Exercise

1. Read through the following dialogue and identify (a) the issue being debated and (b) the two sides of the debate. See if you can spot any of the following features within the dialogue: (i) The use of critical questioning (ii) counter-arguments or examples and (iii) refutation. (This extract refers to Damien Hirst's *Adam and Eve Under the Table*, 2005)

    Jed: All I can say is that's not art!

    Kate: So what is, then?

    Jed: Not that rubbish!

    Kate: You don't know anything about art. You never go into a gallery. You never look at a picture intelligently. And yet you pick up a paper, see a picture and make rude comments about it as if you are an expert or something.

    Jed: You don't have to be an expert to know that shoving two skeletons under a pub table is not real art. It doesn't take any skill to do that. It's also disrespectful to the dead. After all, they were real people. It's not like the unmade bed or the pile of bricks. It's tasteless.

    Kate: The trouble with people like you is you think art has got to be pretty scenery and sunsets. But why shouldn't art be disrespectful sometimes? And skill's got nothing to do with whether it's art. You can be skilled at something and not produce art. My brother's an engineer but no one would say he produces art.

    Jed: I never said he did.

    Kate: But you just said skill was what made something art.

    Jed: No I didn't. What I said was that it didn't take any skill to make that thing.

    Kate: Well you implied it. It was the same with Picasso. People used to say 'my child could do better than that'. He upset people. But everybody thinks *Guernica* is a masterpiece nowadays. Surely you're not going to say that Picasso's not art.

Jed: But there's a major difference. Picasso put shapes and colours on the canvas and created his own effects. Hirst didn't create anything. He just got some objects and plonked them on the floor any old how.

Kate: But that's because he's a conceptual artist. For him art's all about ideas, not objects or how they're made. I think artists should have the right to see things in their own way and try and get other people to see things differently. As long as they do that and make people think, that's all that really matters.

Jed: Ever think you've been taken for a ride?

Kate: Yeah, sure, me and thousands of others, including critics and collectors and all those kinds of people. But you know better of course!

Jed: Well, I know what's good and what isn't!

(DOCUMENT B (New GCE Critical Thinking for First Teaching 2008: version 1.1, approved July 2007))

EMBEDDED AND DIRECT ARGUMENT

embedded argument – A report or summary of an argument rather than the argument itself.

extract – An **embedded argument** needs to be extracted before it can be treated as an argument in its own right.

The final section of this chapter looks at **embedded** or 'indirect' arguments. These are simply 'reports' of arguments rather than the arguments themselves. They are contrasted with the 'direct' arguments that we have looked at so far in this chapter. Embedded arguments occur when an author wants to summarise or explain someone else's argument rather than put forward their own. If I were to report that John believes 'animal testing should be made illegal because it is both cruel and unnecessary', this no more commits me to John's belief than the claim 'John likes custard on his sardines' means I like custard on mine! The original, embedded version obviously contains an argument, but before we can treat it as one, we first need to **extract** it by separating the argument from its author. This leaves us with: (premises) 'Animal testing is cruel' and 'Animal testing is unnecessary'; (conclusion) 'Animal testing should be made illegal.'

The following, taken from Anne Thomson's *Critical Reasoning: A Practical Introduction*, provides us with a slightly trickier example of how this can be done:

> Sir: Martin Kelly ('Fishy Business in Loch Ness', 28 March) reports Dr Ian Winfield as saying that the fish stocks in Loch Ness are not big enough to feed a monster, therefore a monster does not exist. He confuses cause and effect.
>
> It is perfectly obvious to me that the reason why the fish stocks are low is because the monster keeps eating them. (Peter Stanton, Letters to the Editor, *The Independent*, 31 March 1995)

Here, the embedded argument (originally put forward by Dr Ian Winfield) is as follows:

Conclusion: The Loch Ness monster 'does not exist'.

Premise: Because 'the fish stocks in Loch Ness are not big enough to feed [it]'.

Once we have extracted this argument, we can treat it directly (i.e. as an actual argument rather than a report of one), and, in fact, the author of the letter does just this, putting forward the counter-argument that:

Conclusion: The author (Dr Ian Winfield) is mistaken (because he 'confuses cause and effect').

Premise: The fish stocks are low because the monster keeps eating them!

Here we have successfully extracted two arguments from a single piece of reasoning and we can now treat them directly (i.e. as arguments in their own right).

Summary questions . . .

1. Explain what is meant by the term 'embedded argument'.
2. How do we go about 'extracting' an embedded argument in order to treat it as an argument in its own right?

END OF CHAPTER ACTIVITY

Extract the embedded argument from the following example:

> In his recent book, *The God Delusion*, the evolutionary physicist Richard Dawkins argues that the idea of God as the divine creator of the universe is incoherent. This is because, if such a being existed, it would have to be more complex than its creation. This would explain nothing because we would then require a further, more complex explanation for the cause of God.

SUMMARY CHECKLIST

Points you need to remember:

✔ What is an argument

✔ What are the key features of reasoned argument

✔ What are reasoning indicators and what they allow us to do

✔ What we mean by the term 'explanation' and what the difference is between an argument and an explanation

✔ What are dialogues and what are the key features of 'dialogic' reasoning

✔ What are embedded arguments and how we go about extracting them

Mission Critical (San Jose State University) provides some excellent examples of argument and a range of interactive activities that can be used to sharpen your skills of analysis.

UNIT 1 **FOUNDATION UNIT**

Chapter 2: Areas of discourse

LEARNING OBJECTIVES ✔

By the end of this chapter you should:

✔   Understand what is meant by the expression 'area of discourse'.
✔   Be able to identify the area of discourse to which a particular debate belongs.
✔   Understand the specific features of particular areas of discourse.

Reasoning does not take place in a vacuum. It has a specific form which is dictated by the context within which it occurs. Before you can begin the task of evaluating an argument (the central focus of Chapters 3 and 6) you will first have to work out what kind of form this is.

To do this, you will need to identify the **area of discourse** to which it belongs. Reasoning in different disciplines has different characteristics requiring different kinds of evaluation. Historical discourse, for example, raises questions about the past; mathematical discourse, about number, calculation and measurement; psychological discourse, about the mind and motives for human behaviour, and sociological discourse, about the social structure of human interaction. In short, there are as many areas of discourse as there are subjects of study. Sometimes these will overlap – as with the previous dialogue we looked at regarding the legalisation of cannabis (Chapter 1) which involved moral questions (whether or not smoking this drug was wrong) and legal ones (whether or not the drug should be outlawed).

This chapter will focus on three of the most common: ethical (relating to the rightness or wrongness of action); aesthetic (relating to art and beauty), and scientific (relating to our understanding of how the physical world operates)

area of discourse – The area of discourse to which an argument or debate belongs indicates the type of reasoning that it employs – for example, moral, legal, scientific etc.

as a means for introducing you to the kinds of reasoning that each employs. This last point is important because, when analysing a particular piece of reasoning, it is important to do so on its own grounds. The question of whether or not it is wrong to smoke cannabis is *not* the same question as whether or not it is *legal* to smoke it or whether it really damages your health (although many, unreflectingly, confuse these issues!). Even if the drug *were* illegal, this does not automatically make smoking it immoral (many people suffering from critically dehabilitating diseases use the drug as effective pain-relief, for which one could, perhaps, make out a special moral case). For similar reasons, the fact that an action is legal does not imply that it is *moral* to carry it out (it is currently legal to have an affair, but it is certainly not *moral* to do so!).

ETHICAL DISCOURSE

ethical discourse – An ethical discourse carries with it implications for how we ought to behave.

The following example of **ethical discourse** from David Bain confronts us with an intriguing moral dilemma:

> Should we kill healthy people for their organs?
>
> Suppose Bill is a healthy man without family or loved ones. Would it be ok painlessly to kill him if his organs would save five people, one of whom needs a heart, another a kidney, and so on? If not, why not?
>
> Consider another case: you and six others are kidnapped, and the kidnapper somehow persuades you that if you shoot dead one of the other hostages, he will set the remaining five free, whereas if you do not, he will shoot all six. (Either way, he'll release you.)
>
> If in this case you should kill one to save five, why not in the previous, organs case? If in this case too you have qualms, consider yet another: you're in the cab of a runaway tram and see five people tied to the track ahead. You have the option of sending the tram on to the track forking off to the left, on which only one person is tied. Surely you should send the tram left, killing one to save five.
>
> But then why not kill Bill?

This reasoning gets us to consider whether, at the expense of saving several lives, it would be ethical to kill (or cause the death of) a single life. The debate is moral because it carries with it implications for how we *ought* to behave. If the debate were purely numerical, i.e. 'five lives versus one', then in all three cases, killing one person to save five would be the correct thing to do. The fact that most would regard killing Bill for his organs as wrong, whilst in the runaway train case, allowing five people to survive at the expense of one innocent death would be right, shows us that there is more to consider than mere number. One of the principal difficulties with this type of debate is that moral claims cannot be *proved* in the same way that scientific ones can. Saying 'killing a human for his organs is wrong' is not like saying 'Bill is a human.' There seems to be an awkward 'gap' between a *fact* (which can be *shown* to be true) and a *value* (whose seeming 'rightness' cannot be proved scientifically). But this is not to say that moral claims have the same status as subjective opinions.

To resolve these kinds of disputes, critical thinkers usually appeal to one of two kinds of principle, either: (a) what is known as the 'deontological' view – that certain actions, such as killing, rape and promise breaking are always wrong regardless of their consequences; or (b) what is known as the 'utilitarian' principle whereby an action is morally justified if the consequences it brings about are more favourable than those that would be brought about by not doing it.

Exercises

1. Using the two principles above, come to a decision about what (a) a deontologist and (b) a utilitarian would do in each of the three scenarios presented in the 'Kill Bill' passage.

2. Stretching activity: Which position do you think offers the better response? Why?

AESTHETIC DISCOURSE

Whereas moral discourses focus on the rightness or wrongness of action, **aesthetic discourses** focus on the 'beauty', 'ugliness' and/or 'artistic merit' of an object. They are similar inasmuch as they both contemplate questions of *value* rather than fact (claiming the *Mona Lisa* is beautiful is very different from claiming that she depicts a woman). They differ, however, insofar as moral discourses focus on *action* whereas aesthetic ones focus on *contemplating* objects or artworks (these might include landscapes, the human face and

aesthetic discourse – An aesthetic discourse contemplates questions of value – for example, those focusing on the 'beauty' or 'artistic merit' of a particular artwork or object.

Identifying the area of discourse to which an argument or debate belongs will help you decide how to evaluate it. There is a difference, for example, between arguing that an action is morally wrong, and arguing that it is legally wrong – not least of all because it is only the second of these that can be proved.

animal movement as well as paintings, sculpture, music, architecture etc.). The following example should give you an idea of some of the questions this type of discourse seeks to address:

Conceptual art: What's the idea?

Every time the Turner Prize comes around, there is a debate about whether conceptual art is real art. But what is conceptual art – and what isn't 'proper' about it?

Conceptual art is concerned with ideas and meanings, rather than forms and materials. The making of the art object is seen as something incidental that could be assigned to assistants or abandoned entirely.

However, it is hard to see how art can ever be *just* an 'idea'; art only really works when it is a visual experience of some kind. Of course, this visual experience represents ideas, but not pure ideas as are found in speech or writing.

Much of the criticism of 'conceptual art' today is levelled at works that are not really conceptual art at all. The label of conceptual art is liberally bandied around, and stuck on to any piece of modern art that somebody wants to discredit. Most of the art in the Saatchi Gallery or the Turner Prize, for example, couldn't really be described as conceptual. Some of the pieces in the Turner Prize involve significant craftsmanship, and most aim to create a striking visual effect.

There is little point in opposing the art in the Turner Prize and elsewhere with some fixed idea of 'proper' art. The Stuckists, a group who demonstrate against the prize every year, show how this position easily slips into absurdity. Proper art is paint and canvas, they say – which ends up with a ridiculous fixation on the medium. It is as if they attribute paint with almost magic qualities, so that you only need take a few brushstrokes in order for it to be real art. The conclusion must be that, while every primary schoolchild produces art, Damien Hirst does not.

In actual fact, painting is just one medium among many – arguably no better or worse than video art, readymades* or installations. Rather than demonstrating outside Tate Britain calling for a return to painting, it would be far better to head inside. (Josie Appleton, www.spiked-online.com)

* 'readymades' are objects the artist obtains rather than creates

Very often, as we see with the above piece of reasoning, aesthetic discourses revolve around problems of definition: 'What do we mean by "art"?' and value:

'Does art have to be beautiful or skilfully manufactured in order for us to appreciate it?' They are often resolved by coming to an agreement about how these terms should be employed. If, for example, it was agreed that neither beauty *nor* craftsmanship are necessary features of art, then objecting to 'conceptual' art because it lacks either of these will not be acceptable.

Exercises

1.
   - Identify the main conclusion (final paragraph) of the above passage.
   - What reasons does the author give in support of this claim?
   - How does the author define 'conceptual art'?
   - What is conceptual art being compared to and how is this defined?

2. Stretching activity: How convincing do you find the author's reasoning and why?

The issue of moral claims is taken up in detail in Ch. 3: 'Value judgements' and 'Statements of principle'.

SCIENTIFIC DISCOURSE

Scientific discourses differ from moral or aesthetic ones because their subject matter is factual rather than value based. Moral considerations may well impinge upon scientific reasoning (as, for example, when we debate about whether 'designer babies' or genetically modified crops breach a moral principle) but the two lines of enquiry must always be kept separate (claiming such research is immoral could never be established scientifically!). Scientific arguments are used to support *theories* or *hypotheses* and they appeal to *evidence* and *data* in order to do this. They generally proceed from singular observations (for example, instances of white swans) to general hypotheses (the inference 'all swans are white') and aim to do so objectively (i.e. by actively seeking out counter-examples [non-white swans] in order to test the hypothesis in question).

On 6 August 1996, NASA issued a news release:

scientific discourse – This supports a theory, hypothesis or causal explanation. It appeals to evidence and data of a factual nature and tends to move from singular observations to general hypotheses/ explanations. Unlike ethical and aesthetic discourses, its subject matter is factual rather than value-based.

For more on this theme, see Ch. 3: 'Value judgements'

Meteorite from Mars points to possibility of life on other planets, 1996

NASA has made a startling discovery that points to the possibility that a primitive form of microscopic life may have existed on Mars more than three billion years ago. The research is based on a sophisticated examination of an ancient Martian meteorite that landed on Earth some 13,000 years ago.

The evidence is exciting, even compelling, but not conclusive. It is a discovery that demands further scientific investigation. NASA is ready to assist the process of rigorous scientific investigation and lively scientific debate that will follow this discovery.

The issue of identifying and evaluating scientific claims is taken up in greater detail in the next chapter. In the meantime, see if you can complete the following exercise.

Exercise

1.

- What 'startling discovery' has NASA made?
- What evidence is given in support of this claim?
- Why is NASA 'ready to assist the process of rigorous scientific investigation and lively scientific debate'?

Summary questions . . .

1. Briefly explain what is meant by the expression 'area of discourse'.
2. Identify the common characteristics of moral, aesthetic and scientific areas of discourse.

END OF CHAPTER ACTIVITY

1. Identify the area of discourse to which each of the following pieces of reasoning belongs.
2. See if you can spot some of the 'identifying characteristics' of each (you might find rereading the initial section of this chapter helps you to do this).

Lay out your answer in the following way:
  *) _____ is a _____ discourse because_____.

(a) Freud's book, *The Interpretation of Dreams*, published 1900: In 1897 Sigmund Freud began his famous course of self-analysis. He had already noticed that dreams played an important role in his analysis of neurotic and 'hysterical' patients. As he encouraged them to free-associate, that is, talk about whatever came into their minds, they often referred to their dreams, which would set off other associations and often illuminate other important connections in their past experience. Freud also had noticed that hallucinations in psychotic patients were very much like dreams. Based on these observations, Freud [argued that] sleeping dreams were nearly always, like day-dreams, wish fulfilment. (www.pbs.org)

For more on this topic, see Ch. 3: 'Definitions' and 'Value judgements'.

(b) Antibiotics transformed medicine. The discovery of antibiotics began by accident. On the morning of September 3rd, 1928, Professor Alexander Fleming was having a clear up of his cluttered laboratory. Fleming was sorting through a number of glass plates which had previously been coated with staphylococcus bacteria as part of research Fleming was doing. One of the plates had mould on it. The mould was in the shape of a ring and the area around the ring seemed to be free of the bacteria staphylococcus. The mould was penicillium notatum. Fleming had a life-long interest in ways of killing off bacteria and he concluded that the bacteria on the plate around the ring had been killed off by some substance that had come from the mould. (adapted from www.historylearningsite.co.uk/antibiotics.htm)

For more on necessary conditions, see Ch. 11: 'Confusing necessary and sufficient conditions'.

(c) Legalising 'voluntary euthanasia' on the basis of excruciating 'hard cases' would result in its being routinely practised on a large scale. Bad cases do not make good law. One leading medical ethicist said more than twenty years ago *'We shall begin by doing it because the patient is in intolerable pain but we shall end up doing it because it is Friday afternoon and we want to get away for the weekend.'* The precedent of abortion is chilling: 'Aging Advisory Services' would offer a 1-stop shop where you could pop in your inconvenient relatives and, for a suitable fee, euthanase them in your lunch-hour. (www.starcourse.org)

For more on this theme, see Ch. 3: 'Hypotheses' and 'Causal explanations'.

(d) Durkheim was concerned primarily with how societies could maintain their integrity and coherence in the modern era, when things such as shared religious and ethnic background could no longer be assumed. In order to study social life in modern societies, Durkheim sought to create one of the first scientific approaches to social phenomena. Along with Herbert Spencer, Durkheim was one of the first people to explain the existence and quality of different parts of a society by reference to what function they served in maintaining the quotidian, and is thus sometimes seen as a precursor to functionalism. Durkheim also insisted that society was more than the sum of its parts. Thus unlike his contemporaries Ferdinand Tönnies and Max Weber, he focused not on what motivates the actions of individuals (methodological individualism), but rather on the study of social facts, a term which he coined to describe phenomena which have an existence in and of themselves and are not bound to the actions of individuals. He argued that social facts had an independent existence greater and more objective than the actions of the individuals that composed society and could only be explained by other social facts rather than, say, by society's adaptation to a particular climate or ecological niche. (Wikipedia – Durkheim)

(e) Those who cannot remember the past, are condemned to repeat it. (George Santayana)

The BBC website offers a range of interesting discussions on a variety of interrelated subject matters. These can be used to sharpen your understanding of the different areas of discourse and also your skills of analysis and evaluation. The section on ethics is particularly good.

SUMMARY CHECKLIST

Points you need to remember:

✔ What is meant by the term 'area of discourse'.

✔ The different *areas* of discourse; in particular moral, aesthetic and scientific.

✔ The 'identifying characteristics' of each of these.

FOUNDATION UNIT

Chapter 3: Claims

LEARNING OBJECTIVES

By the end of this chapter you should:

✔ Understand what critical thinkers mean by the term 'claim'.
✔ Be able to identify different types of claim from a wide variety of contexts; most importantly, predictions, hypotheses, statements of principle, definitions, causal explanations, recommendations, allegations and value judgements.
✔ Have developed a basic understanding of how each type of claim can be assessed.

Because **claims** are so fundamental to every aspect of critical thinking (they form the basic components of *all* reasoning), understanding what they are and how to assess them is an essential skill that you will need to acquire. But what are they? Put simply, claims assert or deny that something is the case. They form the basis on which arguments are built and come in many different forms. Some express facts:

- Britain declared war on Germany on 3 September 1939.

Others opinions:

- 'Never in the field of human conflict was so much owed by so many to so few.' (Churchill's speech, 20 August 1940)

Or value judgements:

- 'If the British Empire and its Commonwealth last for a thousand years, men will still say, "This was their finest hour."' (Ibid.)

> **claims** – Claims form the basis of all reasoning. They assert or deny that something is the case. There are many different types of claim and each needs to be analysed and evaluated on its own terms.

recommendation –
A recommendation
advocates a particular
course of action.

Sometimes they are used to make **recommendations**:

*   'Whoever fights monsters should see to it that in the process he does not become one.' (Nietzsche)

Whilst others are used to make predictions:

*   'Most scientists agree that even if we ceased production of greenhouse gases today, the average temperature in the UK would continue to rise for the next 100 years or so.' (*Rising Temperatures*, Channel 4)

At times it is not always clear whether a claim expresses a fact or opinion:

*   'I am the greatest. Not only do I knock 'em out, but I pick the round.' (Muhammad Ali)

What is clear is that the ability to come to such a decision is an important skill that you will need to develop. This is because a claim (and subsequently an argument) cannot be assessed until you are clear about what type of claim is being made. An argument is a chain of reasoning and a chain is only as strong as its weakest link. The following represent a list of the types of claim you might expect to encounter in an exam and some thoughts on how each can be assessed.

PREDICTIONS

prediction – A claim
made about the future
based upon something
else being true in the
present or past.

A **prediction** is a claim made about the future based on something being true in the present or past:

*   He's lied to you before, he'll do it again.
*   'I've never been a man to make predictions. Never have been, and never will be.' (!) (Paul Gascoigne)
*   The Conservative Party have a current lead of 19% in the opinion polls therefore we can comfortably predict they will win the next general election.
*   'Join the 12 million other women around Britain. Try Danone Activia for 14 days and beat that bloated feeling.' (Advert)

Predictions do not express facts, but rather beliefs about what will happen in the future. They can be confirmed (proved) or refuted (disproved) at some later date, but at the time they are made, they are neither true nor false.

Evaluating predictions

Whilst predictions can never be 100% certain, they can be strong or weak. Generally speaking, the greater the amount of evidence in support of a prediction, the greater the likelihood that it will turn out to be true. Whilst it would be unwise to reject the credibility of a politician who had lied on one occasion, one who did so regularly could reasonably be expected to carry on doing so. For similar reasons, if every time a party had held a 19% lead in an opinion poll they had gone on to win an election, then it would be reasonable to predict that, in this instance, the Conservatives would be successful. Alongside evidential support, a prediction may also be strengthened or weakened by the method used to reach it, how clearly or vaguely it is expressed, and by the expertise of the author or reliability of the source from which it stems. For this reason, we would have greater reason to trust the 'scientific' astronomer's prediction that:

> The next lunar eclipse will occur on the 9th February 2009 and will affect Eastern Europe, Asia, Australia and the Pacific Ocean. (Lunar Eclipse Preview 2001–20: Fred Espenak [astronomer])

than the 'mystic' astrologist's prediction that:

> Later, the moon checks into your relationships chart and you can talk to a partner on a much deeper level. (*The Sun*, Horoscopes, December 2008)

This last claim is unscientific, stems from a questionable source and is vague enough to be applicable to a whole range of situations.

> To assess the strength of a prediction, you will need to think about how much evidence there is in support of it; how clearly it is expressed, and how reliable/well informed its source is.

> For a more detailed discussion on reliability and expertise of sources, see Ch. 15 – in particular 'Motive and agenda' and 'Sources'.

Exercise

1. Taking into account, where appropriate:
    - the type of claim being made
    - the reliability of the method or evidence used to make the prediction
    - how clearly the prediction is expressed
    - the expertise (i.e. relevant skill) and/or reliability (i.e. whether they/ it are trustworthy) of the author/source of the claim

organise the following examples on a scale of reliability (from most to least reliable) giving reasons for your answer:

(1)   It should be a drier than normal January, with probably fairly lengthy spells without precipitation. (BBC Weather forecast)

(2)   The new Critical Thinking teacher looks good. I'm confident results will improve this year. (Headmaster)

(3)   The Centre for Economics and Business Research (CEBR) predicts the economy will shrink by 2.9% in 2009 – more than at any time since the 1940s. (BBC News)

(4)   The blood of the just will commit a fault at London, burnt through lighting of twenty threes the six: The ancient lady will fall from her high place; several of the same sect will be killed. (A claim made by Nostradamus which some have argued predicted the Great Fire of London in 1666)

(5)   Clearasil will give you clearer skin in just 3 days ... guaranteed. (Advert)

HYPOTHESES

hypothesis – A claim put forward for testing which attempts to explain why something has occurred/occurs. Once a hypothesis is accepted/confirmed, it will then be regarded as a theory or explanation.

Hypotheses are claims put forward for testing which attempt a possible explanation of a particular event or events. For example, if I were to leave my house one morning and notice my car wasn't in the drive, I could offer a range of hypotheses to account for this. For example:

•   My wife had taken the car.
•   I have been acting very absent-mindedly of late and perhaps I left the car at work yesterday.
•   The car had been stolen. (etc.)

Whereas explanations proper are accepted as true, hypotheses can only ever be speculative (provisional), requiring further investigation before their truth or falsity can be established. Once a hypothesis has been confirmed (or refuted), it ceases to be a hypothesis and becomes an accepted theory or explanation (or gets rejected!). For this reason, a hypothesis cannot be regarded as factual.

Evaluating hypotheses

One of the most important features of this type of claim is that it should be testable. This means that we need to be clear about what evidence would prove or disprove it. If I had ruled out my wife taking the car (by asking her) or my absent-mindedly parking the car elsewhere (by going out and checking) then I might reasonably conclude that the third hypothesis (the car having been stolen) must be the correct one. I could not, for example, hypothesise that the car had simply vanished into thin air – for how could I ever test this?!

If a hypothesis cannot be tested, then it is not a valid hypothesis (the creationists' claim that the existence of fossils is not so much evidence of evolution as of God 'testing' our faith, is often rejected on these grounds. Such a claim could never be proved true or false). It is also important that a hypothesis be backed up by a range of evidence. The seventeenth-century physician Francesco Redi wished to refute the commonly held belief at that time that maggots 'spontaneously generated' in decomposing meat. Instead, he hypothesised that maggots were produced by flies. In order to test this hypothesis, he filled four jars with various types of meat and placed a lid on each. He did the same with a further four jars, but left these open. When worms appeared only in those jars freely exposed to air, he believed his hypothesis had been confirmed. Supporters of the previous 'spontaneous generation' hypothesis, however, were not convinced and suggested 'contaminated air' as an alternative explanation for the worms' appearance. In order to refute this, Redi conducted a further experiment where one set of jars was left open as before, whilst another set was covered with gauze, so as to let air, but not flies, in. When, once again, flies appeared only in the freely exposed jars, his hypothesis was confirmed and later became an accepted theory.

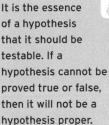
It is the essence of a hypothesis that it should be testable. If a hypothesis cannot be proved true or false, then it will not be a hypothesis proper.

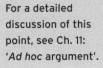
For a detailed discussion of this point, see Ch. 11: 'Ad hoc argument'.

Exercises

1. Provide your own hypothesis for each of the following:
   (a) The increase in student numbers studying Critical Thinking.
   (b) The dinosaurs becoming extinct.
   (c) The rise in sun cancer amongst young Australians.
   (d) The fact that life-expectancy (for both men and women) has increased by over fifteen years since 1960.

2.
- What evidence would be required to confirm (or refute) each of your hypotheses?
- Suggest an alternative hypothesis for each example you have given.

3. Stretching activity: For each example, come to a reasoned decision about which hypothesis offers the best explanation. Make sure you give reasons/evidence in support of your answer.

CAUSAL EXPLANATIONS

causal explanation
– Explains an event or action in terms of the prior event which brought it about. Scientific discourses frequently make use of this type of claim. A **causal explanation** differs from a **plausible** one because it provides an *actual*, rather than just *probable* explanation for why a particular event has occurred.

A **causal explanation**, unsurprisingly, explains why something is as it is in terms of what caused it to be so. A gambler's addiction might be explained in terms of his having inherited a gambling gene; a car engine's backfiring might be explained in terms of a faulty distributor cap; John doing cartwheels across the room might be explained in terms of his happiness, his happiness in terms of a lucky bet on a horse etc. In all such cases, a later event is explained in terms of a special relation to a prior event which brought it about. These claims usually take the form of 'b because a':

- John hit the ground at a greater velocity than Mary *because he neglected to wear a parachute*.
- Slugs shrivel up when you apply salt to them *because the external concentration of sodium exceeds the internal concentration, thus causing excess water to rise to the surface of their skin*.

Or 'a causes/caused b':

- *Ultraviolet light from sunbeds or sunlight is the major cause of* skin cancer.
- *Gravitational interaction between the Earth and Moon is responsible for* the Earth's tides.

They can be singular (i.e. apply to a specific event or process – 'a caused b'):

- John contracted lung cancer *because he smoked forty a day*.

Or general (i.e. 'whenever a, then b'):

- *Smoking causes* lung cancer.

In each example, the section underlined represents the causal explanation, and the section not underlined, the thing being explained.

Evaluating causal explanations

It is not always true that one event regularly following or occurring at the same time as another (referred to as a 'correlation') implies a causal connection. If, for example, every time I sneezed, my mobile phone rang, I couldn't say with certainty that my sneezing was the cause of the phone ringing – no matter how many times one event followed the other! In order to establish whether a causal link is genuine, we need to rule out the possibility of coincidence; it is not enough to show *that* event b follows event a, we need to show *why* it does. Even if we can establish a causal link between two particular events (John's smoking forty a day, rather than a predisposition towards cancer running in the family, as being the *cause* of his contracting lung cancer), this, on its own, is not enough to determine a *common* link (that smoking *in every case* causes lung cancer). For this we need an explanation:

- Smoking causes lung cancer because there are over sixty carcinogenic (i.e. cancer-producing) chemicals in tobacco smoke.

Backed up by a substantial amount of evidence:

- In a scientific study which observed the results of over 100,000 smokers, it was found that around 8% contracted lung cancer.

From as wide a range of sources as possible:

- The study took place between 1980 and 2000 and involved male and female smokers from America, Europe, Asia and Africa.

Which rules out coincidence as a possible alternative explanation:

- This contrasted with the 1% of non-smokers who contracted the disease.

Only then can the claim be regarded as acceptable in the strong sense (although, of course, it might be *reasonable* to accept a causal claim without this amount and range of evidence!). It is also important that causal explanations don't understate or overstate the scale of the causal link. The claim 'smoking causes cancer' would be better translated as 'smoking *often* causes cancer'. It would be just as unacceptable to say 'smoking *always* causes cancer' as it

Two events regularly occurring together, either at the same time or in direct succession, do not always establish a causal link. To do this an explanation is needed for *why* event a causes event b – it is not enough just to say *that* it does.

For a detailed discussion of the range of ways in which causal explanations can misfire, see Ch. 11: 'Cause-correlation fallacy' and also Ch. 17.

would be to say that 'smoking *rarely* causes cancer'. Expressions such as 'always', 'usually', 'sometimes' and 'rarely' are important features of causal explanations and need to be chosen with care.

Exercises

1. Suggest *two* possible causes for each of the following effects (the first two are singular, the second two general):
    (a) A person outside wearing a duffel coat.
    (b) 'Flashing lights' in the sky.
    (c) Belief in God.
    (d) Childhood obesity.

2. State whether the following are examples of (a) causation (b) correlation or (c) not enough evidence to decide. Make sure you give reasons for your answer:
    (a) Night following day.
    (b) Alka Seltzer curing a hangover.
    (c) Going out for a meal at a cheap restaurant and contracting food poisoning.

3. Read through the following four examples and decide how convincing they each are by inserting 'always', 'usually', 'sometimes' and 'rarely' next to each:
    (a) Eating lots of sugary food without brushing your teeth _____ causes tooth decay.
    (b) Eating beef _____ causes mad cow disease.
    (c) Smoking cannabis _____ causes schizophrenia.
    (d) Heat _____ causes metal to expand.

4. Stretching activity: Explain the type of evidence that would be needed to back up the following example (which would also rule out coincidence as a possible explanation):
    • 'Faulty MAOA gene* causes some people to become aggressive drunks' (Rebecca Smith, Medical Editor, *Daily Telegraph*)

(* The MAOA gene is responsible for breaking down chemicals in the brain responsible for mood.)

DEFINITIONS

A **definition** is a claim made about the meaning of a concept or expression; it offers an explanation or clarification of what a word or phrase means. Some are simple and precise:

- A triangle is a three-sided shape.

Others are more intricate, reflecting the complexity of the term involved:

- 'Plagiarism is the act of literary theft. [It] occurs when a writer duplicates another writer's language or ideas and then calls the work his or her own.' (*The American Heritage New Dictionary of Cultural Literacy,* 3rd Edition).

Definitions are formed of two parts: the part being defined (sometimes referred to as the *definiendum*) and the part doing the defining (referred to as the *definiens*):

Term being defined (*definiendum*)	Definition (*definiens*)
God	'is an omniscient (all knowing), omnipotent (all powerful), supremely good and loving being' (Cluett, McAdoo, Rawlinson and Sidoli, *AQA Philosophy*, 2008)
Critical thinking	'is the intellectually disciplined process of actively and skilfully conceptualising, applying, analysing, synthesising and/or evaluating information gathered from, or generated by, observation, experience, reflection, reasoning or communication, as a guide to belief and action' (Scriven and Paul, *Defining Critical Thinking*, 1987)
Manslaughter	is 'the unlawful killing of a human being without malice' (Webster's Dictionary of Law)

Evaluating definitions

Disputes, as we have already seen, may often arise when two or more people have conflicting views on how a term should be used. Such disagreement can often be resolved when the parties involved come to a mutual decision about

> **definition** – A definition offers a clarification or explanation of what a concept, term or expression *means*.

> Disputes, particularly in dialogic reasoning, often turn on how a particular word or expression is being used. Identifying and clarifying such examples is often the key to their resolution.

For a more detailed discussion of circularity, see Ch. 11: 'Begging the question/ circularity'.

how a term should be used. This is often the *aim* of a debate. But what do we need to think about in order to decide whether a definition is acceptable?

Some definitions are described as 'circular' because the term being defined also forms part of the definition:

- Critical thinking is the act of thinking critically.
- A causal explanation is one that explains something causally.

It is easy to see that such examples, although undeniably true, are also boringly uninformative!

Others are too broad, laying themselves open to obvious counter-examples. The Greek philosopher Plato once offered the following definition of what it is to be human:

- Man is a featherless biped [creature with two legs].

To which his fellow philosopher Diogenes wryly responded by presenting him with a plucked chicken!

Yet others are too narrow. Suppose that Plato tried to tighten up the definition:

- A human is a featherless biped with the ability to think rationally.

This would unfairly deny humanity to one-legged and/or irrational humans. A central problem here is that trying to provide a perfect definition makes it difficult to handle such tricky, borderline cases. The questions you need to ask to test the adequacy of a definition are: 'What is being defined?' 'How is it being defined?' 'Does it cover all particular cases or are there *obvious* counter-examples which could be used to question the definition?' Perhaps more practically: 'Does the definition suit the task in hand?' 'Does the definition fit with our normal use of the term?' (Alec Fisher, *Critical Thinking: An Introduction*, Cambridge, 2001) To give an example, the philosopher Kant defined art as:

> A kind of representation that is purposive in itself and, though without an end, nevertheless promotes the cultivation of the mental powers for sociable communication. (Kant, *Critique of Judgement*, 44)

Such a definition, whilst acceptable for professional philosophers, would hardly be a suitable definition for a child – nor does it correspond with our everyday understanding of this word!

Exercises

1. Read through the following excerpt from a dialogue (specimen assessment material AQA) and answer the follow-up questions:

    > Kate: But that's because he's a conceptual artist. For him art's all about ideas, not objects or how they're made. I think artists should have the right to see things in their own way and try and get other people to see things differently. As long as they do that and make people think, that's all that really matters.

    (a) What is Kate trying to define?
    (b) How does she try and define it?
    (c) Stretching activity: How satisfactory do you find her definition? Why?

2. Taking into account the following points:
    - Is the definition circular?
    - Can you imagine any counter-examples?
    - Does it correspond with our normal usage?

    Decide whether or not each of the following examples provides a satisfactory definition:

    (a) A square has four equal sides.
    (b) Depressed: suffering from depression (adapted from *The American Heritage Dictionary of the English Language*).
    (c) Happiness is a cigar called Hamlet. (Advert)
    (d) Art is the creation of beautiful artefacts.

3. For each example that does *not* provide a satisfactory definition, explain *why* it doesn't and suggest an alternative/modified definition to make it more precise.

4. Try and offer a clear definition, in your own words, for each of the following:
    (a) Love
    (b) A car
    (c) Democracy
    (d) A definition!

VALUE JUDGEMENTS

value judgement – A non-factual claim which assigns a value to (i.e. says something positive or negative about) an object, event, action or person's worth.

Recommendations, statements of principle and allegations have each been covered in this chapter. Ethical and aesthetic discourses are covered in Ch. 2.

As we saw in Chapter 2 (pp. 31–3) a **value judgement** is not founded on the same basis as a factual statement (e.g. a causal explanation or an accurate definition). Broadly speaking, a factual statement asserts something that is true whereas a value judgement assigns a value to (i.e. says something positive or negative about) an object, action, event or person's worth. 'Smoking causes cancer' is a factual statement; 'smoking is a vile habit' is a value judgement. Unlike the former, the latter cannot be verified as true or false. To claim something is good or bad; right or wrong; desirable or undesirable etc. is to make a value judgement. Recommendations and statements of principle can express value judgements. Allegations often involve them too, while moral and aesthetic discourses usually revolve around such claims. Here are some examples:

- Picking your nose is a filthy habit.
- The world is an awful place.
- 'The problem with being teetotal is you wake up in the morning and that's as good as it gets.' (George Best)
- 'I spent 90% of my money on women, drink and fast cars. The rest I wasted.' (Ditto)
- That's a terrible hat!
- 'History is a nightmare from which I am trying to awake.' (James Joyce)
- 'Football isn't a matter of life and death. It's much more important than that.' (Bill Shankly)

Generally speaking, a value judgement on its own would not strongly support a conclusion, but when combined with factual evidence or a statement of principle (see below) it can lend further weight to an argument. For this reason, an argument like:

- Broccoli is disgusting; therefore we should ban it from the college menu.

cannot be regarded as a strong argument, but it could be made stronger by appealing to further evidence:

- Broccoli is disgusting and it also contains goitrogens – naturally occurring substances in certain foods that can interfere with the functioning of the thyroid gland (www.whfoods.org). Therefore we should ban it from the college menu.

Whilst still fairly weak, this example is nevertheless stronger than the previous one!

Evaluating value judgements

Value judgements are often, but not always, subjective, revealing more about the beliefs of the person making them than they do about the thing being judged. When I say 'broccoli is disgusting' what I really mean is 'I don't like broccoli'. If broccoli were truly disgusting (in the same way that broccoli is green) then everyone would presumably agree about this. The fact that they don't shows us that being 'disgusting' is not something that can be true in the same way that being 'green' can. But this is not to say that there is no more to value judgements than their being unjustifiable, subjective assertions. If this were so, then it would be difficult to see how any importance could be attached to them, nor how they could possibly be a subject for debate (for on this view, you have your values, I have mine and that's an end to it!). The fact is that we do, quite naturally, distinguish between claims like: 'Broccoli is disgusting', which does seem down to the individual, and others like: 'Torture is evil', which seem to transcend individual opinions. To decide whether a value judgement is acceptable, we need to think about:

- Whose judgement it is: the opinion of an expert will usually carry greater weight than that of a layperson – for example, someone who might criticise a Picasso portrait for 'not looking like a normal human face'!
- Whether the judgement expresses a merely subjective opinion which it would be easy to disagree with (broccoli should be banned), or one that it would be hard/absurd not to agree with (torture should be banned).
- Whether it corresponds with popular belief. However, note that popular belief is not always reliable. One would like to think, for example, that few would argue that torture, on any grounds, was an acceptable practice. But this is not always the case.
- Whether there is evidence to back it up (although it is worth bearing in mind that such evidence could never constitute 'proof') – for example, the appalling effect torture has had on those who have experienced it.
- Whether it is supported by a strong principle – for example, torture is evil 'because it breaches our basic human rights' (more of this below).

Evaluating value judgements is a topic to which we will return in the next two chapters in particular and throughout the text as a whole. In the meantime, see if you can work through the following activities:

> Value judgements, whilst neither true nor false, often express more than just unjustified, subjective opinion. To evaluate a value judgement, we need to consider whose judgement it is, how easy it would be to disagree with, whether it corresponds with widely held beliefs, whether there is evidence to back it up and whether or not it is supported by a strong principle.

> Value judgements crop up, in one form or another, throughout the book. For further guidance on how to analyse, evaluate and incorporate them into your own reasoning see Ch. 2: 'Ethical' and 'aesthetic' areas of discourse; Ch. 4; Ch. 7; Ch. 12: 'Comparative evaluations', and Ch. 13.

Exercises

1. Decide which of the following claims state facts and which express value judgements:
    (a) If you want to get to school on time, you should take an earlier train.
    (b) Stephen Hawking is a genius.
    (c) Stephen Hawking has an IQ of over 160.
    (d) April is the cruellest month. (T.S. Eliot)

2. Taking into account:
    - the author and nature of the judgement
    - whether it corresponds with popular belief and/or a strong principle
    - whether it is (or could be) backed up by evidence

    (a) Identify the value judgement being made in each of the following examples and (b) come to a decision about how acceptable it is:
    (i) When I read something saying I've not done anything as good as *Catch-22* I'm tempted to reply, 'Who has?' (Joseph Heller – famous author)
    (ii) States like these [Iran, Iraq and North Korea], and their terrorist allies, constitute an axis of evil, arming to threaten the peace of the world. By seeking weapons of mass destruction,* these regimes pose a grave and growing danger. (George Bush, State of the Union Address, 29 January 2002) (*Only North Korea had such weapons.)

3. England haven't played that well since winning the World Cup in 1966. (Football pundit)

4. My kid could paint better than that! (Internet blog about Picasso)

RECOMMENDATIONS

Recommendations are prescriptive rather then factual; they are claims about what should (or should not) be done in any given situation. The claim 'the Government should ban smoking completely' is different from the claim 'the Government has banned smoking in all enclosed public spaces'. The latter claim is true whilst the former claim is neither true nor false: it recommends a particular course of action. Recommendations come in a wide variety of forms as the following examples should make clear:

- We ought to promote the teaching of Critical Thinking in schools and colleges across the UK.
- 'If you're not ready to die for it, take the word "freedom" out of your vocabulary.' (Malcolm X, *Chicago Defender*, 28 November 1962)
- 'Teenagers should be banned from drinking any alcohol before driving, to cut the number of accidents and deaths, public health experts have said.' (*Daily Telegraph*, December 2008)
- 'And so, my fellow Americans: ask not what your country can do for you – ask what you can do for your country.' (Inaugural Address by John F. Kennedy, 20 January 1961)
- 'The government should ban the teaching of religion in schools never mind creationism.' (Letter to the *TES*, November 2008)
- Save human lives, test on animals.

Evaluating recommendations

Recommendations in themselves then, are neither true nor false. We can, however, bring in further evidence of a truthful nature in favour of, or against, such claims. If it could be proved that studying Critical Thinking significantly raised student achievement in other subjects, then its promotion *should* be encouraged. If banning teenagers from drinking before driving substantially lowered road deaths, then arguably we *ought* to impose such a ban (but this ban clearly shouldn't be restricted to teenagers alone). If animal testing has successfully contributed to providing cures for numerous diseases (which it has) then this is a powerful argument for allowing it; but here we might have to appeal to a moral principle (see next section) such as 'human life is of greater value than animal life' in support of this claim. Alongside evidential support, we also need to think about what the various consequences would be if we followed a particular recommendation. If these can be regarded as broadly positive (and there is evidence to support this), then a recommendation can be regarded as acceptable; if not, then it can't.

As with value judgements, recommendations are neither true nor false. To evaluate them, you will need to consider what the consequences would be if you were to follow them. If these are broadly positive – and there is evidence to support this – then a recommendation will be acceptable. If not, then it won't.

Exercise

1. Thinking about:
    *   the type of evidence that could be brought in to strengthen or weaken the recommendation
    *   what the consequences would be if we followed it

    assess the persuasiveness of each of the following examples:

    (a)

    I ASKED HER WHAT SHE'D RECOMMEND AND SHE SAID THE RESTAURANT DOWN THE STREET WITH THE FOODSAFE EXCELLENCE CERTIFICATE ...

    (b) (Hotel review)

    Hotel Catalonia

    11/12 found this review helpful

    We just got back from the Hotel Catalonia a couple of days ago. First I want to say that I would definitely recommend this to my friends and family.

    Overall we had a great time at this resort. It was our first time here and 3rd time in Mexico

    (c) I wouldn't recommend sex, drugs or insanity for everyone, but they've always worked for me. (Hunter S. Thompson)

    (d) The proverb warns that 'You should not bite the hand that feeds you.' But maybe you should, if it prevents you from feeding yourself. (Thomas Szasz)

    (e) Everybody should eat five portions of fruit and veg a day.

STATEMENTS OF PRINCIPLE

A **statement of principle** is a basic rule, usually accepted as self-evidently true, which acts as a guideline for how we ought to behave.

Whereas recommendations are specific (and hence not like laws: they apply only to particular situations) a statement of principle applies to all situations. When I tell my son: 'It is wrong to throw jigsaw pieces at Nursery School staff' I am referring to a particular event. When I tell him: 'It is wrong to harm others (unnecessarily!)' I am making a general claim – i.e. one that applies beyond a particular circumstance. For this reason, statements of principle usually act as a justification for specific value judgements. Here are some further examples:

- 'That the only purpose for which power can be rightfully exercised over any member of a civilized community, against his will, is to prevent harm to others.' (John Stuart Mill's 'Harm Principle', *On Liberty*, Chapter 1)
- 'Happiness is the supreme good towards which all other human action should be directed.' (Paraphrased from book IV of Aristotle, *Nicomachean Ethics*)
- 'One should not behave towards others in a way which is disagreeable to oneself. This is the essence of morality.' (The Hindu *Mahabharata*)
- 'Thou shalt not kill, commit adultery [nor] steal.' (Old Testament, Exodus 20: Commandments 7, 8 and 9)
- 'Every man has the right to life, liberty and property.' (Paraphrased from John Locke's *Second Treaty on Government*)

The issue of principles is taken up in greater detail in Ch. 4 – see 'The principle of charity' – and also Ch. 13, where a discussion of how to incorporate these into your own reasoning is given.

statement of principle – A basic rule, usually accepted as self-evidently true, which acts as a guideline for how we ought to behave

Evaluating statements of principle

Because different principles require different methods of assessment, the first question you will need to ask yourself is 'What *kind* of principle is it that we are dealing with?' This isn't always as clear as it could be. Sometimes a principle may remain hidden or assumed and thus will need drawing out:

- Smoking is bad for your health so you should quit.

Here the reasoning only works if we supply the implied but hidden principle that 'if something is bad for your health, you shouldn't do it'.

In order to evaluate a principle, you will need to think about whether or not it admits of exception. The fewer of these that can be found, the stronger the principle will be.

At other times, the same principle can be understood in more than one way. Whereas:

- One should not commit adultery.

is clearly a moral principle, but not necessarily a legal one:

- One should not kill.

is a principle which has both moral *and* legal connotations and would need to be evaluated accordingly. The farmer Tony Martin, who in 1999 unintentionally shot dead a teenager attempting to burgle his house, received a ten-year custodial sentence for his actions (commuted to three years on appeal). There was a public outcry over the verdict as many thought the deed was morally, if not legally, justified. Killing on a battlefield, on the other hand, may well be regarded as a legal, but not a moral, act. The conscientious objectors of World War Two objected to going to war on these grounds. Often the only way to settle a dispute about which way a principle is being used is to think about the context in which it is being applied. Here you will have to use a bit of common sense.

A second issue that you will need to think about is this: because a statement of principle is a general claim which applies not just to specific, but to all, cases (when I say 'killing is wrong' I do not mean 'killing is wrong in this instance', I mean killing is wrong, full stop) in order to evaluate it you will need to judge how well it applies to other situations beyond the one in hand. The principle:

- One should *always* tell the truth.

could be objected to because, in certain situations, lying may well be the appropriate course of action. For example, responding in the negative to the question 'am I putting on weight?' so as to avoid hurting someone's feelings; a doctor telling a patient suffering from a fatal disease 'you're going to be fine'; a captured soldier who lies to the enemy about the position of troops in order to save lives. These are all examples of cases where lying might be regarded as 'acceptable' (although some may disagree!) and reflecting on such cases may well force us to reconsider our original principle. Generally speaking, the harder it is to find exceptions for a principle, the stronger that principle will be.

Exercises

1. Explain the following principles in your own words:
    (a) I may not agree with what you say, but I will defend with my life your right to say it. (attributed to Voltaire)
    (b) Every individual has the right to a fair trial. (Human Rights Act article 6)
    (c) **Golf course attire**
         Members and Guests are expected to wear the appropriate golf attire. MEN – Men are to wear slacks and shirts with collars or turtlenecks or mock turtlenecks. Shirts must be tucked in on the Golf Course and all practice areas. Shorts are permitted on the Golf Course as long as they are no shorter than five inches (5") above the bend at the back of the knee or nineteen inches (19") in total length and no longer than the bottom of the kneecap. Billed hats must be worn bill forward. (Santa Ana Golf Course dress code)
    (d) Do unto others as you would have them do unto you. (Jesus)
    (e) It is allowed on all hands, that the primitive way of breaking eggs, before we eat them, was upon the larger end; but his present majesty's grandfather, while he was a boy, going to eat an egg, and breaking it according to the ancient practice, happened to cut one of his fingers. Whereupon the emperor his father published an edict, commanding all his subjects, upon great penalties, to break the smaller end of their eggs. (Jonathan Swift, *Gulliver's Travels*)

2. What kind of principle is it – e.g. Moral? Legal? Religious? Etc.

3. Try to provide at least one counter-example for each principle and refine the principle itself in light of this.

ALLEGATIONS

An **allegation** is a claim which is (usually) used to accuse someone of something, the truth of which has yet to be proved. You will often come across examples of these in newspapers or news reports when it is believed someone is guilty of something, but this has not been established:

> **allegation** – A claim made to accuse somebody of something, the truth of which has yet to be established.

The Independent Police Complaints Commission has today provided an update on the investigation into allegations made in BBC TV's 'The Boys who Killed Stephen Lawrence'. The IPCC is investigating two allegations made in the documentary. The first is that 1 <u>an officer, or officers, who worked on the original murder investigation may have been involved in a corrupt relationship with the father of one of the murder suspects</u> and, secondly, that 2 <u>this claim had been reported to the Metropolitan Police Service but not investigated or passed on to the Stephen Lawrence public inquiry</u>. (IPCC, 5 April 2007)

Here, the allegations (underlined) must have *some* evidence to support them, but this is, as of yet, inconclusive.

Evaluating allegations

In order to test whether an accusation is strong, we need to think about the nature and amount of evidence there is in support of it. A claim made on the basis of hearsay or rumour, for example:

- 'I heard the boss is taking out Jenny from accounts on Friday. She must be looking for a promotion!'

will clearly be weaker than the claim:

- 'Nicolás Leoz, a Fifa executive committee member and long-serving president of Conmebol, the South American football confederation, is said to have been sent bribes totalling SFr211,625 (£90,000) in two separate payments in January and May 2000.' (*The Guardian*, 26 October 2006)

The first claim lacks substantial support. Even if the first part of the allegation could be proved, it wouldn't automatically follow that Jenny was only going out with the boss because this might further her chances of promotion. Maybe she was at a loose end and had nothing better to do. The second claim, on the other hand, is specific, has substantial evidential support (documents received by *The Guardian* showing bank payments received by Nicolás Leoz made by the company in charge of television rights for the 2002 and 2006 World Cups) and was made by a Swiss magistrate whose credibility would be at stake if the allegation were shown to be unfounded.

Similarly to predictions and hypotheses, to evaluate an allegation you will need to think about how precisely it is stated; whether or not there is substantial evidential support to back it up, and, finally, the reliability of the source making the claim.

The issue of credibility is taken up in greater detail in Ch. 15: 'Motive and agenda' and 'Sources'.

Exercises

1. Taking into account:
    *   the nature and amount of support
    *   the author/source of the claim
    place the following allegations in order of their plausibility:
    (a) The recent revelation about MPs' expenses shows that MPs are only interested in feathering their own nests, not running the country.
    (b) Some of the world's top climate scientists have been accused of manipulating data on global warming after hundreds of private emails were stolen by hackers and published online. (*Daily Telegraph*)
    (c) He's wearing a long beard so he must be a terrorist.
    (d) A report by a former consultant to the Afghan Ministry of Mines and Industry regarding the Aynak Copper Tender has generated allegations that Afghanistan's Mines Minister took either a $20 million or $30 million bribe to award the development of Aynak to a Chinese firm. (www.mineweb.com)

2. For each example, explain what evidence would be required in order to validate the allegation.

SOME CONCLUDING COMMENTS

The specification points out that:

> in practice, claims often overlap. For instance, a hypothesis may consist of a prediction or an explanation ('We can confidently expect numbers in Critical Thinking will continue to rise due to the number of Universities that now require students to sit a CT entrance exam'); an allegation may involve a value judgement' ('you stand accused of the heinous crime of attacking a defenceless old lady') and so on. Nor is this an exhaustive list.

As you continue with your studies, you will need to develop and refine your vocabulary to take these points into account.

Summary questions . . .

1.   What is meant by the term 'claim'?
2.   Offer your own, brief explanation for each of the following types of claim:
   • a prediction
   • a hypothesis
   • a statement of principle
   • a definition
   • a causal explanation
   • a recommendation
   • an allegation
   • a value judgement

END OF CHAPTER ACTIVITY

Read through the following passage (adapted from I. Loudon, *Ignaz Phillip Semmelweis' Studies of Death in Childbirth*, 2002) and identify:

1.   A prediction
2.   A hypothesis
3.   A causal explanation
4.   A definition

In 1846, Ignaz Phillip Semmelweis (1818–1865), who was born in Hungary, was appointed to what was then by far the largest maternity hospital in the world: the Vienna Maternity Hospital, which was divided into two clinics. Doctors and medical students were taught in the first clinic, midwives in the second, and patients were allocated to the clinics on alternate days. There was no clinical selection of cases for either clinic. From 1840 through 1846, the maternal mortality rate in the first clinic was 98.4 per 1,000 births, while the rate in the second clinic, the midwives clinic, was only 36.2 per 1,000 births. Almost all the maternal deaths were due to puerperal fever, a fever which is brought about by an infection of the uterus following childbirth or abortion. The alarmingly high mortality in the first clinic had defied explanation until Semmelweis was appointed and postulated that the excess deaths in the first clinic were due to the routine procedures carried out in the courses attended by doctors and medical students. Each day started with the carrying out of post-mortems on women who had died of puerperal fever. Then, without washing their hands, the pupils went straight to the maternity wards where they were required, as part of their training, to undertake vaginal examinations on all the women. The pupil midwives in the second clinic did not, of course, carry out post-mortem examinations, and did not undertake routine vaginal examinations.

This was many years before the role of bacteria in diseases was discovered, and Semmelweis suggested that the training procedures of the first clinic resulted in the transfer from the corpses of what he first called 'morbid matter', and later 'decomposing animal organic matter', on the hands of the students. In 1847, he therefore introduced a system whereby the students were required to wash their hands in chloride of lime before entering the maternity ward. This, he claimed, would significantly lower the death rate caused by the transferal of bacteria. The result was dramatic. In 1848, the maternal mortality rate in the first clinic fell to 12.7 in the first clinic compared with 13.3 in the second clinic. The process of admission to the two clinics on alternate days produced, by accident rather than design, a controlled trial, and the large numbers of deliveries (from 1840 through 1846 there were 42,795 births and 2,977 maternal deaths in the two clinics) mean that chance could confidently be excluded as a possible explanation for the differences observed.

5. The claim: 'Almost all the maternal deaths were due to puerperal fever, a fever which is brought about by an infection of the uterus following childbirth or abortion' can be understood in two different ways; what are they?

6. How convincing do you find the final claim in the passage – that chance could be excluded as a possible (causal) explanation for the differences observed? Give reasons for your answer.

7. 'Semmelweis' observations were clinically astute and potentially of great practical importance. But Semmelweis was a complex, difficult, and dogmatic man.' (Ibid.) What sort of claim does the second half of this statement make?

8. Provide your own statement of principle which could be used to explain Semmelweis' desire to eradicate this disease.

Newspaper articles offer an excellent source of material for this section of the course. www.paperarticles.com contains links to thousands of articles on a variety of topics, all listed alphabetically. You can use these to practise identifying, analysing and evaluating claims from a wide range of contexts.

SUMMARY CHECKLIST

Points you need to remember:

✔ What is meant by the term 'claim'.

✔ The different types of claim that can be made: predictions, hypotheses, statements of principle, definitions, causal explanations, recommendations, allegations and value judgements.

✔ How you must go about assessing each of these.

FOUNDATION UNIT

Chapter 4: Analysing and interpreting arguments

LEARNING OBJECTIVES

By the end of this chapter you should:

✔ Be able to analyse the underlying structure of an argument by placing it into diagrammatic form.
✔ Understand the two ways in which reasons function dependently and independently of each other ('T' diagrams and 'V' diagrams).
✔ Understand the difference between 'simple' and 'complex' arguments.
✔ Be able to apply the above skills of analysis to more authentic 'real/live' arguments.
✔ Understand what is meant by the term 'principle of charity' and when to apply it.

Before you can evaluate a particular argument, you will first need to analyse its underlying structure. This will reveal the reasoning involved and indicate how it should be processed. The simplest method of doing this is to list the premises and separate them from the conclusion using a horizontal line:

[P1] Socrates is a man

[P2] All men are mortal

_____

[c] Therefore Socrates is mortal

But this, on its own, doesn't show us how the premises actually *function* – whether they work *together* or *independently* of one another and how they bring about the conclusion of the argument.

THE STRUCTURE OF SIMPLE ARGUMENTS

A better way of exposing the hidden structure of reasoning is to lay it out in diagrammatic form. For our example above, this can be done as follows:

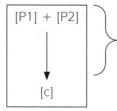

Here the '+' sign tells us that premises [P1] 'Socrates is a man' + [P2] 'All men are mortal' are *dependent* upon each other and hence *jointly* support the conclusion. If either of these were missing, the inference [c] 'Therefore Socrates is mortal' could not be drawn. To see why this is so, try to see if either P1 or P2 support the conclusion on their own. For example, does the premise 'Socrates is a man' support the conclusion that he is mortal? You will quickly find that it only does this if you build in the premise that 'all men are mortal' (P2). Conversely, arguing 'all men are mortal', therefore 'Socrates is mortal' only works if we build in the premise 'Socrates is a man'. Such examples, for obvious reasons, are often referred to as 'T' diagrams.

If we were to change our initial argument, like so:

[P1] Socrates gets no exercise

[P2] Socrates drinks excessively

_____

[c] Therefore Socrates is unhealthy

We can then reveal the second way in which premises are used to support a conclusion:

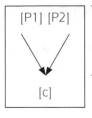

Here, what makes such premises different from the first kind is that each one can support the conclusion on its own, quite independently of the other premise – although the other functions to reinforce the conclusion. We could, in fact, subtract either premise, and the inference, though weakened, would still be acceptable. Such examples are often referred to as 'V' diagrams, although obviously more than two premises can feature in this type of argument, or even just a single premise, as we have seen.

The difference between these two types of argument is important when it comes to assessment. With 'T' diagrams, because both premises are *dependent* upon one another, if one of them is false, then the argument will fail. With 'V' diagrams, on the other hand, because the premises work independently of one another, it is still possible for one of these to be false without affecting the overall validity of the argument, as long as the other premise/s are sufficiently strong. For example, if Socrates went to the gym every morning, then P1 would be false, even though the conclusion might still be true thanks to the truth of P2.

Exercises

1. Put the following two arguments into diagrammatic form (one is a 'T' and the other a 'V' type argument):
    (a) The treating of smoking-related illnesses has become a tremendous drain on NHS resources. This money would be better spent elsewhere. We need a complete ban on cigarettes.
    (b) Banning smoking in public spaces infringes on the civil liberties of smokers. It also unjustifiably demonises a minority group. We need to resort back to the good old days where smokers could indulge in their habit wherever and whenever they liked.

2. Create your own simple argument for each of the diagrams:

THE STRUCTURE OF COMPLEX ARGUMENTS

The above examples are straightforward. They both contain premises which *directly* support (either dependently or independently) the conclusion that the argument is trying to get us to accept. Arguments, however, are often more complex than this, involving **sub-arguments** and **intermediate conclusions** which then go on to act as support for the main argument, the conclusion of which is the ultimate point an argument is trying to get us to accept:

> Most prospective parents would prefer to have sons. Therefore, if the choice is made available, due to advances in technology, it is likely that eventually there will be many more males than females in the population. This would result in serious social problems, so we should prohibit the development of techniques which enable people to choose the sex of their children. (AQA specification)

Here, the initial premise:

> P1: Most prospective parents would prefer to have sons.

only *indirectly* supports the final conclusion. It *directly* supports an intermediate conclusion:

> IC: If the choice is made available … it is likely that there will be many more males than females in the population.

which then goes on to act as support, alongside a further premise:

> P2: This would result in serious social problems.

for the *main* conclusion:

> MC: So we should prohibit the development of techniques which enable people to choose the sex of their children.

which is the *main* point the argument is trying to get us to accept. As such, the argument is *complex*. This should become clearer if we present its structure in diagrammatic form:

sub-argument – Offers *direct* support for an intermediate conclusion which in turn goes on to offer support for a main conclusion.

intermediate conclusion – The conclusion of a sub-argument which goes on to offer support for the main conclusion - the ultimate point the argument is trying to get us to accept. For this reason, an intermediate conclusion functions both as a conclusion (for a sub-argument) and as a premise (for the main argument).

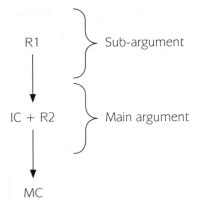

You should be able to see that the reasoning presents us with two arguments. The first, referred to as the 'sub' argument, is used as a foundation for the main argument. The initial conclusion from the sub-argument is referred to as the 'intermediate' (or sometimes 'interim' or 'subordinate') conclusion because it is not what the passage is *ultimately* trying to persuade us of, but rather a link in a longer 'chain of reasoning'. The intermediate conclusion then itself becomes a reason which acts as *support* for the main conclusion of the argument. A very useful method for discriminating between an intermediate and a main conclusion (and hence a sub-argument from a main one) is to place each conclusion alongside each other in order to see which supports which. One combination will make little sense because it puts the cart before the horse:

- We should prohibit the development of techniques which enable people to choose the sex of their children.

Therefore ...

- If the choice is made available ... it is likely that there will be many more males than females in the population.

Whereas the second combination clearly creates an argument:

- If the choice is made available ... it is likely that there will be many more males than females in the population.

Therefore ...

- We should prohibit the development of techniques which enable people to choose the sex of their children.

Once you have understood (a) the two ways in which reasons (premises) function, (b) the difference between intermediate and main conclusions, sub-arguments and main arguments and finally (c) how to analyse the structure of these arguments by presenting them in diagrammatic form, you will then be able to apply this knowledge to more complex chains of reasoning. This is an essential first step to beginning the process of evaluation which we will develop in Chapter 6.

Exercises

1. Analyse the reasoning involved in the following two arguments by putting it into diagrammatic form:

    (a) When the mathematical laws of probability are applied to the known facts of biology, the odds against the incredible, organised complexity of our biological world evolving through blind chance, plus time, are so astronomical in size that, for all practical purposes, evolution is mathematically impossible. In fact, the more we discover about the incredibly intricate, organised complexity of the biological world which exists at the molecular level, the more amazing it is that the evolutionist can actually believe it is all a product of pure blind chance over time. The 'intelligent design' model, based upon a Divine Creator, makes much more sense. (Frank L. Caw Jr, *A Short Summary of Fundamental Scientific Arguments Against Evolution*: www.frankcaw.com/science.html)

    (b) At the end of the 1990s, Dr Valerie Curtis of the London School of Hygiene and Tropical Medicine began to survey people in different countries to find out what things they found disgusting. Curtis uncovered some interesting cultural peculiarities. For example, food cooked by a menstruating woman was a frequent cause of disgust in India, while fat people scored highly as disgusting in the Netherlands.

    Although culture had a small role to play in what we find disgusting, overall, people kept reporting the same things as revolting wherever they were from. Curtis concluded that responses to disgust were therefore not culture specific, but rather universal. It seems that whether we live in Islington or Isla Pinta, Margate or Marrakech, we are all disgusted by:

- Bodily secretions - faeces (poo), vomit, sweat, spit, blood, pus, sexual fluids
- Body parts - wounds, corpses, toenail clippings
- Decaying food - especially rotting meat and fish, rubbish
- Certain living creatures - flies, maggots, lice, worms, rats, dogs and cats
- People who are ill, contaminated

2. Create your own 'complex' argument for each of the following diagrams. R = reason, IC = intermediate conclusion and MC = main conclusion (challenging!):

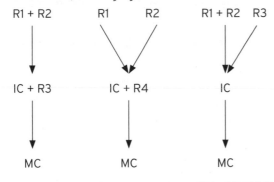

'REAL' OR 'LIVE' ARGUMENTS

Many of the examples we have looked at so far have been engineered for the purposes of clarity and simplicity. However, arguments, as we encounter them in real life, are rarely this simple. That is not to say 'real' arguments don't exhibit a similar kind of structure to the ones we *have* been looking at; nor is the value of the examples that we have been looking at in any way lessened by their artificial nature (we all need to start somewhere!), but what it shows is that, as your reasoning skills develop, you will need to learn how to apply them to more authentic and complex texts both inside and outside the classroom. It is beyond the scope of this book to reveal fully how this is done (Alec Fisher's *The Logic of Real Argument* (Cambridge, 2004) does an admirable job here) but looking at an example will help you understand both the method of analysis and the importance of this enterprise.

The following is adapted from *Nuclear Power: The End of the War against Japan* by Professor Duncan Anderson on the nuclear bomb dropped on Hiroshima, Japan, by America in 1945 which appears, in full, at http://www.bbc.co.uk/history/worldwars/wwtwo/nuclear_01.shtml.

(1) The first to arrive on the scene witnessed 'thousands of hideously burnt people … huddled in shanties, coughing up and urinating blood … waiting to die'. (Anderson)

(2) John Hersey, a journalist reporting for *The New Yorker* in Japan at the end of the conflict, told the story of the devastating events through a study of the plight of six survivors.

(3) His story was published in 1946, the same year that the United States Army Air Forces published a report on the effects of strategic bombing on Japan. It found that Japan had already been severely weakened by conventional attacks.

(4) The report stated: 'it is the Survey's opinion that certainly prior to 31 December 1945, and in all probability prior to 1 November 1945 (well before the date of the invasion) Japan would have surrendered even if the atomic bombs had not been dropped'.

(5) By the mid-1960s, influenced by the onset of the Cold War, the Vietnam conflict and the US's development of the hydrogen bomb, academics, including Gar Alperovitz, were challenging the legitimacy of the use of the atomic bomb in their work.

(6) Alperovitz and others maintained that the test firing of the first atomic bomb was a demonstration of power by Truman, who was negotiating with the Russians. Truman, to ensure the Japanese would not capitulate before the bombs could be used, refused the demands of the Japanese that he guarantee the emperor's safety.

(7) They argued 'it was not the bombs that produced Japan's surrender … but the Soviet invasion of Manchuria on 9 August. Truman and his administration, then, had been guilty of an act of callous, wanton brutality … to no purpose other than to intimidate the Soviet Union.'

> ## Exercise
>
> 1. **Stretching activity:** See if you can extract the argument presented in paragraphs 3-7 by (a) identifying the intermediate conclusion and the reasons used to support it and (b) the main conclusion and the reasons used to support it. Once you have done this, check your analysis with the one offered below (don't look before you've had a go!). Remember that asking 'what is this passage trying to get me to accept?' will help you to identify the conclusions, whilst asking 'what grounds are provided for why I should be persuaded?' will lead you to the reasons. The main conclusion will be the ultimate point of which the argument is trying to persuade, whilst the intermediate conclusion will provide further support for this claim.

Without going into too much detail (you will not be required to analyse a passage such as this in the exam!) the overall conclusion that this passage attempts to get us to accept is that the *real* reason for America dropping the bomb (contrary to the American justification that it was 'a necessary step to end the Second World War') was to:

MC: intimidate the Soviet Union

Working backwards, the premises offered in support of this claim (the *main* argument) are:

R1: The test firing of the first atomic bomb was a demonstration of power by Truman, who was negotiating with the Russians.

R2: Truman, to ensure the Japanese would not capitulate before the bombs could be used, refused the demands of the Japanese that he guarantee the emperor's safety.

R3: it was not the bombs that produced Japan's surrender but the Soviet invasion of Manchuria on 9 August.

The main argument is supported by a sub-argument, the conclusion of which *predicts*:

IC: Japan *would* have surrendered even if the atomic bombs had not been dropped.

And the reason and evidence provided in support of this claim are:

R1: the United States Army Air Forces published a report on the effects of strategic bombing on Japan [evidence].

R2: It found that Japan had already been severely weakened by conventional attacks.

Don't let this example put you off! It is only offered to show you that the skills we have been practising can be applied to longer, more authentic and complex passages. See if you can break down the following, more simple examples into reasons and conclusions (they are all genuine). You might find that summarising these in your own words simplifies this task. You will also need to apply the principle of charity (see next section) to the final example:

- 'Our greatest primary task is to put people to work. This is no unsolvable problem if we face it wisely and courageously.' (Franklin D. Roosevelt's 'we have nothing to fear but fear itself' speech)
- 'If you are living comfortably while others are hungry or dying from easily preventable diseases, and you are doing nothing about it, there is something wrong with your behaviour.' (Peter Singer, 'Humility Kills', *Jewcy*, May 2007)
- 'South Africa preaches separation and practises separation. America preaches integration and practises segregation. This is the only difference. They don't practise what they preach ... I have more respect for a man who lets me know where he stands, even if he's wrong, than one who comes up like an angel and is nothing but a devil.' (Malcolm X, Oxford Union Debate, 3 December 1964)

THE PRINCIPLE OF CHARITY

A critical thinker is an objective thinker whose thoughts do not become clouded by emotion, self-interest or dogmatism. Yet regrettably, as was pointed out at the start of the book, the desire to win arguments often trumps the obligation to get at the truth. When this occurs, as we shall see with the 'straw-man fallacy', reasoning backfires.

The **principle of charity** is an implicit rule that critical thinkers need to abide by in order to avoid this happening. The principle states that, when confronted with a piece of reasoning that allows for more than one interpretation, we ought always choose the more charitable or persuasive one and assume its author, being a rational individual, would have intended it so:

> We make maximum sense of the words and thoughts of others when we interpret in a way that optimises agreement. (Donald Davidson, *Inquiries into Truth and Interpretation*, Oxford, 1984, Ch. 13)

To condense, we must treat the arguments of others as we should like them to treat our own. But how is this principle applied? Well, sometimes we will stumble across examples of reasoning that, at first blush, appear to contain no argument whatsoever – at least not in the *critical* sense:

JL: But, just say that there is a God, what color is he? White or black?

Larry: Well, if it is a God … I wouldn' know what color, I couldn' say – couldn' nobody say what –

JL: But now, jus' suppose there was a God –

Larry: Unless'n they say…

JL: No, I was jus' sayin' jus' suppose there is a God, would he be white or black?

Larry: He'd be white, man.

JL: Why?

Larry: Why? I'll tell you why. 'Cause the average whitey out here got everything, you dig? And the nigger ain't got shit, y'know? Y'unnerstan'? So – um – for – in order for that to happen, you know it ain't no black God that's doin' that bullshit.

This is an extract taken from an essay by the linguist William Labov (*Lanuage in the Inner City*, Philadelphia, 1973, p. 217). The words are spoken by 'Larry', a young black gang-member, who is providing a justification for his **'hypothetical'** claim that '*if* God exists, he must be white'. Superficially, it appears to be nothing over and above a foul-mouthed rant, but when analysed charitably it actually contains quite a powerful argument:

principle of charity – The principle of charity dictates that, when an argument admits of more than one interpretation, we should always choose the more charitable/ persuasive one.

It directly contrasts with the 'straw-man' fallacy – see Ch. 11 – which deliberately sets up an argument in its weakest form in order to knock it down. It is a classic example of a 'statement of principle' – see Ch. 3.

hypothetical claim – This takes the form of an if … then … statement. Hypothetical claims are a useful tool because they allow us to consider the consequences of an argument without having to establish the truth of its premises. For example, we can understand the content and implications of the claim that 'if God exists then he must be white', without having to prove God's existence.

> R1: The white man has everything.
>
> R2: The black man has nothing.
>
> C: In order for that to happen, and assuming he exists, God cannot be black (hence he must be white).

which we need to make an effort to expose. Interestingly enough, Larry's reasoning is contrasted with that of 'Charles', a middle-class, well-educated, 'standard-English' speaker. The reasoning Charles presents is superficially more eloquent, well structured and powerful than Larry's, but when analysed carefully, actually contains no argument whatsoever! Looks can often be deceiving:

> CR: Do you know of anything that someone can do, to have someone who has passed on visit him in a dream?
>
> Chas M: Well, I even heard my parents say that there is such a thing as something in dreams, some things like that, and sometimes dreams do come true. I have personally never had a dream come true. I've never dreamt that somebody was dying and they actually died (Mhm), or that I was going to have ten dollars the next day and somehow I got ten dollars in my pocket. (Mhm.) I don't particularly believe in that, I don't think it's true. I do feel, though, that there is such a thing as – ah – witchcraft. I do feel that in certain cultures there is such a thing as witchcraft, or some sort of science of witchcraft; I don't think that it's just a matter of believing hard enough that there is such a thing as witchcraft. I do believe that there is such a thing that a person can put himself in a state of mind (Mhm), or that – er – something could be given them to intoxicate them in a certain – to a certain frame of mind – that – that could actually be considered witchcraft.

A second way in which the principle can be applied is to ensure that we do not read an argument into a piece of reasoning that was not intended. It might be the case, for example, that an author merely wishes to express an opinion, commend a particular course of action, make an accusation etc. These may well bear a passing resemblance to argument (i.e. we might read them as drawing an inference from a premise or set of premises) but, if the author did not so intend, then such an interpretation would violate the principle of charity:

Astronomy is not astrology. Astrology is nonsense. The idea that our lives can be affected by the flight of planets is not even slightly plausible. (Conn Iggulden and Hal Iggulden, *The Dangerous Book for Boys*, London, 2007.)

Here, claiming the authors are presenting a case for the absurdity of astrology would be doing them a disservice. It would be more charitable to suppose, and no doubt more in line with their *actual* intention, that this latter point is assumed and thus does not need arguing for. As such, the passage should not be read as an argument.

The principle can also be applied to ensure we interpret an opponent's reasoning in its strongest possible form. This is often not the form in which a claim or argument is originally presented. If we look back to one of our previous examples from an exam:

Jed: All I can say is that's not art.

We could interpret this claim in one of two ways. Firstly, in its literal sense, we could take it to mean that Jed really believes the example (two skeletons under a pub table) is not an artwork. But this would be absurd. The fact that it is presented in an art exhibition, created by a renowned artist etc. should be enough to convince us of this. A more charitable interpretation might be that what Jed is *really* saying is that it's not *good* art. There is a clear difference. Because this first interpretation is so easily refuted, the principle of charity forces us to accept the second, more sympathetic one. This is no doubt more in line with Jed's original intention. Examples such as these are rife:

- I hate you. (Uttered to a parent by a hysterical toddler!)
- Abortion is wrong. (But in every case?)
- Animals should be given equal rights. (The same rights as humans? To vote? Own property?!)

And are usually fairly easy to interpret:

- I am angry with you.
- Aborting a potentially healthy child, which prevents no health risks to the mother, is wrong.
- Animals should be given the right to protection.

> This point is of particular significance when a word or expression is 'vague' or 'ambiguous' – see Ch. 9.

The principle of charity can often be applied to 'live' arguments (see this chapter), 'embedded' arguments (see Ch. 1) and 'dialogic reasoning' (ditto) where the reasoning employed often lacks the kind of clarity and precision that we come to expect of arguments that have been carefully constructed on paper (or engineered for the purposes of critical thinking!).

Ultimately, the principle involves actively seeking out weaknesses in one's own reasoning by looking at the strongest arguments against the views that we hold and a generosity of interpretation towards the reasoning of others. This is the essence of thinking objectively.

Summary questions . . .

1. Briefly explain what is meant by the terms 'T' and 'V' diagram. How are they different?
2. What is the difference between a simple and a complex argument? How do intermediate conclusions help us distinguish between the two?
3. Explain the principle of charity. When should it be applied?

END OF CHAPTER ACTIVITY

Read through the following examples and offer (a) an uncharitable interpretation and (b) a charitable one. Which do you think most satisfactorily captures the author's intention? Why?

1. The weather forecast always gets it wrong.
2. If Germany invades Poland, we have no option other than to go to war.
3. The anti-social behaviour of young people on this Midlands estate shows that we live in a broken society.

SUMMARY CHECKLIST

Points you need to remember:

✔ How to analyse an argument into diagrammatic form.

✔ The difference between 'T' and 'V' arguments/diagrams.

✔ The difference between simple and complex arguments.

✔ What the principle of charity is and when/how it should be applied.

www. criticalthinking. org.uk/ not only has a range of good explanations, examples and activities to work through, but there are also links to a range of 'live' documents and articles that you can use in order to practise your skills of analysis.

UNIT 1   # FOUNDATION UNIT

Chapter 5: Assumptions

LEARNING OBJECTIVES ✔

By the end of this chapter you should:

✔ Understand what is meant by the term 'assumption'.

✔ Understand why some assumptions are unproblematic but why others force us to question the legitimacy of a piece of reasoning.

The final thing we need to look at before addressing the all-important task of evaluating arguments is the nature of '**assumption**'. An explicit assumption is a claim put forward which lacks evidential support. These claims often function as essential premises in an argument:

> [P1] Most people in England believe in God.
>
> [C] Therefore we ought to promote the teaching of religion in English schools.

The 'reasonable' assumption here: 'most people believe in God', is explicit and is used to support the conclusion that religion should be taught in schools. But the initial claim is only stated; no evidence or reasons are provided to support it. Of course, such material *could* be provided (for example, in the last national census, 72% of Britons declared themselves 'Christian'), in which case it would no longer be an assumption. But this point is left *tacit*; it is merely *assumed*. Not all assumptions are explicit though (in fact most aren't). If we think about the inference 'therefore we ought to promote the teaching of religion in schools', we can ask if this really follows from the initial premise. In fact, the 'implicit' (i.e. unstated) assumption that

assumption – An (often unstated) part of an argument which is needed for the conclusion to be drawn. Many assumptions are **legitimate** (i.e. acceptable and unproblematic). When an argument depends upon an **illegitimate** (i.e. unacceptable) assumption, we have good reason for rejecting its inference.

For more on this topic, see Ch. 8: 'Additional evidence'.

For more on this topic, see Ch. 11 – the fallacy of 'appealing to popular opinion'.

An *explicit* assumption appears as a *stated*, but *unsupported*, part of an argument. An *implicit* assumption, on the other hand, will be unstated. This distinction is important as you could be required to identify either in an exam.

Identifying assumptions and judging whether or not they are legitimate is key to the process of argument analysis and evaluation. Many questions in the exam will ask you to 'identify an assumption' and 'assess whether or not it is legitimate'.

it *does* follow is even *less* convincing than the previous explicit one for it would only be valid if we accept the implicit premise that: 'the majority of people believing in something is evidence enough for the promotion of that thing being taught'. But this is not so. Many predominantly religious countries, for example France and Turkey, promote secularism (non-religion) in matters of education and politics. That the majority of people believe in God no more entails that religion should be taught in schools than it entails that God exists! Majority views are often unreliable. That the majority of people, until a few hundred years ago, believed that the Earth was flat and at the centre of the universe should be enough to convince us of this! For the above inference to be valid then, alternative grounds need to be provided which offer more stable foundations.

THE IMPORTANCE OF ASSUMPTIONS

The importance of identifying assumptions should not be overlooked. This is because, if a piece of reasoning depends upon an illegitimate assumption (or assumptions), then clearly we have solid grounds for rejecting it. That doesn't mean that the conclusion it presents us with will necessarily be false, nor that legitimate reasons might not be provided that *would* provide adequate grounds of support, but rather that assumptions, in their untested state, are insufficient for doing this.

But what constitutes adequate grounds here? The majority of arguments depend upon assumptions that are so obvious they hardly need stating. For example:

- Smoking is bad for your health.
- Therefore you should quit.

The reasoning here depends upon the assumption (usually referred to as a 'suppressed' middle premise) that:

- If something is bad for your health, you quit it.

But this is all but self-evident. If this were the only assumption on which the reasoning depended, then it would be difficult to understand why so many people in the world *do* continue to smoke despite the health risks (or drink alcohol, eat unhealthy food etc!). But it isn't. There are other, more subtle and questionable assumptions at play here that undermine the argument's general legitimacy. These include:

- That smokers value their health *more* than they value the pleasures of smoking.
- That the desire for good health is greater than the addiction to nicotine.
- That smoking is a *rational*, rather than a *compulsive*, habit (etc.)!

and these are far more problematic. If we were to lay the original argument out, making such assumptions explicit, like so:

[P1] Smoking is bad for your health.

[P2] If you value your health more than you value the pleasures of smoking and

[P3] Your desire for good health is greater than your addiction to nicotine and

[P4] Smoking is a rational, rather than compulsive habit (etc.)

[C] Then you should quit!

We can see that the original argument is considerably weakened! Identifying assumptions, then, is one of the most effective ways of testing whether or not an inference is valid. It is not surprising, however, that authors often fail to draw our attention to these. This is because they often undermine the position being argued for. If an author fails to expose and test his or her assumptions (either intentionally or unintentionally) then it is the job of the critical thinker to do so on their behalf.

Summary questions . . .

1. What is meant by the term 'assumption'?
2. Why is the identification of assumptions an important task when judging whether or not a piece of reasoning is effective?

To identify an assumption, you will first need to judge whether an argument (a) contains an inference which follows unproblematically from the premises provided or (b) depends upon further 'hidden' premises not supplied. If (b), then identifying these premises will reveal the assumptions.

To assess whether an assumption is legitimate you will need to consider whether the assumption is (a) so obvious it does not need stating, (b) unstated but unproblematic (i.e. it would be easy to provide grounds of support for) or (c) unstated *and* problematic (i.e. it would be difficult to provide grounds of support for) – see activity 1.

The issue of assumptions is taken up again in the end of unit exam chapter.

END OF CHAPTER ACTIVITY

1. For each of the following examples, identify (a) at least one assumption being made and (b) come to a reasoned decision about whether or not it is acceptable. Remember, some assumptions are so obvious and acceptable that they do not need stating ('get down, he's shooting!') whilst others are more subtle and problematic ('he hasn't got a decent alibi, he must be guilty'). It is this latter type for which we need to be on guard.

   • Smoking cannabis causes dangerous physical and psychological side effects, so it should be kept illegal.

   • Homosexuality violates the laws laid down in the Bible, therefore it is immoral.

   • 'Look out, there's a polar bear behind you!'

   • The majority of Britons are opposed to the death penalty so it should not be reinstated.

   • Homer Simpson: 'Not a bear in sight. The "Bear Patrol" must be working like a charm!'

2. Stretching activity: Read through the following (adapted from the Law Schools Admissions Test [LSAT]) and answer the question presented at the end of the passage:

   Studies of fatal automobile accidents reveal that, in the majority of cases in which one occupant of an automobile is killed while another survives, it is the passenger, not the driver, who is killed. It is ironic that the innocent passenger should suffer for the driver's carelessness, while the driver often suffers only minor injuries or none at all.

   Which of the following is an assumption underlying the reasoning in the passage above?

   (a) In most fatal automobile accidents, the driver of a car in which an occupant is killed is at fault.

   (b) Drivers of automobiles are rarely killed in auto accidents.

   (c) Most deaths in fatal automobile accidents are suffered by occupants of cars rather than by pedestrians.

   (d) Auto safety experts should increase their efforts to provide protection for those in the passenger seats of automobiles.

   (e) Automobile passengers sometimes play a contributing role in causing auto accidents.

SUMMARY CHECKLIST

Points you need to remember:

✔ The nature and role of assumptions.

✔ The difference between explicit and implicit, legitimate and illegitimate assumptions.

✔ The importance of assumptions in determining whether or not a piece of reasoning is legitimate.

The following websites offer a detailed explanation of assumptions coupled with a range of illustrative examples: www.criticalthinking.org/articles/ct-distinguishing-inferencs.cfm; www.criticalthinking.org.uk/unit2/fundamentals/elementsofarguments/assumptions/.

For some excellent exercises on identifying assumptions, see: http://philosophy.hku.hk/think/arg/hidden.php.

6

Chapter 6: Evaluating arguments

The issue of argument evaluation is taken up in greater detail in Ch. 19: judging what can (and cannot) be **safely inferred** from a given body of information/ evidence.

LEARNING OBJECTIVES

By the end of this chapter you should:

✔ Understand that different types of argument *exhibit* varying degrees of certainty.

✔ Understand why different types of argument *require* varying degrees of certainty.

✔ Be able to evaluate an argument by applying the above points.

We encounter arguments in one form or another on a daily basis, but how can we tell apart the good from the bad? In essence, such evaluation involves judging whether or not the premises of an argument are acceptable and whether or not they adequately support the conclusion they are intended to bring about (learning how to do this is a priority if you wish to avoid being hoodwinked or bullied by dubious reasoning!). If they are and do, the argument is said to be 'sound', if they're not and don't, it isn't. But what is meant by the terms 'adequate' and 'acceptable' here? This is not an easy question. Different types of argument require varying standards of adequacy (and hence evaluation). It might be *adequate*, for example, to say of a computer that it is reliable if it only crashed once a year, but the same could not be said of an aeroplane! Standards of adequacy shift from context to context. You will need to become sensitive to this as your reasoning skills develop.

VARYING STANDARDS

Making sure that the standards you use to *judge* an argument correspond with the *context* in which it is presented is the key to determining whether or not an inference is acceptable.

To draw a parallel, suppose you were walking in the park and saw some young children vandalising a park bench. In this situation, getting angry and ticking them off would be an appropriate course of action. Looking the other way and ignoring them would *not* be. Nor would battering them to within an inch of their lives (for similar reasons to the inappropriate response given above)! The first reaction seems to fit the circumstances. The second strikes us as insufficient and the third as excessive.

We need to apply a comparable sense of appropriateness to argument. In essence, we need to make sure that the level of certainty *displayed* by an argument matches the level of certainty we should *require* it to display. For this reason:

- What a load of nonsense all this talk about global warming is. It was rather chilly today. (Adapted from *Viz Letterbox*)

is obviously an inadequate argument. A day's chilliness might provide adequate grounds for wearing a jumper, but not for drawing the inference 'global warming is nonsense'! Here the criterion appealed to is obviously far too loose. But for similar reasons, requiring irrefutable evidence before accepting global warming as a possibility would be far too strict. It should be clear that the degree of evidence required lies somewhere in between!

Whilst some arguments can be presented with *absolute* certainty (such arguments are often referred to as '**deductive**' – where the truth of the premises absolutely guarantees the truth of the conclusion), such as:

> **deductive argument** – An argument where the truth of the premises absolutely guarantees the truth of the conclusion.

- Theft is the deprivation of property. If a man is guilty of theft, he must also be guilty of the deprivation of property. (Adapted from Hume's *Enquiries*)

the majority of arguments need only be established 'beyond reasonable doubt' (i.e. with substantial, but not complete, proof – as is often the case in a court of law):

- All observed ravens have been black; therefore, all ravens are black. (Nevertheless, a non-black raven remains a possibility.)

Often arguments can only be presented with a degree of *uncertainty*:

• Dave's got flu. There's no way he'll be able to give that presentation tomorrow! (But what if he doses up on medication and delivers it anyway?!)

And this is reasonable enough. A degree of uncertainty is an acceptable feature of most arguments and does not, on its own, provide adequate grounds for rejecting an inference. For this reason, the question 'is it reasonable to *accept* that?' is often more practical than the question 'can it be *proved* that?' when judging whether or not an inference, and thus an argument, is adequate. In order to judge what is reasonable, you must consider what is at stake should the inference prove wrong. Brazil's winning the World Cup on four consecutive occasions, for example, might provide adequate grounds for drawing the inference that 'we ought to put a small wager on them doing so again'. It would not provide adequate grounds for selling up everything one owns in order to place a much larger bet – as the specification points out: a favourable weather forecast might provide adequate grounds for the planning of a barbecue, but not a space launch!

Exercises

1. For the following premises, draw (a) a reasonable and (b) an unreasonable inference:
    • All young children benefit from playing.
    • Cheap air travel brings foreign holidays within easy reach.

2. For each of the following inferences, offer (a) reasonable and (b) unreasonable grounds of support:
    • There should be British jobs for British people.
    • There should be an 8 o'clock curfew for anyone below the age of eighteen.

EVALUATING ARGUMENTS

Once you have identified the reasons and conclusion of an argument, there are only two questions you will need to address in order to evaluate it. Firstly, do the premises present plausible claims? Secondly, do the premises add relevant and adequate support to the argument's inference? The first point is important because, no matter how persuasive an argument's inference, if the claims that support it are implausible, false or irrelevant, the question of whether or not the conclusion is valid will be redundant and the argument should be rejected. The following example illustrates this point:

- Paris is the capital of England.
- All capitals have a population of more than 1,000 people.
- Therefore Paris has a population of more than 1,000 people.

Whilst this conclusion is both true and logically follows from the premises (hence the argument is said to have a '**valid**' form), because the premises are false (Paris is obviously not the capital of England and Adamstown, the capital city of Pitcairn Island, currently has a population of 46!) the argument is unsound. Because the truth and plausibility of premises is a topic we have already dealt with and will return to in later chapters, we will leave the issue here for the time being.

Once you have identified the premises of an argument and come to a decision about whether or not they present plausible claims, you will then need to decide whether the reasoning employed to move from premise to conclusion is acceptable. This is because the truth and/or plausibility of premises on their own will not guarantee an argument's soundness. Note that the same kinds of principles underlie *all* acceptable arguments. You will probably have noted by now that some examples in this book are slightly frivolous and others more serious. All, however, are subject to the same principles of validity and so will be equally useful for sharpening your powers of analysis. The following example should make this clear:

- Those who shave daily stand a lower than average chance of developing a stroke in later life.
- Those who shave less than once a day stand a 70% greater chance of developing a stroke in later life.
- Therefore, failing to shave on a daily basis increases the risk of a stroke by 70%! (Adapted from BBC News/Health)

Believe it or not, both of the premises of this argument are true. But the inference that it is *the failure to shave* that increases the likelihood of suffering a stroke, rather than some other cause (for example a hormonal imbalance or lower testosterone levels) is inadequate. It depends upon the largely illegitimate assumption that if two events regularly occur together – failure to shave and

valid argument – A valid argument (see **deductive argument** above) is one whose premises entail the conclusion of an argument regardless of whether or not they are true. A **sound** argument is a valid argument with true premises and hence a true conclusion.

For more on truth and plausibility of premises, see Chs 3, 5 and 6: ('Varying standards').

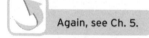

For a more detailed discussion of this point, see Chs 3: 'Causal explanations', 5 and 11: Cause-correlation fallacy.

For more on this point, see Ch. 6: 'Varying standards'.

Again, see Ch. 5.

For more on this, see Ch. 8.

For a detailed account of each logical fallacy, see Ch. 11: 'Logical fallacies'.

The general issue of evaluating arguments is picked up again in Chs 8, 9, 15: 'Motive and agenda' and 'Sources', but perhaps most importantly (and in most detail) in the two end of unit exam chapters.

increased likelihood of a stroke – then the former *causes* the latter. For this reason, it would be more reasonable to suggest that it is *possible* (although not very likely) that the failure to shave increases the likelihood of a stroke, rather than just asserting that it does.

There are a range of ways in which an inference can be called into question. Firstly, as indicated above, you will need to think about how strongly an inference is stated (with certainty, probability or as a mere possibility) and whether the evidence or reasons provided justify the strength of the assertion. Secondly, you will need to decide whether an inference depends upon any unstated assumptions and if it does, whether these are acceptable. Thirdly, you will need to think about whether there are any counter-examples, alternative explanations or pieces of evidence that could be brought to test whether the inference is a valid one. And finally, you will need to ask whether the argument commits any **logical fallacies** which invalidate the reasoning employed. For simplicity's sake, a good argument is one that presents us with plausible premises which offer both adequate and relevant support for the conclusion they are intended to bring about. If an argument fails on either of these counts, we have solid grounds for rejecting it.

Summary questions . . .

1. What do we need to think about in order to determine the level of certainty required by an argument? Why?
2. What questions do we need to ask in order to evaluate an argument? Why?

END OF CHAPTER ACTIVITY

Thinking about (a) whether the premises present plausible claims and (b) whether they adequately support the conclusion they are intended to bring about, come to a reasoned decision about how acceptable each of the following arguments are (giving reasons for your answer):

1. My brother George is a cat. All cats are pink. Therefore my brother George is pink.
2. Playing a musical instrument helps to relieve stress. Hazel is a very relaxed person so she must play a musical instrument.

3. There are seven days in a week and twenty-four hours in a day, so that means there must be twelve months in a year.
4. The Thames is the longest river in the world. All rivers flow from north to south so the Thames flows from south to north.
5. All humans are mammals. All mammals are warm-blooded. Therefore all humans are warm-blooded.

SUMMARY CHECKLIST

Points you need to remember:

✔ Why different types of argument require varying degrees of certainty.

✔ How to determine the level of certainty required by an argument by considering what's at stake should its inference prove wrong.

✔ The qualities of a good argument and how to go about evaluating these.

The following website has an excellent synopsis and range of activities on evaluating argument: www.class.uidaho.edu/crit_think/ctw-m/eval.htm.

The following website is more challenging, but offers a detailed overview of the process of argument evaluation: http://academic.cuesta.edu/acasupp/as/403.htm.

logical fallacy – A general term which refers to a set of common errors in reasoning. If a piece of reasoning is said to be **fallacious** (i.e. if it commits a logical fallacy), we have solid grounds for rejecting it.

UNIT 1 **FOUNDATION UNIT**

Chapter 7: Considering consequences

LEARNING OBJECTIVES

By the end of this chapter you should:

✔ Understand why thinking through the consequences of an argument may allow us to determine whether or not it is acceptable.

'What would happen if we all did that?' 'If Johnny jumped off a bridge, would you do too?' We have all, at some point in our lives, been asked questions such as these! Whilst superficially annoying ('Not everybody *will* do that.' 'Johnny wouldn't *jump* off a bridge, he's not an idiot!') they nevertheless get us to reflect upon the consequences of our actions. A similar approach can be applied to argument. The strengths or weaknesses of an argument can often be drawn out by considering the consequences that would follow from accepting or rejecting it.

This is a point that we have already touched on but now need to develop in greater detail. A simple example will help you understand how this is done:

- The consumption of alcohol is responsible for high crime rates, poverty, death and a general lowering of the quality of life, both physically and psychologically.
- Therefore, the government has a duty to ban it.

An argument like this was used to defend the American Prohibition (banning of alcohol) Act of the 1920s (see the 18th Amendment, 18 December 1917). At face value, it looks quite convincing, but what would follow were we to accept the reasoning it presents us with? Well, first of all, it would be difficult

> Considering consequences is a theme which has already been touched upon in Ch. 3 – see 'Statements of principle' and 'Recommendations'.

to see how such an argument could be limited to alcohol use alone. Any activity, for example gambling or smoking, which had a similarly negative effect should surely also be banned. But what about other potentially 'negative' activities that many might regard as relatively harmless? Eating junk food, for example, or watching too much television. Might the government be justified in placing limits on each of these too? If so, where could we draw the line? You should be able to see that each of these questions raises doubts about whether the initial argument, as it stands, is acceptable.

A more sophisticated example comes from a classic defence of freedom of speech. In Chapter 2 of the book *On Liberty*, the philosopher John Stuart Mill presents us with the following, now famous, piece of reasoning (enshrined in the first amendment to the American constitution):

> If all mankind minus one were of one opinion, and only one person were of the contrary opinion, mankind would be no more justified in silencing that one person than he, if he had the power, would be justified in silencing mankind. (Mill, *On Liberty*, Chapter 2)

In plain English, Mill argues that there is no condition, bar that which would lead to the direct physical harm of another human being, which could be appealed to in order to restrict how people express themselves. But just how convincing is this? Mill attempts to justify his position by considering some of its consequences:

- Many beliefs that were suppressed in the past later turned out true (for example the church suppressing the belief that the Earth was round and at the centre of the universe). We have no way of knowing the same won't hold true of future beliefs, so we ought not to suppress them.
- Allowing for freedom of speech and expression would reduce the persecution of minority groups (for example those discriminated against or silenced on grounds of gender, race, sexuality or religion).
- We have no way of knowing how strong an accepted practice or belief is until we question it. To use a modern example, it was only when the suffragette movement of the early 1900s challenged the view that women were 'too emotional' to vote, that this belief was overturned (1928) and women were given equal voting rights to men.

And each of the above 'positive' consequences strengthens Mill's position. But the argument doesn't stop there. Mill believed the suppression of *any* belief or practice, no matter how repugnant, would damage the general applicability of this law. His reasoning was later echoed in Martin Luther King's famous claim that 'injustice anywhere is a threat to justice everywhere' (Letter from Birmingham Jail). Because of this, Mill argued there could be *no* circumstance (bar the direct causing of physical harm to *another* individual) under which freedom of speech, thought or expression could be limited. But this was quite a bold claim! There are a range of practices that most would regard as completely unacceptable that would, if we were to accept the consequences of his reasoning, be permissible on Mill's grounds. For example, people would be free to:

- take drugs
- be as obscene or offensive as they liked as long as this caused no *direct* physical harm to another individual
- preach religious fundamentalism
- preach religious, racial or sexual intolerance
- share military secrets
- watch and share pornographic material of an extreme nature as long as they did not produce it.

And each of these possible outcomes, assuming we agree they are unacceptable, would weaken Mill's position. Considering consequences, then, not only allows us to reach a decision about whether or not an argument is acceptable, but also to think about ways in which an argument could be modified in order to make it *more* so. The political and social philosopher Joel Feinberg adapted Mill's 'harm' principle to take into account the above points. He argued for an 'offence principle' which meant that personal freedoms could be restricted if they are used to cause harm and/or offence (which Mill thought was acceptable) to another individual.

Summary questions . . .

1. In your own words, summarise how thinking through the consequences of an argument allows us to determine whether or not it is acceptable.

END OF CHAPTER ACTIVITY

1. Thinking through the consequences of accepting each of the following arguments, come to a reasoned decision about how acceptable they are. Try to modify any examples you find unacceptable.

    (a) A disillusioned teacher who argues, along the following lines, that a lifetime of teaching sixteen-year-olds has taught her that none of them have enough understanding of the realities of life to be given the vote. Indeed, she thinks that it is rare enough to find an eighteen-year-old with such understanding, let alone planning to give people even younger the right to have a say in the running of the country.

    (b) Coming out of the darkest and raunchiest ghettos of New York and LA, gangster rap music has quickly metamorphosed into the worst and most satanic form of music in the world. It promotes hatred and violence of the worst sort, a kind of evil that kids are being exposed to at an increasingly younger age ... I urge the authorities to ban gangster rap ... Your time and consideration would be greatly appreciated. (Extracted from 'ban gangster rap' petition)

    (c) Fox hunting should NOT be banned. Foxes are vermin who kill farmers' livestock for fun. Hunters are just trying to protect the livestock of the farming community. They are also a pest in the town. They have terrorised my dog and tried to eat my guinea pigs. They are just evil pests out to cause trouble for people all over the country. If hunting is stopped then not only farmers will be in danger our economy will be in a lot of trouble as well. DON'T BAN HUNTING. (Overheard on a local radio chat show)

2. Stretching activity: For something really different, try the same exercise on the savage political irony of the eighteenth-century satirist Jonathan Swift, who, in 'A Modest Proposal' (1721) suggested that the related problems of starvation and overpopulation in Ireland at that time might both be solved at a stroke, if the rich were to eat the children of the poor!

    > I have been assured by a very knowing American of my acquaintance in London, that a young healthy child well nursed is at a year old a most delicious, nourishing, and wholesome food, whether stewed, roasted, baked, or boiled; and I make no doubt that it will equally serve in a fricassee or a ragout.
    >
    > I do therefore humbly offer it to public consideration that of the hundred and twenty thousand children already computed, twenty thousand may be reserved for breed, whereof only one-fourth part to

be males; which is more than we allow to sheep, black cattle or swine; and my reason is, that these children are seldom the fruits of marriage, a circumstance not much regarded by our savages, therefore one male will be sufficient to serve four females. That the remaining hundred thousand may, at a year old, be offered in sale to the persons of quality and fortune through the kingdom; always advising the mother to let them suck plentifully in the last month, so as to render them plump and fat for a good table. A child will make two dishes at an entertainment for friends; and when the family dines alone, the fore or hind quarter will make a reasonable dish, and seasoned with a little pepper or salt will be very good boiled on the fourth day, especially in winter.

SUMMARY CHECKLIST

Points you need to remember:

✔   Why thinking through the consequences of an argument allows us to determine whether or not it is acceptable.

The following website contains thirty arguments. Thinking through the consequences of each will help sharpen your evaluative skills: http://grammar.about.com/od/developingessays/a/topicargumt07.htm.

FOUNDATION UNIT

Chapter 8: Additional evidence, counter-examples and analogies

8

LEARNING OBJECTIVES

By the end of this chapter you should:

✔ Be able to understand what is meant by and consider the impact the following have on argument:
  • Additional evidence
  • Counter-examples
  • Analogies
✔ Be able to apply this knowledge to both exam material and your own arguments.

We have seen that thinking through the consequences of a particular argument is an effective method for deciding how strong (or weak) it is, but it is not the only one. Another way is to consider the impact **additional evidence**, **counter-examples** (used to challenge a general claim or argument) and **analogies** (appealing to a parallel or similar case in order to shed light on the first) have on a particular piece of reasoning. Let us deal with each in turn.

ADDITIONAL EVIDENCE

Arguments can be strengthened or weakened by bringing in further evidence of a factual nature. In Arthur Conan Doyle's 'The Adventure of the Norwood Builder', Sherlock Holmes is dealing with what seems like a pretty cut-and-dry case. John McFarlane, a young lawyer, is accused of murdering one of his clients – a builder named Jonas Oldacre. He had a motive, was in the area at the time the murder was committed and, perhaps most damningly, his stick was found at the scene of the crime. We might summarise this in argument form as follows:

- McFarlane stood to gain a considerable amount of money from Oldacre's death (R1).
- He was in the area at the time the crime was committed (R2).
- His stick was found at the scene of the crime (evidence).
- Therefore, he is guilty of the murder of Jonas Oldacre (C).

Even Holmes is swayed by this reasoning but nevertheless has his doubts. When a further piece of evidence is discovered:

- McFarlane's bloody thumbprint (found on a wall in Oldacre's house).

Lestrade, the police inspector investigating the crime, believes the case to be conclusive. However, Holmes, who had completed a thorough investigation of the house the day before and found no such thumbprint, is able to use this evidence to establish McFarlane's innocence. He reasons as follows:

- There was no thumbprint on the wall in Oldacre's house the day prior to its discovery (R1).
- McFarlane was locked up in gaol overnight (R2).
- Whoever placed the thumbprint there could not have been McFarlane (R3).
- So somebody is trying to frame McFarlane for murder (IC/R4).
- And *this* person, rather than McFarlane, must be the real culprit (MC).

The issue of bringing in additional evidence to support your own reasoning will be taken up in greater detail in both of the end of unit exam chapters.

With this additional piece of evidence, Holmes is able to flush out the real culprit (the very much alive Jonas Oldacre who had been running a revenge campaign against McFarlane!) and establish McFarlane's innocence. Additional evidence, then, can be used to strengthen, weaken, confirm or refute an argument, hypothesis or explanation. In order to test the effect that additional evidence might have on an argument, we need to ask ourselves the question: 'if the following were true, would it (a) strengthen/confirm, (b) weaken/refute or (c) have no effect on the argument in question?' The following example will show you how this is done:

We should support the introduction of new identity cards that will contain biometric data, such as fingerprints and iris scans [part of the eye]. The pattern on the iris is a unique record of each individual that cannot be guessed or forged. This means that it will be very difficult for criminals to forge or steal someone else's identity – a process often called identity theft. These stolen identities are valuable to criminals as they can be used to buy goods and cover other illegal activities.

Which of the following, if true, would *most strengthen* the above argument?

    A New identity cards will be no bigger than a conventional credit card.

    B The cost of the technology required to produce the cards will reduce over time.

    C Current security, such as passwords and pin numbers, fails if people forget their passwords.

    D Current security, such as passwords and pin numbers, fails to prevent over 100,000 identity thefts a year. (Critical Thinking 2006 Question paper OCR)

The correct answer is D. This is because, if we accept the evidence that current security measures are ineffective (i.e. they 'fail to prevent over 100,000 identity thefts a year') then finding a way to make them *more* effective (by using a 'unique record of each individual that cannot be guessed or forged') adds strength to the inference 'we should support the introduction of new identity cards that will contain biometric data, such as fingerprints and iris scans'. It provides us with a reason for accepting this claim. Answer A (new identity cards will be no bigger than a conventional credit card) *has no effect on* the argument. This is because the size of the cards is largely irrelevant to the question of whether or not they are a good idea. Answer B (the cost of technology required to produce the cards will reduce over time), if anything, *weakens* the argument. It implies that such cards will be initially expensive to produce and cost *is a* relevant factor for deciding whether or not identity cards are a good idea. If their production is too expensive, then perhaps government money would be better spent elsewhere. Finally, answer C (current security, such as passwords and pin numbers, fails if people forget their passwords) *looks* like it might strengthen the argument (if current security fails when people forget their passwords and pin numbers then perhaps we need to implement a new system) but if it does so, it does so weakly. This is because C highlights a problem with *people*, rather than security, and because of this, the point is of limited relevance.

Exercises

1. Bearing in mind what we have just looked at, bring in your own example of a piece of evidence that would (a) strengthen and (b) weaken each of the inferences drawn in the following arguments (you may find that breaking the examples down into premises and conclusion will help you to do this):

    • 'No one has anything to fear from giving the police random stop-and-search powers so long as they have nothing to hide. Opponents of these powers can only be helping to protect the guilty.' (AQA specification)

    • 'The Earth's climate is always changing and this is nothing to do with humans. Even before the industrial revolution, when humans began pumping carbon dioxide into the atmosphere on a large scale, the earth experienced warm periods such as the medieval warm period.' (Royal Society, *Misleading Argument 1: Climate Change has Nothing to do with Humans*)

2. Stretching activity: Read through the following passage (taken from Law Schools Admissions Test [LSAT]) and then answer the questions below:

    An ingredient in coffee, known as RTC, has been found to inactivate common cold viruses in experiments. In previous experiments, researchers found that inactivated common cold viruses can convert healthy cells into cancer cells. It can be concluded that the use of coffee can cause cancer.

    Q: Identify which of the following options (a) strengthens (b) weakens and (c) has no effect on the argument. Make sure you explain your answer.

    (a) Several teams of scientists performed the various experiments, and all of the teams had similar results.

    (b) The carcinogenic effect of RTC could be neutralised by the other ingredients found in coffee.

    (c) If chemists modify the structure of RTC, RTC can be safely incorporated into medications to prevent the common cold.

COUNTER-EXAMPLES

Counter-examples function in one of two ways. Firstly, they can be used to question or refute a *general* claim or argument and, secondly, they can be considered and then responded to in order to strengthen one's own reasoning. A general claim is one that is intended to hold true in *every* case. They tend to involve reasoning indicators such as 'all', 'every' or 'always', or when phrased negatively, 'none', 'no' or 'never'. If such a claim is correct, it will be impossible to find exceptions. This is especially true of general claims that are true by definition, such as '*all* bachelors are male'. Here, a counter-example (i.e. a non-'male and unmarried' bachelor) would be impossible. But the majority of general claims do not display this degree of certainty. Because such claims as:

- All swans are white.
- All second-hand car dealers are dishonest.
- All knowledge comes from experience.

are meant to hold true in *every* case, all that would be required to refute them would be *one* counter-example – i.e. a non-white swan, an honest second-hand car dealer and an instance of knowledge that did not come from experience. For this reason, counter-examples often force us to limit the force of our conclusion. The above claims would be better phrased as:

- *Most* swans are white.
- *Some* second-hand car dealers are dishonest.
- *The majority of* knowledge comes from experience.

The harder it is to provide a counter-example for a general claim, the greater the likelihood that it will be true. Conversely, the more counter-examples that can be provided against such claims, the less plausible they will be. Because arguments often depend upon general claims for their effectiveness (although these are often left implicit) looking for counter-examples is an effective method for testing whether or not an inference is valid:

- The Bugatti Veyron is the fastest (253mph and 0–60 in under 2.5 seconds) and most expensive (£880,000) production car ever built.
- It *has* to be the greatest vehicle on the road.

Here, the reasoning only works if we accept the (assumed) general principles that:

The issue of counter-examples has been discussed in Ch. 3 – see 'Statements of principle' and 'Recommendations'. The theme is also developed in both of the end of unit exam chapters.

1. An expensive product is *always* better than an inexpensive one.

2. A faster vehicle will *always* be better than a slower one.

And more generally:

3. That in *all* cases speed and price are what determine how good a car is.

But it is easy to find counter-examples for each of these. For the first principle, we would need to bring in an example of an inexpensive product that was superior to an expensive one – I recently, for example, bought a pricey new bottle opener that was significantly inferior to the cheaper one I already owned. Price is clearly not always a good indication of quality! For the second, we would need to find an example of a slower vehicle that was superior to a faster one – a Rolls-Royce Silver Shadow, widely regarded as one of the greatest cars ever made, has a top speed of 115mph: certainly *slower than*, but not *inferior to*, the majority of modern, less expensive cars on the market. And for the third, we would need to show that speed and price do not always determine how good a vehicle is. A popular car magazine recently listed fuel consumption, safety, comfort, ease of handling and cost of insurance as being the decisive factors for doing this, none of which the Veyron is likely to score highly on. Whilst none of these points fully refutes the inference drawn, they nevertheless cast doubt upon the reasoning used to enforce it. Looking for counter-examples, then, is an essential step for determining how strong an argument is.

Exercises

1. (a) Try and provide counter-examples for each of the following general claims and (b) if no counter-examples can be found, insert 'all' or 'always' in the blank space. If a few counter-examples can be found, insert 'most' or 'usually', and if many counter-examples can be found, insert 'some' or 'occasionally':
   - Lying is _____ wrong.
   - Water _____ boils at 100°C (at sea level!).
   - _____ emeralds are green.
   - _____ men are liars.
   - _____ people should be held responsible for their actions.
   - Drinking alcohol _____ causes cirrhosis of the liver.

2. Look at the following example and (a) identify the general claim being made and (b) provide at least one counter-example against it:

   - All politicians are corrupt because they would not be in politics if they were not.

   Counter-examples can also be an effective tool for *strengthening* your own arguments (more of this in Chapter 12). They can be used to (1) anticipate and (2) overcome an opponent's criticism in order to strengthen one's own reasoning (see underlined):

   > Importantly, girls in single-sex schools are more likely to pick traditionally male subjects such as maths and science, demonstrating that single-sex schools break down gender barriers. (1) <u>Some have argued that these schools are in some way discriminatory – perhaps thinking that the success of girls' schools is to boys' disadvantage.</u> (2) <u>This is simply not the case and is typical of the views of those who want girls and boys to be treated exactly the same</u> – presumably including shared changing rooms and toilet facilities. ('Single Sex Success', OCR Critical Thinking AS-level exam)

   In this respect, counter-examples are an important feature of objective reasoning. If we fail to consider these when arguing a case, we risk giving a 'one-sided' account.

3. Identify the counter-example in the following piece of reasoning. How is it responded to?

   > Many people argue that taking embryonic cells, even from a placenta, is morally wrong because it is killing a 'child'. But, in all honesty we need to ask ourselves: is an embryonic cell really a foetus? It's hard to think so. While life may begin at conception, life at that point is not far enough along in development to consider it a baby. (Mary Pagay, *In Favor of Stem Cell Research*: www.associatedcontent.com/article/61833/in_favor_of_stem_cell_research.html)

For more on 'one-sidedness' (bias) see Ch. 15: 'Motive and agendas'.

ANALOGIES

Analogies can be used as an effective shortcut for getting to grips with a difficult idea. For example, in the introduction to this book I compared an argument to the human body:

The human body is not just a single unit, but, rather, a complex one which can be broken down into many separate parts. Each of these parts has a function: the heart pumps blood around the body; the eyes provide us with sight, and the ears, sound etc. and these individual functions combine to contribute to the body's functioning as a whole. An argument is like this, composed of separate parts, each with a specific role.

Here I drew a comparison between an idea that might be new to you and fairly complex (that of argument) and one that you should all be familiar with (the body). Because there are suitable similarities between the two things being compared this was a legitimate way of communicating a difficult idea. Here are some further examples for you to think about:

- The eye is like a camera.
- 'Darkness cannot drive out darkness; only light can do that. Hate cannot drive out hate; only love can do that.' (Martin Luther King)
- Religion 'is the opium of the masses'. (Karl Marx)
- 'When they debate as to what the sound of the SLR engine was akin to, the British engineers from McLaren said it sounded like a Spitfire. But the German engineers from Mercedes said "Nein! Nein! Sounds like a Messerschmitt!" They were both wrong. It sounds like the God of Thunder, gargling with nails.' (Jeremy Clarkson, when driving the McLaren Mercedes SLR through a tunnel)
- 'I'd give each one of 'em a stick and, one for each one of 'em, then I'd say, "You break that." Course they could real easy. Then I'd say, "Tie them sticks in a bundle and try to break that." Course they couldn't. Then I'd say, "That bundle ... that's family."' (Alvin in David Lynch's film, *The Straight Story*)

Analogies are often appealed to in arguments because, if we accept that something holds true in one case, then it should also hold true in parallel cases (i.e. those which are suitably similar). Perhaps the most famous example of this type of reasoning was put forward by William Paley who argued for the existence of an 'intelligent designer' (God) by drawing an analogy with a watchmaker:

In crossing a heath, suppose I pitched my foot against a *stone* and were asked how the stone came to be there, I might possibly answer that for anything I knew to the contrary it had lain there forever; nor would it, perhaps, be very easy to show the absurdity of this answer. But suppose I had found a *watch* upon the ground, and it should be inquired how the watch happened to be in that place. I should hardly think of the answer which I had before given, that for anything I knew the watch might have always been there. Yet why should not this answer serve for the watch as well as for the stone? Why is it not as admissible in the second case as in the first? For this reason, and for no other, namely, that when we come to inspect the watch, we perceive – what we could not discover in the stone – that its several parts are framed and put together for a purpose ... [The requisite] mechanism being observed ... the inference we think is inevitable, that the watch must have had a maker. Every observation which was made in our first chapter concerning the watch may be repeated with strict propriety concerning the eye, concerning animals, concerning plants, concerning, indeed, all the organised parts of the works of nature ... [T]he *eye* ... would be alone sufficient to support the conclusion which we draw from it, as to the necessity of an intelligent Creator. (William Paley, *Natural Theology* – adapted from *Stanford Encyclopedia of Philosophy*)

We could simplify Paley's argument as follows:

- A watch displays order (all the parts fit together) and purpose (it has a specific function) and for this to be so, it must have been designed (by a watchmaker).
- Analogically, when we look at objects in the world (the eye, animals, plants etc.) we realise that these too display an order and purpose that is too complex to have come about by chance (as with the stone). They must thus be the product of an intelligent designer (God).

So an analogy is drawn between objects which have been designed for a purpose and the universe. The inference (that the universe too must have a designer) rests upon the assumption that the two cases are suitably alike for the points that hold true of the first to hold true of the second. If we accept this, the analogy works, if we don't, it doesn't. But what grounds might there be for reaching such a judgement? In deciding whether or not an analogy is effective, three things need to be taken into account. Firstly, you will need to be clear about which two things are being compared (in the above example, a mechanism which has been designed, and the universe). Secondly, you will need to consider their similarities and differences (whether or not the universe displays a similar sort of design to the watch; whether something manufactured is suitably similar to something natural etc.). Thirdly, you will need to judge whether the similarities are *significant* enough, and that the two cases do not differ in any *important* aspects, for the analogy to be effective (if the level of design displayed by the watch is significantly different to that displayed by the universe, then the analogy should be rejected). This last point is significant because if, as is often the case, there are noteworthy differences, the example will be guilty of committing the *weak analogy* fallacy:

- 'Using a condom to prevent the spread of AIDS, is like trying to put out a fire with paraffin.' (Cardinal Alfonso Lopez Trujillo [paraphrased slightly])

These words were uttered by one of the leaders of the Roman Catholic Church (BBC, Panorama, 'Can Condoms Kill?'). They were preached alongside information contained in a twenty-page document which urged that condoms, far from preventing the flow of AIDS, actually contributed to it. Trujillo argued that condoms had tiny microscopic holes in them which allowed the transmission of the HIV virus (this has since been scientifically refuted) and this message was taken to Africa, a continent ravaged by AIDS. It should be clear that, although visually powerful, the analogy is a weak one. It attempts to convey the message that condoms are responsible for the spreading of AIDS (it was argued that, not only do condoms not work, but that they also encourage an irresponsible attitude towards sex) in much the same way that paraffin contributes to the spreading of fire! But the differences between the two cases are so substantial, the analogy fails – although its emotional force blinded many people to this. We might summarise these differences as follows:

- Condoms are used to *prevent* AIDS whereas paraffin is used to *encourage* fire.
- The failure rate of condoms is roughly 1.5%; the failure rate of paraffin (to put out a fire) would be 100%.
- Condom use can be regarded as a responsible activity; putting fire out with paraffin, an irresponsible one!

And no doubt there are many others. In fact, it would be difficult to find any *significant* similarities between the two cases that could help the analogy. Contrast this example with the following one:

- Using a condom to prevent the spread of AIDS is like wearing a raincoat to prevent oneself getting wet in a thunderstorm.

Now of course there is at least one important difference here – the threat of contracting AIDS is significantly more dangerous than the threat of getting wet. However, because there are a suitable amount of *relevant* similarities, i.e.:

- Both offer an *effective* method for preventing something happening.
- Both offer protection in the form of a *barrier* from an external threat.

the analogy can be regarded as *fairly* strong. Coming to a decision about whether the relevant similarities between the two things being compared outweigh the differences is the key to evaluating an analogy. The notion of relevance is important here because, whilst it would be *fairly safe* to argue that:

- Your car is a similar make and model to mine and has the same engine, so they probably travel at similar speeds.

because make, model and engine size are all *relevant* factors for determining a car's speed. However, it would be exceedingly *unsafe* to argue that:

- Your car is a similar *colour* to mine, so they probably travel at similar speeds!

Obviously, the colour of a car has no effect on the speed at which it travels.

Summary questions . . .

1. Explain what you understand by the following terms:
    (a) Additional evidence
    (b) Counter-examples
    (c) Analogies
2. How might each of the above be used to strengthen/weaken an argument?

END OF CHAPTER ACTIVITY

Come to a decision about the effectiveness of the following analogies by (a) identifying the two things being compared, (b) listing their *relevant* similarities and differences and (c) coming to a judgement about whether or not the similarities between these two cases outweigh the differences:

- 'Whatever I have accepted as true up until now has come through my senses (experience). But occasionally I have found that my senses have deceived me. It would be unwise to trust a friend who has deceived me even once, so it is unwise to trust my senses.' (Adapted from Descartes' *Meditations*)
- 'My momma always said "life is like a box of chocolates. You never know what you're gonna get."' (Forrest Gump)
- There is no real difference between smoking cannabis and drinking alcohol. Alcohol is legal, so cannabis should be too.

It is important to remember that nothing can ever be conclusively established by analogy because analogies, by their very nature, differ from that which they are analogising. Their purpose is to make things clear, but there is also the danger they can mislead (when this occurs, the example can be accused of committing the 'weak analogy fallacy').

For more on this issue, see Ch. 12.

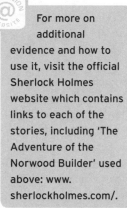

For more on additional evidence and how to use it, visit the official Sherlock Holmes website which contains links to each of the stories, including 'The Adventure of the Norwood Builder' used above: www.sherlockholmes.com/.

The following website has a range of activities on counter-examples: http://arts.monash.edu.au/philosophy/peer-instruction/database/criticalthinking/generalisations.php.

Have a read through the following site which contains twenty-five of the funniest analogies of all time: http://writingenglish.wordpress.com/2006/09/12/the-25-funniest-analogies-collected-by-high-school-english-teachers/.

- Having unprotected sex is like playing Russian Roulette.
- If you enjoyed watching *Star Wars* and *Return of the Jedi*, you'll also enjoy *The Empire Strikes Back*.
- ... skill's got nothing to do with whether it's art. You can be skilled at something and not produce art. My brother's an engineer but no one would say he produces art. (Critical Thinking Exam Paper, AQA)

SUMMARY CHECKLIST

Points you need to remember:

✔ What impact each of the following have on argument and why:
- Additional evidence
- Counter-examples
- Analogies

UNIT 1 **FOUNDATION UNIT**

Chapter 9: Ambiguity, vagueness and clarifying terms

LEARNING OBJECTIVES

By the end of this chapter you should:

✔ Understand what is meant by the terms 'vague' and 'ambiguous' and why vagueness and ambiguity present a problem for reasoning.

✔ Be able to identify and subsequently clarify any instances of vagueness and ambiguity you might come across.

---

vague – A word or expression is **vague** when its meaning is not fixed or clear and **precise** when it is.

ambiguous – A word or expression is ambiguous if it has more than one meaning.

The issue of language is taken up again in Ch. 10

Whether or not we accept a piece of reasoning will often depend upon how clearly it is expressed. This is often unproblematic, but there will be times when clarification is called for. Many of the words and expressions we use on a daily basis are **vague**. We might, for example, say that such and such a person is 'tall' or 'clever' or that such and such a place is 'far away' (but how tall? How clever? How far away?). Sometimes we will use expressions that are **ambiguous**: *Nothing* will take the place of Bill'; 'I *can't tell you* how much I enjoyed this evening'! On a day-to-day basis, these examples are easy to handle. Their meaning is fixed by context. But whilst vagueness and ambiguity may be unproblematic features of everyday language, the same does not hold true of argument. To be effective, arguments require a much greater degree of precision than is to be found in everyday discourse. This is where the notion of clarifying terms comes in.

VAGUENESS

An expression is *vague* if its meaning is not fixed or clear. An expression is *precise* if it is. 'Tall' is a vague expression: it gives us no real indication of the height involved. '6 feet 5 inches' is precise – there can be no disagreement about the level of height we are dealing with. Some expressions are naturally vague. The example often cited is that of a 'heap'. Few would argue that two or three grains of sand constituted a heap or that a thousand grains of sand did not. But at what point, during the process of adding grains of sand together, does a 'heap' emerge? Other expressions such as 'equilateral triangle' are naturally precise. There can be no doubt as to their meaning. In all such cases, we need to be careful not to over- or underestimate the level of precision required. Common sense is as good a guide as any here.

For more on this issue, see Ch. 3: 'Definitions'.

To illustrate the importance of precision, let us look at an example. If you decided to have your room painted and a decorator asked you which colour you would like, the response 'red' would obviously be deficient since it gives no indication of the shade required. Arguments require a similarly appropriate level of precision. For example, if a politician were to argue:

- If we increase taxation on petrol, alcohol and tobacco
- Then non-essential road travel, alcohol consumption and cigarette smoking will decrease

This would be insufficient. There is no explanation of how much 'increase' or 'decrease' we are talking about. The expressions are vague. In order to remedy this (and before we can begin the process of evaluation) we first need to identify and then clarify the meanings of any vague terms involved. Here, it would be better to argue:

- If we increase taxation on petrol, alcohol and tobacco by $x\%$
- Then non-essential road travel, alcohol consumption and cigarette smoking will decrease by $y\%$

And the actual percentage of increase and decrease will determine whether or not the argument is acceptable (a 50% increase in tax, for a 1% decrease in consumption, for example, would obviously be inadequate). The level of precision that an argument requires will, of course, vary from context to context. It might be okay to argue:

- We should book our summer holiday *early* this year
- Because prices are *going up*

even though the terms 'early' and 'going up' are not precise (although, of course, the argument would benefit from making them more so). On the other hand, it would not be acceptable to argue:

- You need to book your heart-bypass operation soon Mr Jones
- Your chances of survival are deteriorating!

because what's at stake demands a much higher level of precision.

Here are some further examples of vagueness:

- I'll meet you there this afternoon (but *where* and at *what time*?).
- 'The moon visits your home chart and makes a family more receptive to your plans so it is worth talking again.' (Mystic Meg Horoscope)
- Any potential job applicants will need to have suitable job qualifications (but what would count as *suitable* here?).
- That party was just great (but how great?).

> ### Exercise
>
> For each of the following examples, (a) identify any vague words or expressions used and (b) offer a more precise definition for each one:
> - George looks a bit under the weather.
> - I'm in a spot of trouble here.
> - Vote for the Peoples' Party for a better tomorrow!

This issue has been dealt with in detail in Ch. 6: 'Varying standards'.

When reasoning depends upon a word or expression which is either vague or ambiguous, disputes can often be resolved by coming to an agreement about how the terms should be used.

AMBIGUITY

A word or expression is ambiguous if it has more than one meaning. Typing the word 'critical' into the Microsoft Thesaurus, for example, reveals that the word can mean 'dangerous', 'significant', 'unfavourable' or 'life threatening'! When used within the context of 'critical thinking', needless to say, it tends to mean 'logical' or 'analytic'. Whenever there is any doubt, we always need to be clear about which meaning of a word is intended and the best guide here is usually context:

- The building is in a *critical* state of repair.
- It is *critical* you understand this.
- Why do you always have to be so *critical*?
- He's still in a *critical* condition.

But it is not just words that can be ambiguous, sentences can be too. Here are some examples of genuine headlines taken from local and national newspapers, all of which contain ambiguities:

- Kids make nutritious snacks
- Miners refuse to work after death
- Milk drinkers are turning to powder
- Juvenile court to try shooting defendant
- Complaints about NBA referees growing ugly
- Panda mating fails; veterinarian takes over
- Man eating piranha mistakenly sold as pet fish
- Hospitals are sued by 7 foot doctors
- Enraged cow injures farmer with axe
- Iraqi head seeks arms

It should be clear that each can be read in one of two ways! Fortunately, it is often the most obvious reading that is correct. Whilst 'man eating piranha mistakenly sold as pet fish' could mean either: (a) a piranha, which is a man-eating fish, was mistakenly sold as a pet or (b) a man who was eating a piranha, was mistakenly sold as a pet fish! – the absurdity of the latter should convince us of the correctness of the former. But not all examples of ambiguity will be as obvious as this. Suppose you were the boss of a company and you came across the following references in response to a job that you had advertised:

1. 'In my opinion, you will be very fortunate to get this person to work for you.'

2. 'I would urge you to waste no time in making this candidate an offer of employment.' (Robert Thornton, *The Lexicon of Intentionally Ambiguous Recommendations [LIAR]*, Minnetonka, 2003 p. 6)

Here, without further information to tell us otherwise, example 1 could mean either:

- This person is perfectly suited for the job and you would be lucky to get him as an employee.

Or

- This person is not suited for the job, and if he is employed, you will be fortunate to get any work out of him!

Example 2 could mean either:

- Do not delay in offering this person a job.

Or

- This person is so ill-suited for the job, any time spent considering him/her would be wasted!

In both examples, the ambiguities are intentional. Their author uses them as an illustration of writing a positive-sounding job reference for a friend or colleague whom you feel is incompetent, but at the same time do not wish to offend!

When analysing a piece of reasoning that contains ambiguity, you will need to (a) identify the ambiguous term/s involved, (b) explain the different ways in which these can be understood and (c) come to a decision (based on context or additional information) about which of these is the correct one. Where no such decision can be made (i.e. when the context of the claim doesn't fix its meaning) judgement should be suspended.

Summary questions . . .

1. Explain what is meant by the terms 'vague' and 'ambiguous'.
2. Why does vagueness and ambiguity present a problem for reasoning?
3. How does one go about resolving such cases?

END OF CHAPTER ACTIVITY

Taking the above into account, analyse the following examples:

- I am a massive fan of yours (said by an admirer).
- I decided to quit drinking on Valentine's Day.
- The next station is Oval (tube announcement).
- Do you smoke after making love?
- Please take advantage of our chambermaid service (hotel sign).
- John gave Andy's passport to his brother.
- The above examples are ambiguous(!).
- A panda walks into a restaurant, sits down and orders a sandwich. He eats the sandwich, pulls out a gun and shoots the waiter dead. As the panda

stands up to go, the manager shouts, 'Hey! Where are you going? You just shot my waiter, and you didn't even pay for your sandwich!' 'Hey, man, I'm a PANDA!' the panda shouts back. 'Look it up!' The manager opens his dictionary and reads: 'Panda: a tree-dwelling mammal of Asian origin, characterised by distinct black and white colouring. Eats shoots and leaves.'

The following link contains some great activities on vagueness and ambiguity: www.sjsu.edu/depts/itl/graphics/vague/vague.html.

SUMMARY CHECKLIST

Points you need to remember:

✔ Vagueness and ambiguity: what the terms mean; how to identify them, and how to clarify any vague and/or ambiguous expressions.

FOUNDATION UNIT

Chapter 10: The use of persuasive language

LEARNING OBJECTIVES

By the end of this chapter you should:

✔ Be able to distinguish between reasoning and the use of persuasive language.
✔ Understand and be able to identify any instances of 'emotive' language and 'doublespeak'.
✔ Be able to clarify (by placing in neutral terms) any instances of the above.

Language serves many purposes. We use it to ask questions, tell jokes, express value judgements, give orders, convey and evoke emotions, describe things as being 'thus and so' and also to *persuade*. We have seen that one way of doing this is to present an argument. Here, a **persuasive** inference is drawn and supported by one or more premises which attempt to bring it about. But this is not the only way. In the absence of reason, language can also be used to persuade via word-power alone. Such a process is referred to as **rhetoric**. It approximates to convincing somebody that something is the case, without providing grounds for *why* this is so. A classic example, often cited in Critical Thinking books, is Winston Churchill's call to arms: 'we will fight them on the beaches' – a rallying cry for the nation to resist Nazi tyranny:

> Even though large tracts of Europe and many old and famous States have fallen or may fall into the grip of the Gestapo and all the odious apparatus of Nazi rule, we shall not flag or fail.

persuasive language – Used either in place of or in supplement to argument in order to convince somebody of something.

rhetoric – An umbrella term which refers to the use of persuasive language, rather than reason, as grounds for persuasion.

We shall go on to the end, we shall fight in France,
we shall fight on the seas and oceans,
we shall fight with growing confidence and growing strength in the air,
we shall defend our Island, whatever the cost may be,
we shall fight on the beaches,
we shall fight on the landing grounds,
we shall fight in the fields and in the streets,
we shall fight in the hills;
we shall never surrender, and even if, which I do not for a moment believe, this Island or a large part of it were subjugated and starving, then our Empire beyond the seas, armed and guarded by the British Fleet, would carry on the struggle, until, in God's good time, the New World, with all its power and might, steps forth to the rescue and the liberation of the old.

Few would deny the power of such words, nor the persuasive potency of the speech itself, but no *argument* is being presented. Its persuasive power rests solely upon the emotional language used to express it rather than in the provision of reasons illuminating *why* we should be so swayed. Expressions such as 'fall into the grip of', 'odious', 'flag or fail', 'go on to the end' etc. are highly charged, rhetorical devices that illuminate just how powerful and persuasive a tool language can be. However, the fact that this type of speech can be used to support ignoble as well as noble causes should remind you just how important is the need for objectivity when analysing such detestable examples as the following:

A devil goes through the land,
It's the Jew, well known to us
as a murderer of peoples,
a race defiler, a child's horror in all lands!
Corrupting our youth
stands him in good stead.
He wants all peoples dead.

Stay away from every Jew,
and happiness will come to you! (Taken from *Der Giftpilz* [*The Poisonous Mushroom*] a book of fascist propaganda by Julius Streicher – aimed at children)

Of course, in everyday discourse, the use of persuasive language is often subtler than this: 'you've *got* to be *kidding*', 'is this some type of *joke*?', 'well you know *best* of course!' and so forth. Nevertheless, the principle remains the same – we are in some way being got at. The ability to discriminate those cases where language is used for rhetorical force from those which present genuine argument is therefore an important one. Where no reasons are presented, we should not allow ourselves to be seduced by the power of words alone. Here is a further example. See if you can identify where language is being used for rhetorical effect:

> Is God willing to prevent evil, but not able?
> Then he is not omnipotent.
> Is he able, but not willing?
> Then he is malevolent.
> Is he both able and willing?
> Then whence cometh evil?
> Is he neither able nor willing?
> Then why call him God? Epicurus (Greek philosopher, 341–270 BC)
> **Atheists: winning since 33 AD**

Rhetoric can be used in a number of less obvious ways than those outlined above. It often trades upon the vagueness or ambiguity of a word or expression. The classic example here is 'one person's freedom fighter is another person's terrorist'. The term 'freedom fighter' is *positively* charged. A questionable activity is paraded as being morally commendable, even heroic. However, the term 'terrorist' is *negatively* charged. It implicitly forces us to consider the actions of such a person as morally reprehensible, regardless of whether this is in fact so. In this respect and depending on wording, such expressions can be said to possess either an **emotive** content – one that is *emotionally* charged – or, by contrast, a *neutral* or *cognitive* content which captures the expression's *actual* meaning. For example, the term 'political activist' might be regarded as a more neutral translation here, insofar as it does not seem to carry the same emotional baggage.

Alongside expressing neutral ideas in an emotive vocabulary, persuasive language can also be used to couch emotionally negative or positive terms in what look like cognitively neutral ones: a practice known as '**doublespeak**'. This is done so as to present a negative issue, event or trait in an acceptable light. Here are some examples:

For more on this topic, see Chs 1 and 15 – in particular 'Motive and agenda' and 'Sources'.

emotive – A word or expression is said to have an emotive content if it is emotionally charged (i.e. its expression has either positive or negative connotations). An emotive content is typically contrasted with a **neutral** or **cognitive** one which captures an expression's *actual* meaning.

This is an issue which has already been covered in Ch. 9.

doublespeak – This occurs when a naturally positive or negative term is expressed in cognitively neutral terms. This is often done so as to present a negative issue, event or trait in an acceptable light.

- '*Friendly fire*': military expression – the accidental shooting or bombing of allied troops.
- '*Incontinent ordinance*': military expression – off-target bombs.
- '*Quantitative easing*': political expression – printing extra money to buy your way out of a recession.
- '*Ethnic cleansing*': political expression – racial genocide.
- '*The final solution*': political expression – the Nazi holocaust.
- '*Downsize/headcount adjustment*': corporate expression – the mass laying off of employees.

Such expressions are used to hide any negative connotations that more literal translations might expose.

Exercise

1. Bearing the above points in mind, identify any instances of 'doublespeak' or the emotive use of language in the following examples. For each, suggest a more neutral/accurate translation:
   - 'Hi learners, I'd like to welcome Mr Weinstein – the new learning facilitator – to the learning environment.' (Head teacher to class)
   - 'I'm afraid you are too vertically, horizontally and facially challenged for the modelling job, Vanessa.'
   - 'We need to neutralise any remaining enemy soldiers.'

RHETORIC IN ARGUMENT

So far we have looked at ways in which language can be used to persuade *in the place of* argument. It is often the case, however, that arguments themselves will employ such a device so as to appear more forceful. Arguments, even sound ones, often fail to convince. When this occurs, the use of rhetoric can increase their persuasive impact by intensifying the strength of the reasons they bring into play. When this occurs, we need to consider the effect that such language has on the overall *strength* of the argument and whether the argument *itself* would still stand without it. Identifying and replacing any emotive terms with cognitively neutral ones will allow us to do this:

- *Little quivering animals* like mice *tremble with fear* as they enter the laboratory *where cruel scientists will perform experiments on them*. The *suffering* of *defenceless little animals horrifies* all *sane* human beings. Therefore we should *punish* all such scientists with a taste of their own medicine and *burn their wicked laboratories to the ground*!

Here, if we were to exchange the italicised *emotive* terms with neutral ones, like so:

- Animals clearly suffer in laboratory experiments.
- It is wrong for animals to suffer.
- We should ban laboratory experiments on animals.

We can see that the original argument loses much of its impact. This process also reveals more clearly the argument's actual content.

Summary questions . . .

1. What is the difference between reasoning and the use of persuasive language?
2. What do the expressions 'emotive language' and 'doublespeak' mean? How do we go about clarifying these?

END OF CHAPTER ACTIVITY

1. Identify any instances of persuasive language in the following extract (taken from Martin Luther King's 'I have a dream' speech).
2. Summarise what is being said in cognitively neutral terms and come to a decision as to whether the speech is still effective without the use of rhetoric.

> One hundred years later, the negro lives on a lonely island of poverty in the midst of a vast ocean of material prosperity. One hundred years later, the negro is still languished in the corners of American society and finds himself an exile in his own land. So we've come here today to dramatise a shameful condition. In a sense, we've come to our nation's capital to cash a cheque. When the architects of our republic wrote the magnificent words of the constitution and the Declaration of Independence, they were signing a promissory note to which every American was to fall heir.

The following website offers a definitive guide to doublespeak, including explanations, examples and activities from a wide range of contexts: www.damronplanet.com/doublespeak/.

The following website offers a clear overview of the emotive use of language and where you are most likely to find it: http://library.thinkquest.org/C008200F/page9.htm.

The following website has two interactive activities on the above example (www.monash.edu) which get you to identify and process examples of the emotive use of language: www.monash.edu.au/lls/llonline/writing/arts/sociology/2.3.2.xml.

This note was a promise that all men – yes, black men as well as white men – would be guaranteed the inalienable rights of life, liberty, and the pursuit of happiness. It is obvious today that America has defaulted on this promissory note in so far as her citizens of colour are concerned. Instead of honouring this sacred obligation, America has given the negro people a bad cheque, a cheque which has come back marked 'insufficient funds'.

But we refuse to believe that the bank of justice is bankrupt. We refuse to believe that there are insufficient funds in the great vaults of opportunity of this nation. So we have come to cash this cheque, a cheque that will give us upon demand the riches of freedom and the security of justice. (Martin Luther King)

SUMMARY CHECKLIST

Points you need to remember:

✔   The difference between reasoning and the use of persuasive language.

✔   What is meant by the expressions 'emotive language' and 'doublespeak'.

✔   How to change emotionally charged terms with cognitively neutral ones.

FOUNDATION UNIT

Chapter 11: Flaws

LEARNING OBJECTIVES ✔

By the end of this chapter you should:

✔ Understand what is meant by the expression 'logical fallacy'.

✔ Be able to recognise and identify what is wrong with each of the following fallacies:

> *ad hominem*, *tu quoque*, straw-man, slippery-slope, cause-correlation and *post hoc* fallacies, overgeneralisation and anecdotal evidence, false dichotomy/false dilemma, begging the question/circularity, confusing necessary and sufficient conditions, *ad hoc* arguments, argument from ignorance and confusion/equivocation.

✔ Understand what is meant by the expression: 'fallacious appeal'.

✔ Be able to recognise and identify what is wrong with each of the following appeals: to authority, popular/majority opinion, emotion, sympathy and precedent.

Many exam questions will require you to *identify* a logical fallacy and show *why* the reasoning which employs it (either explicitly or implicitly) is insufficient. This is often key to the process of argument analysis and evaluation (AOs 1 and 2).

An argument is **flawed** if, for whatever reason, the conclusion it presents us with doesn't follow from the premises provided. There are a range of ways in which this can happen – some of which we have already looked at. If an argument *is* flawed, this doesn't mean its conclusion will necessarily be false, but rather that the reasons offered do not provide adequate grounds for our acceptance of it. For example:

flawed argument – An argument is said to be flawed if, for whatever reason, its conclusion doesn't follow from the premises given.

- In a recent study, it was found that women taking combined HRT (hormone replacement therapy) had a much lower rate of coronary heart disease than those that didn't.

- So, HRT prevents coronary heart disease.

Puzzled by the findings of this seemingly convincing case, scientists conducted a range of controlled experiments (see Ch. 3: 'Causal explanations') to try and establish why this was so. These revealed that women taking HRT tended to be from a higher social group with a better than average diet and exercise routine than those who didn't and it was *this*, rather than the HRT, that was responsible for the low rate of heart disease. So the initial argument is flawed in at least two ways. Firstly, it assumes that correlation implies causation (see 'Cause-correlation fallacy', this chapter) – that two events regularly occurring together, HRT and a low rate of CHD, imply the former causes the latter. Secondly, it fails to seek out 'alternative explanations' to test whether or not the hypothesis presented in the conclusion is acceptable. It merely assumes it to be. In cases such as these, an argument is said to have committed a 'logical fallacy' and this provides us with grounds for rejecting it.

See Ch. 18.

LOGICAL FALLACIES

The term 'fallacy' can be understood in one of two ways. Firstly, it can simply mean 'false' – as when we say 'it is a fallacy to believe that women have equal rights to men'. Secondly, it can mean an error in reasoning – as when we say, 'it is a fallacy to believe that HRT lowers the risk of coronary heart disease in women'. It is the second, more technical interpretation, that we will be using here.

The deliberate use of fallacious reasoning is both widespread and effective. More often than not, fallacies are used as a deliberate ploy to get us to accept something that we would in truth otherwise not accept – at least not without further evidence. All politicians, as we shall see, are adept at using these; the majority of adverts contain them in one form or another, and newspapers, particularly tabloids, employ them extensively to convince us that a particular view is correct. The ability to identify such examples and evaluate any reasoning that contains them are clearly important. The philosopher Aristotle identified thirteen of these; modern logicians have identified in excess of a hundred; for exam purposes, you will need to identify twelve.

Ad hominem

Ad hominem arguments are the tools of scoundrels and blackguards. Therefore, they are invalid. (James W. Benham: http://pages.csam.montclair. edu/~benham/funstuff/logical.html)

The **ad hominem** fallacy (from the Latin 'to the man') involves 'attacking the person' rather than the argument they present. The idea here is that, if an arguer has been shown to be defective in some way, then so too has their argument:

At its simplest, the *ad hominem* takes the form of a 'personal attack' – 'why did you listen *him*, he's an idiot!' – but is often far subtler than this. When confronted by a set of hippies protesting against the Vietnam War and waving *'make love not war'* placards, the ex-American president Richard Nixon responded: 'By the looks of them, they couldn't do either'! *Ad hominem* attacks can be used in a variety of ways, the most common of which is the 'abusive' or 'name-calling' *ad hominem*, where the attacker insults or belittles their opponent in place of paying attention to the substance of their argument:

- Well of course you *could* vote for councillor Jones, if you *wanted* a former alcoholic with a penchant for chasing young ladies running your Town Hall.

and the 'circumstantial' *ad hominem*:

- 'Tobacco company representatives should not be believed when they say smoking doesn't seriously affect your health, because they're just defending their own multi-million-dollar financial interests.' (Wikipedia)

where a person's personal circumstances are appealed to in order to indicate a natural bias. In both cases the reasoning is fallacious because, even if the arguer has such a bias or undesirable personal characteristic and this can be *shown*, unless it has a direct bearing on their *argument*, then it should be dismissed as irrelevant. In all such cases, it is the *argument* rather than the person presenting it that should be the object of the attack. For example, arguments are often unfairly challenged by the aggressive question: 'Who are *you* to say such and such?!' when the question that really needs to be asked is: 'What are your *reasons* for saying such and such?'

> **ad hominem** – The *ad hominem* fallacy attacks the arguer rather than the argument they present.

> For more on this issue, see Ch 15: 'Motive and agenda' and 'Sources'.

Tu quoque *(two wrongs make a right/you too fallacy)*

> Wherever we look, we find the US as the leader of terrorism and crime in the world. The US does not consider it a terrorist act to throw atomic bombs at nations thousands of miles away, when it would not be possible for those bombs to hit military troops only. These bombs were rather thrown at entire nations, including women, children and elderly people and up to this day the traces of those bombs remain in Japan. The US does

not consider it terrorism when hundreds of thousands of our sons and brothers in Iraq died for lack of food or medicine. So, there is no base for what the US says and this saying does not affect us. (CNN, March 1997, Interview with Osama bin Laden (taken from fallacyfiles.org)

tu quoque – The *tu quoque* fallacy is used to deflect attention from attacked to attacker, accusing one's opponent of being guilty of the very same charge they condemn in you.

The **tu quoque** (literally 'you too') fallacy exemplified by Bin Laden's defence above, is another version of the *ad hominem* type, directing itself at the person or establishment making the claim rather than the claim itself. It is typically used, when responding to a particular criticism, to accuse one's opponent of being guilty of the same offence. When applied in debate, this fallacy is particularly effective because it forces the plaintiff to jump on the defensive, deflecting the focus of attention from *attacked* to *attacker*. Colloquially it uses the approach that 'those in glass houses shouldn't throw stones' – a person has no right to condemn in others that of which they themselves are guilty. To do so is both inconsistent and hypocritical. For example:

- It is all very well barrister Jones accusing *me* of speeding whilst under the influence m'lud, but as he himself managed to notch up twelve points on his driving licence, I find it a trifle hypocritical to say the least!
- It is deeply inappropriate that the opposition government accuse us of introducing a 'stealth' tax when in fact it was *they* that secretly introduced this scheme when they were in power.

This type of claim is fallacious because, whether or not the accuser is guilty of the same offence as the accused, it is irrelevant to the truth of the original claim and so does not excuse it. As the saying goes, two wrongs don't make a right!

Straw man

Not one of 800 sexologists at a recent conference raised a hand when asked if they would trust a thin rubber sheath to protect them during intercourse with a known HIV infected person … And yet they're perfectly willing to tell our kids that 'safe sex' is within reach and that they can sleep around with impunity. (James C. Dobson, quoted in fallacyfiles.org)

straw-man fallacy – This fallacy unfairly presents a piece of reasoning in an absurd or deliberately weakened fashion. This is done so as to make it easy to refute.

The **straw-man fallacy**, exemplified by this 'put-down' argument, is committed when an opponent's argument is presented in such a way that it becomes easy to knock down – hence the title of this fallacy: a straw man (a traditional target in archery) is easier to defeat than a real one! A position is attributed that is either (a) *not* the one the opponent actually holds or (b) a deliberately weakened or absurd interpretation of the one they *do* hold with the sole intention of tearing it down after its erection. This is usually done so the perpetrator can then go on to present his or her argument in its place, or at least claim to have successfully refuted the original. Such an approach can be directly contrasted with the principle of charity which requires us to present or interpret an opponent's reasoning in its most favourable light. Here are some examples:

- So, this government favours a decommissioning of nuclear weapons. I cannot understand why they would wish to leave our country defenceless and at the mercy of terrorist organisations.
- Do evolutionists seriously expect us to believe that a species as intelligent as that of humans beings is descended from monkeys?
- How can creationists seriously believe that the world was created in seven days by an old man with a white beard?

The 'straw man' belongs to a group of fallacies known as 'red herrings' (the scent of which was used to distract a pack of hounds from a fox's trail). These are fallacies of reasoning which deliberately aim to mislead us about the position an opponent is arguing for. The straw man is fallacious because the position destroyed is not the one held, so the original argument remains intact – hence the expression 'to burn a straw man'. Remedying this type of fallacy requires that, when attacking an opponent's position, we observe the principle of charity and ensure that the position being attacked is also the one argued for.

> The straw-man fallacy directly contrasts with the principle of charity – see Ch. 4.

Slippery slope

> If I'm gonna be an old, lonely man, I'm gonna need a thing … so I figure I'll be Crazy Man with a Snake. Kids will walk past my place, they will run. 'Run away from Crazy Snake Man,' they'll shout! (The character Chandler, in the TV series *Friends*)

The **slippery-slope** fallacy involves moving from one 'moderate' and acceptable conclusion to an 'extreme', unacceptable and/or undesirable one. It can do so in stages where each 'step' on the slope is justified by its predecessor (if a then b, b then c etc.); or *directly* (i.e. without the 'middle

> **slippery-slope** – The slippery-slope fallacy moves from one moderate and acceptable conclusion to an extreme and unacceptable/undesirable one.

For a reminder about what analogies are and how they function, see Ch. 8.

steps'): 'Give someone an inch, and they'll take a mile.' We looked at one such example of this type of fallacy earlier on. This moved from a seemingly acceptable inference about the legalisation of euthanasia: 'We shall begin by doing it because the patient is in intolerable pain' to an extreme and unacceptable one: 'We shall end up doing it because it is Friday afternoon and we want to get away for the weekend.'

The fallacious nature of this type of argument can be shown via analogy. If, for example, somebody was selling a second-hand car for £1,000, and you offered them £999, the likelihood is that they would accept. You could then go on to suggest that, if they would be willing to accept £999, then there is no reason for them not to accept £998, given there's no real difference between the two. But of course, it wouldn't stop there. There's no real difference between £998 and £997; £997 and £996 etc., and if you were to carry on like this, soon the car would have to be given away free! Responding to this fallacy, then, requires us to judge the point at which the inference becomes unacceptable (the minimum price, as it were). Failure to reach such a judgement leaves us vulnerable to 'sliding' all the way down the slope and accepting a position which we in truth ought not to accept. Here are some further examples of this fallacy. See if you can spot where to draw the line in each case:

- If you don't do your homework, you'll fail this course. Fail this course and you'll flunk out of college. Flunk out of college and you won't get a job. No job, no money. No money, no house. If you don't have a house, you'll wind up sleeping on a park bench, drinking methylated spirits and you'll be dead before you're thirty! (This type of example is often used by parents and teachers!)
- This government has already banned cigarette smoking, next thing you know it'll be alcohol. Banning alcohol is just a short step away from banning unhealthy foods and before you know it, we'll be living in a totalitarian state where people aren't allowed to do anything unless given expressed permission to do so by the state. (This is the type of slippery-slope argument employed by politicians!)

Cause-correlation fallacy

I don't know whether my wife left me because of my drinking or if I started drinking 'cause my wife left me. (Nicholas Cage aka Ben Sanderson, *Leaving Las Vegas*)

When two events occur together it is sometimes difficult to judge whether one event *caused* the other (and if so, which one!) or whether their simultaneous occurrence is merely coincidental. This is called **cause-correlation fallacy**. We looked at one such example earlier, on p. 27, where the view that there was no such thing as the Loch Ness monster was supported by the argument that the fish stock in Loch Ness was not big enough to feed such a giant creature. This same fact was taken by believers in the monster to demonstrate its existence. The reason the fish stock was low, they argued, was precisely because the monster kept eating them!

There are times, of course, when such a judgement will be easy to reach. If every time I sneezed the telephone rang, I would not infer that the former event caused the latter! At other times, however, reaching a decision can be more difficult:

<aside>
cause-correlation fallacy – This occurs when a causal connection is illegitimately inferred (see 'Causal explanations', Chapter 3) between two events because either both events occur together, or one event regularly proceeds the other.
</aside>

- Teens who made more than 15 phone calls and sent more than 15 text messages a day, slept poorly and had more careless lifestyles compared to those who made less than five of each per day. (Conducted by Sahlgren's Academy in Sweden using 21 teenagers. Taken from skepticsdictionary.net)

In this example, we might be inclined to believe, as the authors of the study did, that it was the amount of phone calls made and text messages sent that caused the lack of sleep and careless lifestyles. But how do we know this? Perhaps excessive phone-calling and texting aren't a cause, but rather the effect, of such a lifestyle (if I can't sleep, I might as well give somebody a call or send a text message!). Perhaps there was some other causal factor responsible for both excessive phone use and poor lifestyle (depression maybe). Maybe the correlation was purely coincidental. The examples below highlight the three ways in which correlation can lead us astray:

<aside>
Note how the key phrases in this example: 'slept poorly' and 'careless lifestyles' are vague (see Ch. 9) and that twenty-one teenagers hardly represents an adequate sample (see Ch. 3: 'Causal explanations').
</aside>

1. **Kukkurrik:** Kukkurrikkukkurrriku!

   Narrator: Every day before dawn, the rooster Kukkurrik uttered a mighty volley of crows, watched the sun come up, and said to himself…

   Kukkurrik: I've done it again! (Oscar Mandel, *The Kukkurrik Fables*)

This type of example, sometimes referred to as 'reverse causation', is fallacious because it inverts the true causal relation of the two events (the sun's rising causing the cockerel's crow). It implies that event b causes event a, when in fact the converse is true. Looking at a trickier example will help make this

For more on 'bringing in additional evidence', see Ch. 8.

clear! When psychologists claim that 'playing violent video games leads to aggressive behaviour', it might not be clear whether these games are responsible for the aggressive behaviour, or whether naturally aggressive individuals are predisposed to playing violent video games. Unless further evidence can be provided, we have no right to judge either way.

2. There is a direct correlation to be drawn between going to bed fully clothed, and waking up with an extreme headache. So sleeping fully clothed causes headaches! (Adapted from Wikipedia)

This version of the fallacy fails to take into account the further causal factor, namely the drinking of alcohol, which is responsible for *both* events. In this respect, going to bed fully clothed and waking up with a hangover are both effects of the same cause – getting drunk!

3. You may be interested to know that global warming, earthquakes, hurricanes, and other natural disasters are a direct effect of the shrinking numbers of pirates since the 1800s. For your interest, I have included a graph of the approximate number of pirates versus the average global temperature over the last 200 years. As you can see, there is a statistically significant inverse relationship between pirates and global temperature. (Bobby Henderson, Open letter to the Kansas board of education, www.venganza.org/about/open-letter/)

Global average temperature vs number of pirates

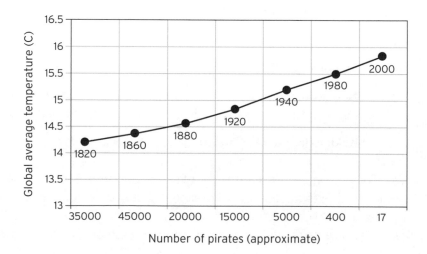

This final 'spoof' example illustrates the third way in which correlation can be deceptive or deliberately fallacious. The relationship between 'global average temperature' and 'number of pirates' is, of course, purely coincidental – similar results could be achieved by appealing to a decline in the use of horse-drawn carts or an increase in the number of Persian cats in south-east England! Nevertheless, such patterns may be used misleadingly to infer a causal link between two sets of events when no such link is known to exist (similar analogous correlations have been discovered between working a night-shift and developing breast cancer; owning a washing machine and dying in a car accident; rising skirt hemlines and increased value of stock-market shares, and prayer and successful impregnation!). Until a plausible justification can be established that explains *why* the link is genuine, all such examples should be treated with caution, if not discarded altogether!

This issue is picked up in greater detail in Chs 17 and 19.

Overgeneralisation

> Batman: When you get a little older, you'll see how easy it is to become lured by the female of the species.
> Robin: I guess you can never trust a woman.
> Batman: You've made a hasty generalization, Robin. It's a bad habit to get into. (*Batman* TV series)

The '**overgeneralisation**' fallacy occurs when a *small* number of observed cases are appealed to in order to support a *general* claim or inference. Sometimes referred to as a 'hasty' or 'rash' generalisation, this form of fallacy has been used to justify all forms of prejudice. The comedian Jack Dee, sceptical of the use of opinion polls in gauging how people will vote in the next general election, gave the following '*reductio ad absurdum*' example (reduction to absurdity) of how such polls work. A man with a clipboard waits at a train station. As the first train pulls in and the commuters begin to disembark, he asks the first two to alight as to whom they will be voting. The first responds 'Conservative' and the second 'Labour' and the man concludes 'the nation is divided'! Whilst humorous, this example illustrates nicely why such generalisations are fallacious. The move from two specific cases to a general conclusion is obviously unwarranted. Such generalisations are only legitimate when two criteria are met. Firstly, a significant amount of evidence needs to be collated (research shows that for opinion polls to be even broadly

overgeneralisation – The fallacy of overgeneralisation (sometimes referred to as '**hasty generalisation**') occurs when a small number of observed cases are appealed to in order to support a general claim or inference.

reductio ad absurdum – Literally, 'reduction to absurdity', is a form of argument which disproves a proposition by showing it to have absurd or ridiculous consequences.

correct i.e. to within a 3% margin of accuracy, at least 2,000 people need to be canvassed) and secondly, this evidence needs to be as widely representative as possible, polling, where appropriate, the views of different genders, cultures, classes, races, religions, ages and locations (if the above sample of 2,000 only represented white, middle-class Londoners, it is unlikely to be proportionate to the views of the nation as a whole!). If either of these conditions are not met, the conclusion will be unreliable. Here are some further examples of hasty generalisations:

- 'After only one year the alternator went out in Mr O'Grady's new Chevrolet. Mrs Dodson's Oldsmobile developed a transmission problem after six months. The obvious conclusion is that cars made by General Motors are just a pile of junk these days.' (Patrick J. Hurley, *A Concise Introduction to Logic*, Wandsworth, 1991, p. 142)
- 'Iraq boasts quite a long history of intermarriage and intercommunal cooperation. But a few years of this hateful dialectic soon succeeded in creating an atmosphere of misery, distrust, hostility, and sect-based politics. Once again, *religion had poisoned everything*.' (Christopher Hitchens, *God Is Not Great: How Religion Poisons Everything*, New York, 2007, p. 27)
- 'We arrived at the park gate at 7:25 P.M., at which time the cashier gleefully took our admission money. Upon entering the zoo and walking across the bridge, we heard the loudspeaker state that the zoo buildings were closing at 8:00 P.M. and that the zoo itself would close at 8:30 P.M. We went to the ticket counter and asked if we could get a pass for the following day. The answer was 'no.' It is easy to see that Calgary is anything but friendly, but, rather, out to rake off tourists for all they can get.' (Ralph H. Johnson and J. Anthony Blair, *Logical Self-Defense*, New York, 2006, p. 70) (The above examples were taken from http://afterall.net/illogic/490543/)
- 'But, to this end, it will not be necessary for me to show that the whole of these are false – a point, perhaps, which I shall never reach; but as even now my reason convinces me that I ought not the less carefully to withhold belief from what is not entirely certain and indubitable, than from what is manifestly false, it will be sufficient to justify the rejection of the whole if I shall find in each some ground for doubt. Nor for this purpose will it be necessary even to deal with each belief individually, which would be truly an endless labour; but, as the removal from below of the foundation necessarily involves the downfall of the whole edifice, I will at once approach the criticism of the principles on which all my former beliefs rested.' (Descartes, *Meditation 1*)

False dilemma/dichotomy

> Either you are with us, or you are with the terrorists. (George W. Bush, Address to Congress, 20 September 2001)

Many things in life are black and white. Humans are either male or female; cardinal numbers, either odd or even; when you take an exam, you will either pass or fail. In each such case there are only two possible options and if one of these is ruled out, then the alternative follows by default. The **false dilemma** fallacy – sometimes referred to as the fallacy of 'restricting the options' – exploits this natural division by presenting us with two alternatives and forcing us to decide between them. For example:

- 'You either turn up on time, or you flunk the course.'
- 'You're either part of the solution, or part of the problem.' (Eldridge Cleaver)
- 'He who is not with me, is against me.' (Jesus Christ, Matthew 12:30)
- 'I thought, "I'm a genius or I'm mad. Which is it? I can't be mad because nobody's put me away. Therefore I must be a genius."' (John Lennon)
- 'If you think education is expensive, try ignorance.' (Derek Bok)

It should be clear, however, that for each dilemma, one of the options isn't really an option at all (siding with the terrorists, flunking the course etc.) so we are forced into accepting the 'alternative'! The false dilemma, then, is an effective method for coercing somebody into accepting something they might otherwise not agree to. The reason why such examples are fallacious is because they fail to consider viable alternatives to those presented (for example, remaining *neutral*; doing a load of extra revision etc.). Drawing attention to these is key to the resolution of such dilemmas.

> **false dilemma/dichotomy** – This fallacy (sometimes referred to as the fallacy of **restricting the options**) presents us with two options, one of which isn't really an option at all, so we are forced to consent to the second.

> 'Appeal to fear' (this chapter) presents us with a similar type of dilemma to this and is equally fallacious.

Begging the question/circularity

> The wonderful thing about tiggers, is tiggers are wonderful things. (A.A. Milne)

An argument or claim is said to be '**question-begging**' or 'circular' if it depends upon the very thing it is trying to prove in order to prove it. In all such cases, the truth of the original claim remains open. The most famous example of this type of fallacy is the kind of simplistic, Christian justification that one sometimes comes across for the belief in the existence of God. It works like this:

> **question-begging** – An argument or claim is said to be question-begging or **circular** if it depends upon the very thing it is trying to prove in order to prove it.

- How do you know God exists?
- Because the Bible tells us so.
- But how do you know the Bible is correct?
- Because it represents the word of God.

Laying the argument out in diagram form should reveal more fully the circularity involved here:

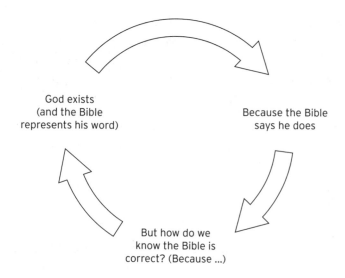

God exists
(and the Bible
represents his word)

Because the Bible
says he does

But how do we
know the Bible is
correct? (Because ...)

It should be clear that, in order to prove God exists, this example already depends upon his existing – hence the circularity! Here are some more examples:

- 'I wouldn't have done it if I didn't believe it was the right thing to do.' (George W. Bush)
- 'I didn't steal it, I'm not a thief.' (Gul Dukat, Cardassian politician, *Star Trek Deep Space 9*)
- But why ...? (Uttered by a curious child). Because ... (Uttered by a tired parent!)

In order to avoid the charge of circularity, an argument needs to avoid assuming the truth of the thing which it is trying to prove. To do this, the premises need to provide independent support for, rather than just reiterate, that which is present in the conclusion.

Confusing necessary and sufficient conditions

> Political commentator: Publicly, Mayor Ellison claims to remain steadfast in his determination to appoint a new police commissioner. However, no determination has yet been made regarding the appointment, so Mayor Ellison's vow is clearly disingenuous. (www.sparknotes.com/testprep/books/lsat/chapter1section7.html)

If x is a **necessary condition** of y, then if x is lacking, y won't come about. If y is a **sufficient condition** of x, then having y guarantees having x. To use a simple example, let us say that passing the Critical Thinking exam requires you to achieve at least 70% (this is purely hypothetical!). Achieving at least 70%, then, would be a necessary condition of passing the exam. Achieving precisely 70%, however, would not be. This is because 71% (or any *other* mark above 69%) would guarantee a pass. 71%, then, can be regarded as a sufficient (i.e. you get 71%, you've passed!) but not a necessary condition of passing the exam. For similar reasons, it is a *necessary*, but not a *sufficient* condition of an argument that it is persuasive – there are other forms of persuasion, for example the use of rhetoric, that are non-arguments. It is a *sufficient*, but not a *necessary* condition of an argument that it contains a single premise and an inference. An argument that contained several premises and inferences would still be an argument, nonetheless.

The fallacy of confusing necessary and sufficient conditions comes about when the debater fails, often inadvertently, to spot the above difference. Let's look at another example of this fallacy from the field of art:

* Beauty is a necessary condition of art. My parents' 'William Morris' wallpaper is beautiful; therefore it is a work of art.

Even if we assume, for the sake of the argument, that both premises are true, the conclusion does not follow on the basis of what went before. Beauty, on its own, may well be a necessary condition for something to be an artwork but here beauty is being confused with being a sufficient condition too and that cannot be right. It is not difficult to find plenty of examples of things that are beautiful but not art – landscapes, faces, animal movement, a pass in football, even a well-constructed argument! And there are examples of non-beautiful objects that *are* art, such as paintings which depict the ugliness of war – like Picasso's famous painting *Guernica*, which employs the broken-glass perspective of a modern art style called 'Cubism' to depict the agony of the Spanish Civil War of the 1930s.

Grasping the difference between necessary and sufficient conditions is quite a challenge. For more information and examples, check the accompanying website.

necessary condition – If x is a necessary condition of y, then if x is lacking, y won't come about.

sufficient condition – If y is a sufficient condition of x, then having y guarantees having x.

Bombed-out buildings, a mother with a dead child in her arms, animals running amok are all painted in oppressive shades of grey, the whole painting being illuminated by a single light bulb that only adds to the terror. If you don't know this painting, search it out. To get around this problem, some have argued that:

- If an object 'is displayed in an art gallery' then such public recognition must be a sufficient condition for it to be an artwork, regardless of whether or not it is beautiful.

The example that is often cited in support of this argument is the famous (or some would say, infamous!) *Fountain* by the twentieth-century French artist Marcel Duchamp. In 1917, Duchamp provocatively displayed a ceramic urinal by this title, in an art gallery in New York. We might not find this very shocking nowadays, but at the time it was regarded as an outrage. However, Duchamp's aim was not primarily to shock, but to make the point that *anything* can be an artwork should the artist so decide, even something which is neither beautiful nor interesting in itself (which had a huge influence on the subsequent history of modern art and can still be felt today in the kind of works that are annually displayed in the Turner Prize competition). On the basis of the above definition then, Duchamp's *Fountain* must be an artwork because, whilst clearly not beautiful, it is, nevertheless, currently on display in Tate Modern. However, once again the fallacy of confusing necessary and sufficient conditions rears its head. Being on display in an art gallery may well be a sufficient condition for something to be considered as an artwork, but this condition can only too easily be confused with its having a necessary role, leading to the fallacious conclusion that anything not on display in an art gallery must be refused the status of artwork. This cannot be the case because there are clearly some works of art, such as Picasso's self-portrait that he kept under his bed, which are nonetheless artworks despite not being in an art gallery.

Ad hoc argument

The issue of hypotheses was discussed in detail in Ch. 3 – see 'Hypotheses'.

Husband to wife: An Englishman on a bus would always give up his seat to an old lady who was standing.

Wife: Nonsense! I see plenty of Englishmen everyday on the buses, sitting while old ladies stand, – even when the old dears are carrying heavy shopping!

Husband: Ah well, those are not *true* Englishmen, are they?!

An argument or claim is said to be ***ad hoc*** (literally, 'for this [specific and limited task]') if it serves the sole purpose of rescuing a theory or hypothesis from refutation. There will be times when such a move is valid. Biologists, for example, having classified *all* living organisms as either unicellular (single-celled) or multi-cellular (many-celled), came across a bothersome, 'fungi-like' organism known as 'slime-mold'. This resisted classification on account of its mutating from unicellular to multi-cellular status at different stages of its development. Rather than reject their initial, rather neat hypothesis biologists instead proposed an '*ad hoc*' clause to modify it: 'all organisms are either unicellular or multi-cellular *except for slime mold*'. Given the organism's unique status, this seemed reasonable enough. But if further such anomalies were discovered, causing further cracks to appear in the original hypothesis, it would be fallacious to go on adding such modifications (i.e. 'all organisms are either unicellular or multi-cellular *except for organisms a, b, c, d, e... etc.*'!). There comes a point where 'patching up' the original claim ceases to be an option and the hypothesis has to be rejected. The refutation of the geocentric (Earth-centred) model of the universe offers a classic example of this. Although it was more or less universally believed until the end of the Middle Ages, this Ptolemaic view (named after the early astronomer, Ptolemy) failed to account for and predict the seemingly erratic movement of the planets. More and more *ad hoc* modifications were therefore attached until it became clear that the original hypothesis could no longer be salvaged. It was eventually replaced by the Copernican 'heliocentric' (Sun-centred) model that we have in place today. Here are some further examples:

- 'Dinosaurs never existed. God put those fossils there in order to test our faith in him.' (Typical creationist response to the existence of fossils as evidence for evolution)
- 'Although we said we had proof that weapons of mass destruction existed, and although we found no evidence that they really did, the war was still justified because the leader was a tyrant.' (http://papyr.com/hypertextbooks/comp1/logic.htm)
- 'Every morning, Chantecleer the cockerel would boast to the assembled chickens that it was his early morning crowing that caused the sun to rise. The more intelligent of the chickens were sceptical, but had to admit that the evidence for this connection was very strong. Then, one morning, Chantecleer overslept and yet the sun still rose high in the heavens. At last, those chickens who were sceptical of the boasting cockerel's claim thought

This cells example shares a similar form to the 'false dilemma' fallacy (this chapter).

ad hoc – An argument or claim is said to be *ad hoc* (literally: 'for this [specific and limited task]') if it serves the sole purpose of rescuing a theory or hypothesis from refutation.

that they could challenge his account. "So how do you explain that the sun still rose, even though you were asleep?" they said. "Ah," said Chantecleer, "I crowed so loudly the day before that its effect carried on over two days! That's why I had a lie-in this morning!"' (traditional tale)

Argument from ignorance

'If *polar bears* are [the[dominant [predator[in the Arctic, then there would seem to have been no need for them to evolve a white-coloured form of camouflage.' (Hugh Montefiore, Anglican Bishop)

For a detailed discussion of the above example, see: http://en.wikipedia.org/ wiki/Argument_from_ ignorance#Examples.

argument from ignorance – This works on the premise that a claim can be regarded as true if not proven false, and false if not proven true.

The **argument from ignorance** (*argumentum ad ignorantiam*) works upon the principle that claims that have *not* been subject to rigorous scrutiny can still be regarded as true if they have yet to be proven false and false if yet to be proven true. In response to the above example, the evolutionary biologist Richard Dawkins, in his book *The Blind Watchmaker*, points out that, if its author had tried to imagine a black polar bear sneaking up on one of its prey in the Arctic, he would understand the evolutionary value of such fur! The argument is fallacious insofar as, far from validating the truth (or falsity) of a claim, lack of evidence is no evidence at all and thus cannot be appealed to as support.

If we were to argue:

- There is no evidence to *prove* that crop-circles are man-made hoaxes; therefore they have to have some form of paranormal explanation.

Or conversely:

- There is no evidence to *prove* crop-circles are the result of paranormal activity; therefore they have to be man-made hoaxes.

Such examples might *appear* convincing, but are fallacious inasmuch as they conflate absence of *disproof* with truth, and absence of *proof* with falsity. Using parallel cases will make this clear:

- I didn't see him smoke a single cigarette on Friday night, so he must have quit.
- There is no evidence to prove there *isn't* gold at the end of every rainbow, so there must be gold at the end of every rainbow.

It is important that these types of example aren't confused with arguments that share a similar form. The theory of evolution, for example, has yet to be *disproved*, despite numerous attempts to do so (creationist arguments, intelligent design, irreducible complexity etc. – you will not be required to know these!) whilst the existence of the Loch Ness monster has yet to be *proved*. However, it does seem far more reasonable to think that, whilst evolution *is* an acceptable theory, the Loch Ness monster clearly isn't. This is because, contrary to our previous examples, rigorous, scientific attempts have been made both to confirm and to refute both of them. A final word of warning! The argument from ignorance would still be fallacious if the inference drawn (for example 'crop-circles are man-made hoaxes') were true. This is because, in *all* such cases, it is not the inference which is at fault, but the reasoning used to enforce it.

Confusion/equivocation

In an episode of *Blackadder* which takes place in a First World War trench, one of the characters, on being asked why he volunteered to fight, says that it was 'because he wanted to see how a war was fought so badly'. Captain Blackadder replies:

> Well, you've come to the right place, Bob. A war hasn't been fought this badly since Olaf the Hairy, high chief of all the Vikings, accidentally ordered 80,000 battle helmets with the horns on the inside!

Sometimes an ambiguous word or expression can be used in such a way that its meaning becomes unclear or confusing. This is sometimes accidental, but more often than not a deliberate ploy to mislead. In the above example, Bob's expression 'so badly' can be understood in one of two ways. Its first use can be taken to mean 'I really wanted to' whilst its second retains the more literal sense of 'very poorly'. Here the ambiguity is played upon for humorous effect and is transparent. Other classic examples include:

The issue of ambiguity has been taken up in greater detail in Ch. 9.

- Nothing relieves headaches quicker than Panadin – so take nothing instead!
- Why is it that your nose runs and your feet smell? (Beer advert)
- Women need not fear man-eating sharks!
- 'One morning I shot an elephant in my pyjamas. How he got into my pyjamas I'll never know.' (Groucho Marx)
- A feather is light. What is light cannot be dark. Therefore, a feather cannot be dark.

fallacy of equivocation – This occurs when an ambiguous word or expression (i.e. one with more than one meaning) is used in order to deliberately mislead.

For more on 'clarifying the meaning of terms' see Ch. 9.

There are numerous websites providing examples, information and activities on logical fallacies. Among the best are: www.sjsu.edu/depts/itl/graphics/main.html; www.nizkor.org/features/fallacies/; www.goodart.org/fallazoo.htm; http://mcckc.edu/longview/ctac/fallacy.htm; www.skepdic.com/refuge/ctlessons/lesson5.html; www.drury.edu/ess/Logic/Informal/Overview.html. My own personal favourite is: www.fallacyfiles.org/.

Most examples that commit this '**fallacy of equivocation**'– i.e. where a piece of reasoning trades upon the ambiguity of its terms – are subtler and correspondingly more difficult to identify than the above:

- 'The publication ban in the Paul Bernardo case ought to be lifted. After all, there is a great public interest in the case and the courts always ought to act in the public interest.' (http://faculty.uccb.ns.ca/philosophy/115/equivocation.htm)

Here the ambiguity arises with the expression 'public interest'. The first use: 'there is a great public interest in the case' simply means that people are curious about what's going on. The second, that the courts 'always ought to act in the public interest', means they have a duty to do what's right by their citizens. The difference is clearly an important one as the argument's validity depends upon the terms functioning *in the same way* – a point the author evidently fails to take into account! Where equivocation occurs, identifying the culprit terms and clarifying their meaning are a necessary first step in the process of evaluation.

A final word of warning before moving on! Where a piece of reasoning, whether unwittingly or not, is guilty of committing a logical fallacy, this does *not* imply that its conclusion will be false. Indeed the belief that it does is fallacious in its own right and has earned itself the title 'the fallacy of a fallacy'! What it *does* mean is that the reasoning used to enforce it is insufficient and should thus be identified and rejected.

Exercise

1. Choose one of the websites and work through the activities.

FALLACIOUS APPEALS

We often make use of appeals in support of our claims. We might appeal to the expertise of a football pundit to support the belief that Arsenal will win the league; we could appeal to popular opinion to support the claim 'the government will not be re-elected'; we may well appeal to human sympathy to support the belief that a charitable donation to the NSPCC would be a worthwhile act, and of course, we could go on like this. As long as these are relevant and well directed and the information provided comes from a reliable source, then they can play an important role in reasoning. When the source appealed to is *not* reliable, nor well directed or relevant to the matter in hand, then any reasoning which depends upon such sources will be fallacious. Once again, this does not entail that the inference they support will be false, nor that adequate grounds which *would* offer legitimate support might not be provided, but rather that the grounds that *are* provided are ineffective in bringing about the conclusion they intend. **Fallacious appeals** fall into one of two camps. Firstly, **misdirected appeals**: these share the same form as legitimate appeals, but are directed at a source whose authority is not relevant to the claim being made. Secondly, **emotional appeals**: these are never legitimate as they appeal directly to the emotions of their audience, rather than to reason or evidence of a factual nature. In the former camp, we would include appeals to authority, popular opinion and precedent; in the latter, appeals to such emotions as fear, sympathy and vanity. We will deal with each in turn.

Misdirected appeals

Appeal to authority

In the absence of knowledge, we often appeal to authoritative sources in an attempt to justify our claims. We might not, for example, understand how antibiotics clear infections, but if we have it on the advice of a good doctor that they do, then this is reason enough to believe it; few of us know how a car's engine functions, but if a reliable mechanic informs us we need to replace the auto-transmission, our belief in the faultiness of this mechanism is justified; we might not know the word for chair in Klingon, but if 'Keith' the local IT technician and avid *Star Trek* fan assures us this is 'DlvI'Hol' then we have no reason for doubting this! Of course, where possible, it is always best to go out and check for ourselves to see whether a claim is true, but when this is *not* possible, and this is often the case, such appeals form an essential part of our reasoning. There are, nevertheless, several ways in which appeals can misfire. Firstly, if the authority appealed to is an expert, but not in the field of our enquiry, then their testimony should be dismissed (some refer to this as an appeal to *illegitimate* authority!):

fallacious appeals
– Fallacious appeals (illegitimately) appeal to emotions, common practices, illegitimate authorities etc. in the place of (legitimate) reasons, sources and evidence in order to convince us that something is the case. For more on this issue, see Chs 1 and 15: 'Motives and agendas' and 'Sources'.

misdirected appeal
– Misdirected appeal petitions the support of an authority or source whose expertise is not relevant to the claim being made. Three of the most common types are the **appeal to authority** (where the authority has expertise, but not in the relevant field of enquiry); the **appeal to popular opinion** (where, if a significant number of people can be shown to believe or do x, then x is regarded as justified/correct/ true), and the **appeal to precedent** (where, because a precedent [standard] has been set in a previous case, then so too it can be applied to *all* cases of a similar nature).

emotional appeal
– An emotional appeal, unsurprisingly, appeals to the emotions rather than reason as a means to influence belief. The most common of these include appeals to fear, pity, spite, vanity, prejudice and loyalty (in fact there are probably as many of these as there are human emotions!).

- Albert Einstein believed in a God that 'revealed himself in the orderly harmony of what exists'. If one of the greatest scientific minds the world has ever produced is convinced of God's existence, then surely God must exist.

But Einstein was a scientist and so not necessarily an authority on religion. An appeal to Einstein might support a particular *scientific* claim (and again here we face problems since much of what Einstein believed has since been scientifically refuted), but on religious matters we need to look elsewhere. Another example of this kind of appeal makes use of celebrities in place of expertise (still a *type* of authority). If someone with great popular appeal – usually a sports star, actor or musician – is affiliated with or endorses a certain product, then this is enough to convince many of its worth. Adverts are the classic offenders here:

- 'It is 50 megabytes, fibre-optic, it is the mother of all Broadband.' (Samuel L. Jackson, actor, advertising a new type of internet connection)
- 'Get a life, get Swiftcovered.' (Iggy Pop, excessive rock star, advertising car insurance!)

But an actor cannot be expected to know much about Broadband, and a rock star with a history of overindulgence hardly offers an appropriate endorsement for car insurance! Once again, if the authority lacks *relevant* expertise, their testimony should be dismissed.

However, note that, insofar as the experts themselves may disagree, even where their expertise *is* relevant, then we may still need to exercise caution.

Scientists sign letter in support of global warming legislation

The evidence in favour of global warming is undeniable. *This is supported by a team of over 600 prominent American scientists* who have all called upon US Congress to pass legislation that will curb its effects. *In the words of the eminent Dr Thomas Lovejoy, president of the H. John Heinz III Center for Science, Economics and the Environment: 'The science is irrefutable not only about the reality of climate change, but also that plant and animal species are already being harmed by it.'* Based on this evidence, it is clear that radical steps need to be taken to halt this process. (www.targetglobalwarming.org/blog/scientistletter)

As compelling as such an appeal is (see the *italicised* phrases) it is seriously weakened by a petition, signed by over 31,000 scientists, who deny the above on the grounds that there is no convincing scientific evidence that human release of carbon dioxide, methane or other greenhouse gases is causing or will, in the foreseeable future, cause catastrophic heating of the Earth's atmosphere and disruption of the Earth's climate. Furthermore, they go on to point out that there is substantial scientific evidence that increases in atmospheric carbon dioxide can produce many beneficial effects upon the natural plant and animal environments of the Earth. (For a full list of these, see: www.oism.org/pproject/.)

It is also important to note that the authority appealed to might have some natural bias or vested interest to distort the truth of a claim. The example above, 'Scientists sign letter in support of global warming legislation', which appeals to the team of *over 600 prominent American Scientists* in support of introducing measures to curb the progress of global warming elicited the following response:

For more on bias, see Ch 15: 'Motives and agendas' and 'Sources'.

Prominent scientists??

Submitted by jpq on Sun, 01/11/2009 – 11:54am.

The signatories are reputed to be 'Prominent Scientists'. However, a review of the list shows them to be a collection of members affiliated with environmental groups [with] pre-conceived agendas.

And obviously, if this is the case, this places doubt over the reliability of such evidence. Equally, one might find that many of the scientists in the global-warming-denying camp may have their research funded by the big petrol firms who stand most to lose from controlling carbon emissions. Guaranteeing the appropriateness of a particular authority is not always an easy task. Generally speaking, as long as (a) the truth of the claim is not one you can easily go out and check for yourself, (b) the authority being appealed to has an expertise that relates to the claim being made and (c) there is no *obvious* controversy surrounding its truth nor bias or vested interest on behalf of its author, then such appeals can be regarded as reliable. If any of these criteria are not met, then a sceptical eye is called for.

Appeal to popular opinion

The appeal to popular opinion can be an effective, persuasive device. It works on the principle that, if the majority of people are favourably inclined towards (or believe/do) x, then x is true (or justified/correct etc.). The reasoning is fallacious because there is a clear difference between people believing something and its actually being true. Consensus and accuracy should not be conflated. Even if, for example, the majority of UK citizens were in agreement that the death penalty should be reinstated, this does not mean that it should be. There were times when the majority of people thought the Earth was flat and at the centre of the universe, but of course, that didn't make it so. We often, and unreflectively, make use of such examples in our reasoning:

- The majority of music is downloaded illegally, so there can't be anything wrong with me doing it.
- Everyone else is going to Glastonbury this year, why can't I?
- 'What, you don't like rice? Tell me Michael, how could a billion Chinese people be wrong?' (*The Lost Boys*)
- Well, everybody else voted for him so he can't be *too* bad!
- Everyone *knows* that cannabis isn't a *real* drug.
- It's the highest grossing movie in recent years; it's got to be worth seeing.
- Everybody knows that appeals to popular opinion are fallacious! (Can you also spot the contradiction here?!)

In all such cases, even if the premises *were* true, they would still need the support of further evidence which did not depend upon popular opinion or behaviour. Here are a couple more examples to give you some idea of how this fallacy works:

- Eight out of ten owners say their pets prefer it. (Popular advert for a well-known brand of cat food)
- In a survey, 87% of those questioned claimed that their hair felt thoroughly replenished and revitalised. Isn't it about time you tried Nutri-Essence-Herbalising-Effect-Hair-Serum-Revita-Lift?

Appeal to precedent

This point is developed in greater detail in Ch. 12.

The appeal to precedent has its roots in courts of law where, if a previous decision has been upheld in a particular case, for example in favour of a female employee being paid the same as a male colleague who performed a similar role, then it should also extend to cases of a similar nature, such as those relating to religion, race or sexuality. A 'precedent' has been set.

However, this type of appeal can become fallacious for a number of reasons. Firstly, when the precedent appealed to in support of a new case is not similar enough to the case in hand for it to warrant the same treatment. Adapting the above example, if we were to appeal to the precedent set in the first case and argue that:

*   Person x, a young employee, has a similar role to that of person y, an older, more experienced one, and should therefore be granted equal rights of pay.

This would be fallacious as it fails to take into account the respective difference in expertise between the two workers. This would be a relevant factor for determining salary. A similar type of reasoning can be found in the 'weak analogy' fallacy where cases x and y are regarded as being similar enough for whatever holds true of x to also hold true of y. If the two cases differ in certain key respects, however, and these are overlooked, the analogy will not hold water. This type of appeal can also be fallacious when the precedent appealed to fails to take into account the fact that circumstances might have changed since its inception – for example, the precedent which endorsed *complete* freedom of speech was no longer regarded as being applicable in today's political climate given the heightened security measures introduced in the wake of 9/11 (see, for example, the new laws banning 'incitement to religious hatred').

For more on weak analogy, see Ch. 8: 'Analogies'.

Emotional appeals

Whilst 'misdirected appeals' can, at least in principle, be modified in order to amend any fallacy they contain, emotional appeals will *always* be fallacious. Emotion can never take the place of reason and factual evidence in the practice of argument construction. There are a range of emotions which this type of fallacy looks to exploit: fear, loyalty, prejudice, pity, vanity and anger being the most common. In each such case, agreement is elicited, not via the presentation of cogent, well-structured argument, but rather by the arousing of non-rational sentiments within the intended audience in order to influence their belief. Such appeals, as the following examples should make clear, can be very persuasive indeed!

Appeal to fear

Fear, with the possible exception of love, is perhaps the strongest of all emotions. Not surprising, then, that its use as a persuasive device is widespread. Appeals to fear share the same form as the 'false dilemma' fallacy; they present us with two choices, one of which will cause alarm/fear/terror so that we are intimidated into accepting the second:

*   Either x or y.
*   Y is alarming/fearful/terrifying.
*   So x.

The following represent just a small sample of examples that commit this type of fallacy. Next time you watch a set of adverts or listen to a politician speak, prick up your ears; you are sure to come across many more!

*   Join our gang or else! (As uttered in the playground)
*   Michael: My father made him an offer he couldn't refuse.
    Kay Adams: What was that?
    Michael: Luca Brasi held a gun to his head, and my father assured him that either his brains or his signature would be on the contract. (*The Godfather*)
*   'For the wages of sin is death, but the free gift of God is eternal life in union with the Messiah Jesus our Lord.' (Romans 6:23)
*   Nutri-glow-miracle-cream or wrinkles – *the choice is yours!*
*   'As I look ahead, I am filled with foreboding. Like the Roman, I seem to see "the River Tiber foaming with much blood". That tragic and intractable phenomenon which we watch with horror on the other side of the Atlantic but which there is interwoven with the history and existence of the States itself, is coming upon us here by our own volition and our own neglect. Indeed, it has all but come. In numerical terms, it will be of American proportions long before the end of the century. Only resolute and urgent action will avert it even now. Whether there will be the public will to demand and obtain that action, I do not know. All I know is that to see, and not to speak, would be the great betrayal.' (Enoch Powell's infamous 'Rivers of Blood' speech – a thinly veiled right-wing piece of propaganda warning of the threat of immigration)
*   'I know today was the coursework deadline, sir, but remember, my father is on the board of governors for the college and I'm sure you can appreciate he would not be happy if you didn't give me an extension.' (Student!)

For more on principles, see Ch. 3: 'Statements of principle'.

- 'The choice is yours, either turn up on time, or leave the course.' (Teacher)
- 'The time has come to make a choice, Mr Anderson. Either you choose to be at your desk on time from this day forth, or you choose to find yourself another job.' (*The Matrix*)

Of course you might be asking yourself why the last two examples are fallacious; after all, it seems reasonable enough that if a student fails to submit homework or an employee fails to turn up for work on time, then their teacher or employer has every right to expel them from a course or sack them. But this misses the point. It is not the principle that's at fault, but rather the method used to enforce it. If we were to argue:

- Turning up on time and completing homework are necessary course requirements.
- Any student that fails to meet either of these conditions should therefore be taken off the course.

There would be nothing fallacious about this. But here, reasons replace fear as the motivating factor that brings about the conclusion.

Appeal to sympathy and vanity

Because all emotional appeals share the same basic form (sentiment rather than reason forms the basis of persuasion), we can cover these last two cases briefly. Appeals to sympathy, as should be obvious, arouse feelings of pity and guilt in the mind of one's opponent/audience in order to bring them round to a particular point of view:

- Many advertisements work on our natural sympathy for innocent suffering as when a pathetic little mongrel dog, scruffy and unloved, stares sadly out at us from the poster, begging us to donate money to the Stray Dogs' Home.
- 'Hath not a Jew eyes? Hath not a Jew hands, organs, dimensions, senses, affections, passions? Fed with the same food, hurt with the same weapons, subject to the same diseases, healed by the same means, warmed and cooled by the same winter and summer, as a Christian is? If you prick us, do we not bleed? If you tickle us, do we not laugh? If you poison us, do we not die? And if you wrong us, shall we not revenge?' (Shylock, Shakespeare's *Merchant of Venice*, Act 3, Scene 1)

See: www.sjsu.
edu/depts/itl/
graphics/adhom/
appeal.html for a
range of explanations,
examples and
activities on fallacious
appeals.

Appeals to vanity, by contrast, *flatter* the intended audience, distracting their attention from the matter in hand by exploiting their natural sense of conceitedness:

- You look an intelligent sort of person, I'm sure that you'll agree with the point I'm trying to make.
- You know you owe it to yourself to spray your hair with luxury Style-O-Curl, the choice of the stars – you deserve it!

For all such cases, unless independent grounds are supplied for what is being argued for, they should be rejected out of hand.

Summary questions . . .

1. What is a logical fallacy? How many of the above logical fallacies can you remember? Try summarising each in a couple of sentences.
2. Explain the two ways in which appeals can be fallacious.

END OF CHAPTER ACTIVITY

Here are some further examples of such appeals to give you a feeling for how they work. See if you can identify which emotion is appealed to in each:

- Come on, John. We went to the same school together. You must give me your support.
- It is simply not cricket to behave like this.
- How can a true British subject have anything but contempt for foreigners?!
- The anger that you must be feeling at this terrible crime will make you cry out for revenge.

SUMMARY CHECKLIST

Points you need to remember:

✔ What is meant by the expression 'logical fallacy'.

✔ How to identify, explain and evaluate each of the following fallacies:

ad hominem, *tu quoque*, straw-man, slippery-slope, cause-correlation and *post hoc* fallacies, overgeneralisation and anecdotal evidence, false dichotomy/false dilemma, begging the question/circularity, confusing necessary and sufficient conditions, *ad hoc* arguments, argument from ignorance and confusion/equivocation.

✔ What is meant by the expression: 'fallacious appeal'.

✔ How to identify, explain and evaluate each of the following appeals: to authority, popular/majority opinion, emotion, sympathy and precedent.

12

UNIT 1 FOUNDATION UNIT

Chapter 12: Drawing comparisons and contrasts

This single stick, which you now behold ingloriously lying in that neglected corner, I once knew in a flourishing state in a forest. It was full of sap, full of leaves, and full of boughs, but now in vain does the busy art of man pretend to vie with nature by tying that withered bundle of twigs to its sapless trunk. It is now at best but the reverse of what it was: a tree turned upside down, the branches on the earth, and the root in the air. It is now handled by every dirty wench, condemned to do her drudgery, and by a capricious kind of fate destined to make other things clean and be nasty itself. At length, worn to the stumps in the service of the maids, it is either thrown out of doors or condemned to its last use of kindling a fire. When I beheld this, I sighed and said within myself, surely mortal man is a broomstick: nature sent him into the world strong and lusty, in a thriving condition, wearing his own hair on his head, the proper branches of this reasoning vegetable, until the axe of intemperance has lopped off his green boughs and left him a withered trunk; he then flies to art, and puts on a periwig, valuing himself upon an unnatural bundle of hairs, all covered with powder, that never grew on his head. But now should this our broomstick pretend to enter the scene, proud of those birchen spoils it never bore, and all covered with dust, through the sweepings of the finest lady's chamber, we should be apt to ridicule and despise its vanity, partial judges that we are of our own excellencies and other men's defaults. (Jonathan Swift, *A Meditation Upon a Broomstick*)

For more on definitions, see Ch. 3: 'Definitions).

We have seen that definitions – claims which involve clarifying what a term or expression means – often do so by distinguishing what is being referred to from items of a similar nature. Similarly, analogies, like the above, are effective to the extent that there are relevant similarities between the objects being compared and defective to the extent of their differences. All such examples require us to reach a judgement which is essentially comparative in nature. For exam purposes, drawing a **comparison** involves judging two things to be alike in certain respects whilst a **contrast** requires us to highlight salient differences. We might say, for example, that football and darts are alike insofar as they are both sports, involve a reasonable amount of skill, are competitive etc., but different to the extent that football is a team sport and requires a high level of physical fitness whereas darts is a game for individual players, none of whom need to be particularly athletic and indeed many of whom have rather large stomachs! In this respect, and for obvious reasons, it would be more reasonable to compare darts to billiards and football to rugby. In all such cases, judging whether the similarities connecting the objects of comparison outweigh their differences will determine the effectiveness of any reasoning which employs them.

For more on analogies, see Ch. 8.

comparison and contrast – Drawing a comparison and contrast requires us to consider the relevant similarities and differences between two (or more) objects of comparison.

Exercise

1. For the following examples (a) identify the two things being compared and (b) come to a decision as to whether their similarities outweigh their differences.
   - The battle of Waterloo was won on the playing fields of Eton!
   - If we give bankers bonuses that will aid the green shoots of economic recovery.

COMPARATIVE EVALUATIONS

For more on value judgements, see Ch. 3.

Often, comparisons will employ value judgements to make a point. For example, it might be said that A is better than B; more attractive than B; braver than B etc. and to evaluate these you will need to identify the way in which the judgement is being used – i.e. how the terms 'better', 'more attractive', 'moral' and 'braver' function. In different contexts, 'better than' might mean 'healthier', 'more moral', 'stronger', 'longer', 'more popular', 'higher quality' and so forth and, in any given context, you will need to settle on which of these is correct before you can decide upon the criteria to be used for comparison. Usually, and assuming the reasoning being analysed is not vague, ambiguous and/or guilty of equivocation an answer to this question will be straightforward. If we were to say, as a mother might to a child when choosing a drink:

For more on vagueness and ambiguity see Ch. 9. For more on equivocation see Ch. 11.

- Orange juice is better than cola.

here, it would be clear that 'better than' refers to 'healthier' i.e. 'better for you'. Given the transparency of the claim, it would not be difficult to list a set of comparative criteria which would allow us confirm its truth. Orange juice contains high levels of vitamin C, no added sugar, caffeine etc. whereas cola does not. The comparison is sound. It would be difficult, however, to try to find similar support for orange juice being a better product, more popular or of a higher quality than cola. Often, comparative evaluations will trade upon this potential for ambiguity in order to mislead us:

- It's official. Sainsways is a more *popular* supermarket than Safeburys!

Here it is unclear how the term 'popular' functions. If, as is no doubt the author's intention, they wish us to believe that Sainsways is preferred by the majority of shoppers, 'the people's choice', then the criteria of comparison would be different to that used to verify the claim 'more people shop at Sainsways'. For the former to be true, a significant amount (i.e. greater than 50%) of people that used *both* stores would have had to have expressed a preference for either the store or its produce (and this would have to be backed up by evidence), whereas the latter would only require that a majority of people *shopped* there. But note how it is probably more beneficial to lead people into believing that the *first*, rather than *second*, of these interpretations is true. It might be the case, for example, that Safeburys is more popular (i.e. has more visitors) simply because the chain has more stores. This does not entail that the majority of shoppers are necessarily happy with the service, nor prefer the produce provided, but rather that they have no choice other than to shop there. Once again, deciding upon the way in which the value judgement is being employed and subsequently the criteria required for comparison is an important first step in the evaluation process. This is no less true when developing your own arguments. **Comparative evaluations** can be an effective way of strengthening your own reasoning, but before you use them, make sure you lay out explicitly how the terms used are to be understood.

> **comparative evaluation** – This evaluation employs value judgements in order to draw a comparison.

Summary questions . . .

1. What is the difference between a comparison and a contrast?
2. What is meant by the expression 'comparative evaluation'?

END OF CHAPTER ACTIVITY

Identify (a) the comparative term being used and (b) come to a decision about how it is being used.

• When it comes to the next election, it is better to vote than not to vote.
• A conscientious objector is braver than someone who joins the army without thinking.
• James' sense of fun makes him more pleasant company than George.

SUMMARY CHECKLIST

Points you need to remember:

✔ How to draw a comparison (and contrast).

✔ What is meant by the term 'comparative evaluation' and how to go about assessing these.

> The following website: www.unc.edu/depts/wcweb/handouts/comparison_contrast.html contains an excellent handout on comparing and contrasting and includes several links to further resources.

13

UNIT 1 FOUNDATION UNIT

Chapter 13: Presenting your own arguments

> The issue of developing your own arguments is developed in detail in both of the end of unit exam chapters.

LEARNING OBJECTIVES

By the end of this chapter you should:

✔ Understand how to present your own argument (on a range of issues) both clearly and concisely.

> Each of these elements has been dealt with in the following chapters:
> Conclusions – Ch. 1.
> Reasons – Ch. 1, and claims – Ch. 3.
> Sub-arguments – Ch. 4.
> Examples and evidence – Ch. 8.
> General (statements of) principle – Ch. 3.
> Counter-examples (etc.) – Ch. 3

In both units of the exam, you may be required to respond to questions concerning claims, arguments and issues by presenting your own arguments. In so doing, you will be expected to:

1. give a clear statement of your conclusion;

2. clearly state the main supporting reasons;

3. where necessary support the main reasons with sub-arguments;

4. introduce examples and evidence (where appropriate);

5. cite general principles in support of your arguments and

6. consider counter-arguments, possible objections etc., and attempt a response to these.

A significant amount of marks are available for doing this so it is a skill well worth honing. We shall start with a deliberately banal example so that, at this stage, you can focus on the general construction of an argument, rather than dealing with its particular content. Let us then imagine (sidestepping the obvious absurdity!) that you have been asked to come to a reasoned decision as to whether *sandy* beaches are preferable to *stony* ones. Here there would be three positions that could be argued for (this will be the case with *all* examples):

1. Sandy beaches *are* preferable to stony ones;

2. Stony beaches *are* preferable to sandy ones;

3. Both sandy *and* stony beaches are of equal or similar merit (or of no merit at all!).

If we were to argue for position 1 (although the same structure applies equally to all three) we might appeal to the following *types* of reason in support of the inference, remembering that there is no such thing as an exhaustive list of relevant reasons here, nor a definitively 'correct' conclusion. What is important, rather, is that your reasoning is pertinent and your position convincing:

1. The superiority in comfort of sandy beaches over stony ones.

2. The superiority in attractiveness of sandy beaches over stony ones.

Each of which could be supported by a sub-argument:

1. You can only hobble over stony beaches, whereas you can run over sandy ones.

2. Sandy beaches have a lovely colour that contrasts with the blue of the sea.

We could also appeal to evidence in support of the main inference (remember, in the exam, you may well be able to extract most, if not all, of the evidence you will need from the documents you will be analysing), for example:

- In a recent survey, 72% of those people polled expressed a preference for sand, rather than stone, as a favoured 'beach-filler'. (!)

Coupled with relevant examples or analogies:

- Lying on a stony beach is like lying on a bed of nails.

Possible counter-examples should be considered:

- However, some might argue that this fails to account for the tiresomeness of getting sand out of hair and clothing when spending any amount of time on such beaches.

Which should be responded to:

- Nevertheless, this is surely a price worth paying when contrasted with the pain and embarrassment of having to 'walk' down a stony beach in order to get to the sea.

And finally we draw the inference that:

- Sandy beaches are indeed preferable to stony ones.

And the argument is complete.

Summary questions . . .

1. What are the key features that need to be present when developing your own argument?

END OF CHAPTER ACTIVITY

1. For one or both of the alternative conclusions above (2 and 3), provide your own argument which mirrors the structure of the one laid out.
2. Stretching activity: Look at the following two examples of 'art' (Figures 13.1 and 13.2) (you may well choose to disagree with this title!) and decide which, if either, has greater artistic merit. Write a reasoned case in support of your position using a similar structure to the one laid out above. You might find that using expressions such as: 'x is of greater artistic merit than y'; 'the reasons for this are ...'; 'it could be argued that ..., however ...' etc. (see 'Reasoning indicators', Chapter 1) will help you to structure your response.

SUMMARY CHECKLIST

Points you need to remember:

✔ How to present your own argument (on a range of issues) clearly and concisely.

Figure 13.1 (Source: Alamy)

Figure 13.2 (Source: Alamy)

14

UNIT 1 FOUNDATION UNIT

Chapter 14: Unit 1 exam guide

For a detailed breakdown of the Unit 1 exam, the scheme of assessment and links to specimen assessment material, past papers and mark schemes see: http://store.aqa.org.uk/qual/gce/pdf/AQA-2770-W-SP-10.pdf.

The format of questions and the mark scheme may well vary slightly from year to year. This is inevitable. It is important that you keep abreast of any developments or changes by checking the syllabus, question papers, mark schemes and examination reports on a fairly regular basis (see the above weblink).

UNIT 1 ASSESSMENT

In the specification, the method of assessment for Unit 1 is laid out as follows:

Candidates will be assessed by means of a written paper lasting 1 hour and 30 minutes. The question paper will be based on a source booklet containing several short documents which may be accompanied by images and/or graphics. These will relate to a single topic or issue, or two or more related topics, and consist of background information and argument. One or more of the documents will be a debate or discussion, or exchange of views. The question paper will have two sections, A and B.

Section A will require short written answers, assessing a range of skills and understanding summarised in the Specification: 3.1–3.14. Not all the points in the list will necessarily be addressed by a specific question in every examination.

There are two main categories of question in this section. The first sets specific tasks or questions, such as:

'Identify an implicit assumption …' or 'Is there a flaw …?'

Questions in the other category are more open and require candidates to select for themselves the point (or points) which are most relevant. These typically ask the candidate to:

'Comment critically …' or 'Critically evaluate …'

Section B will comprise one or two questions which give candidates the opportunity to present their own reasoning on a subject related to the stimulus materials.

No specialist knowledge of the subject matter will be assumed; nor will such knowledge give any advantage to candidates. (AQA specification)

We will deal with each of these sections in turn.

Section A

The first set of questions will relate to Documents A–C and will mainly draw on your skills of analysis (AO1) and evaluation (AO2). It would be a good idea to try and answer these questions on your own before reading through the subsequent commentary (which has been informed by the mark scheme). Rereading the earlier section on 'The examination' (see Introduction) will help you to do this. Expressions in **bold** below either indicate command words relating to these assessment objectives or refer to material covered in previous chapters.

> For a detailed explanation of each of the assessment objectives (AOs) see: http://store.aqa.org.uk/qual/gce/pdf/AQA-2770-W-SP-10.pdf.

Document A

Telegraph.co.uk | Print version

Child use of antidepressants up four-fold

By Graeme Paton, Education Correspondent

(1) The use of antidepressants and other mind-altering drugs among schoolchildren has more than quadrupled in the last decade, it is revealed today.

(2) New figures show that doctors are prescribing pills in record numbers to combat stress, violent behaviour and even tiredness.

(3) The huge increase has been blamed on a rise in childhood mental illness sparked by family breakdown and high-stakes school exams.

(4) The findings come despite the publication of research showing that children given antidepressants run a higher risk of self-harm and are more likely to attempt suicide.

(5) NCH, the children's charity, claims that one child in 10 suffers a significant mental health problem and that rates have doubled since the 1990s.

Source: adapted from Telegraph News, 19 April 2008

Reader's response:

Of course this is not justified. The problem is that due to a poor 'junk food' diet, children are not getting what they need to grow and be healthy. People do not get depressed because they have a lack of Prozac* in their bodies, people get depressed due to deficiencies in amino acids and other fundamental nutritional building blocks. It shocks and saddens me that most doctors only study nutrition for a few weeks of their medical degrees and the powerful drug companies continue to push and peddle unnecessary drugs for problems that can be treated naturally.

Lucy, Northants

---

*Prozac – a drug that is used to treat depression

You will need to read the news article 'Child use of antidepressants up four-fold' before answering the first question.

The first question asks you to focus on the underlying **implication** of the author's reasoning that prescribing children antidepressants is not necessarily a good thing.

(a) Question 1a) asks you to **identify** the information (paragraph 4) which he bases his view on. (*1 mark*)

(b) Question 1b) asks you to **identify** a further assumption that the author needs to make about the relationship between child use of antidepressants and self-harm/attempted suicide in order for this information to support his judgement. (*1 mark*)

Commentary

1a) The answer to this question should be fairly obvious. It merely requires that you **identify** (AO1) and restate the **information** given in the passage – i.e.: 'research showing that children given antidepressants run a higher risk of self-harm and are more likely to attempt suicide'.

1b) This question requires you to **identify** (AO1) an **assumption** in the author's reasoning. In fact there are several. For example, the author needs to assume that there is a *genuine* causal link between taking antidepressants and self-harm/suicide whereas in fact the link could be purely coincidental. The reasoning is also dependent upon (i.e. assumes) the accuracy/fullness/neutrality of the research itself. If, for example, this was in any way slanted, inaccurate or unrepresentative then the legitimacy of the author's judgement could be called into question.

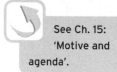

See Ch. 11: 'Cause-correlation fallacy'.

See Ch. 15: 'Motive and agenda'.

You will need to read through the reader's response (that follows the article) in order to answer question 2.

(a) Question 2a) asks you to **identify** Lucy's main conclusion. (*1 mark*)

(b) Question 2b) requires you to **identify** the **two** approaches to combating depression that Lucy contrasts and explain a way in which these approaches are **similar**. (*1 mark*)

(c) Question 2c) requires you to '**comment critically**' on Lucy's use of the phrase 'push and peddle'. To do this you will need to:

* **identify** the implied analogy
* **judge** whether or not it is fair. (*5 marks*)

(d) Question 2d) requires you to 'identify a general principle' which Lucy needs to assume in order for her conclusion (see question 2a) to be legitimately drawn. (*1 mark*)

(e) Question 2e) requires you to **identify** and **explain** the 'straw-man' fallacy in Lucy's reasoning. (*3 marks*)

Commentary

2a) Lucy's main **conclusion** (first sentence) is that the decision to prescribe antidepressants to children 'is not justified' (AO1). This is the point her argument is trying to get us to accept.

2b) The two approaches to combating depression identified in the passage (i.e. Prozac and decent nutrition) are **similar** because they both see depression as having an internal/physical cause rather than an external/environmental one (AO1).

see Ch. 12

2c) This question requires you to do two things. Firstly, to **identify** the **analogy** being made (see Chapter 8 – 'Analogies') and secondly, to **evaluate** it. The analogy, as should be clear, is between drugs companies which legally supply drugs to children (AO1 X 1) and drug dealers who do so illegally (AO1 X 1). You might argue that such a comparison is **acceptable** because in both cases the drugs being supplied are addictive; profitable; mood-altering etc. or alternatively that the analogy is **defective** because prescription drugs are legal; prescribed by trained professionals; used to promote physical and/or psychological well-being (etc.), whereas those supplied by drug dealers are/do not (AO2 X 3).

2d) The **general principle** Lucy needs to **assume** is that natural approaches to combating depression are preferable to non-natural ones (AO1). To see this you will first need to **analyse** the basic **structure of her reasoning** which is as follows:

P1: Depression can be treated naturally

C: Therefore prescribing antidepressants is not justified.

Here it should be clear that such an argument only works if we **assume** that natural treatments are preferable to non-natural ones. Without presuming this, there would be no reason to object to the use of Prozac as an antidepressant.

2e) As with 2c), this question requires you to do two things. Firstly, to **identify** the (straw-man) **logical fallacy** present in Lucy's argument which is that

'People do not get depressed because they have a lack of Prozac in their bodies, people get depressed due to deficiencies in amino acids and other fundamental nutritional building blocks' (AO1). And secondly, to show *why* this type of reasoning is **illegitimate** – in this case, because no serious professional would argue along these lines (i.e. that people who lack Prozac in their bodies need to be prescribed Prozac!). This deliberately distorts/misrepresents the type of reasoning that might be put forward by a doctor prescribing the drug (AO2 X 2).

The next set of questions (3–6) will relate to the following document (B) and will also draw on your skills of analysis (AO1) and evaluation (AO2). Read through the document and try and answer the questions before studying the subsequent commentary.

Document B

JENNY (having just read the article, 'Child use of antidepressants up four-fold')
It's hardly surprising, is it? When you think about the world – everything that's going on. What with the environment. Conflict. Genocides.

NICK But these are all global things. What about the quality of individual people's lives? Surely that's got better.

JENNY It depends what you mean by 'better'.

NICK It means not dying of simple infections. It means your mum not dying in childbirth. It means it not being commonplace for one of your brothers or sisters to die before they're five years old.

JENNY So you're saying that medicine's got better.

NICK And all the rest of scientific progress. Think of the way technology's improved your life. Televisions. Computers. Mobile phones…

JENNY Nuclear bombs! Anyway. All this so-called 'progress' – it just pollutes the world. It's also made us greedier. The more you have, the more you want!

NICK But you're not forced to buy things. What you have these days is choice, like in terms of what you eat. That's got to be an improvement.

JENY But that's irrelevant if it's not making us any happier. We've become too materialistic, too selfish – we don't even care about our own children, let alone society. We're driven by getting richer, owning more things, but none of that is making us any happier.

NICK Well if you want to give everything up and go and live in a cave, that's fine. But leave me your iPod before you go.

JENNY So for you quality of life is all about getting richer and living longer.

NICK At least these things you can actually measure! Look, my main point is this. Have you ever had an operation? Ever taken antibiotics for a serious infection? If so, you probably wouldn't even be alive if this was a hundred years ago. In fact, you probably wouldn't even have been born – almost certainly one of your parents or grandparents would have died for the same reason, or from some other disease that they can now cure, or vaccinate against. So you've got no right to argue that things are worse than they used to be. The fact that you're alive to have this argument proves that's not the case.

JENNY   You've just proved my point!

You will need to read through Document B in order to answer questions 3–6.

The first question refers to the dialogue between Jenny and Nick.

(a) Question 3a) asks you to **identify** an **assumption** that Jenny needs to make about the causes of childhood depression (see the beginning of the dialogue). (*1 mark*)

(b) Question 3b) asks you to **identify** an **assumption** that Nick has to make in return. (*1 mark*)

Commentary

Hopefully you've got the hang of these by now. Once again, see Chapter 5 if you are still unclear!

3a) Jenny's **assumption** is that depression is caused by external/environmental/ sociological factors rather than internal/biological ones (AO1). Were she not to assume this, her inference 'It's hardly surprising, is it?' could not be drawn.

3b) The *explicit* **assumption** Nick makes is that 'Surely [the quality of people's lives has] got better' – there is no evidence to support this (AO1). There are also at least *two* *implicit* **assumptions** in his reasoning. Firstly, that global issues have no bearing on people's quality of life: 'But these are all global things.' And secondly, that quality of life leads to happiness/the absence of depression: 'What about the quality of individual people's lives? Surely that's got better.' (AO1). Both of these points need to be presupposed in order for Nick's reasoning to be effective.

Question 4 refers to Nick's comments on some of the ways in which science and technology have improved life:

> NICK: And all the rest of scientific progress. Think of the way technology's improved your life. Televisions. Computers. Mobile phones.

And the counter-argument Jenny responds with:

> JENNY: Nuclear bombs! Anyway. All this so-called 'progress' – it just pollutes the world. It's also made us greedier. The more you have, the more you want!

You are required to **identify** the **conclusion** which is implicit in Jenny's response. It then asks you to '**explain** and **evaluate** the support she provides' for this conclusion. (*8 marks*)

Commentary

4) This question requires you to do several things. Firstly, to **identify** Jenny's (implied) **conclusion** – that what we refer to as (scientific) 'progress' is not in fact progress/has not led to a better quality of life (AO1). Secondly, to **identify/ explain** the **support** (reasons) she offers in defence of this inference. They are as follows:

(i)   That modern technology has also produced 'Nuclear bombs!' (a counter-example to Nick's reference to televisions, computers and mobile phones as examples of technology that have benefited our lives). (AO1)

(ii) That it merely 'pollutes the world'. (AO1)

(iii) And makes us 'greedier' ('the more you have, the more you want'). (AO1)

Having done this, you will then need to **evaluate** Jenny's reasoning (AO2). To do this you will need to provide your own **reasoning** in **support** of or in **opposition** to each of the points (i–iii) outlined above. For example:

i)   The first reason i) depends upon the (legitimate/illegitimate?) **assumption** that the existence of nuclear bombs has had a *negative* impact on the quality of people's lives. In **support** of this, we might argue that the production of nuclear weapons *has* led to greater global anxiety/depression or that it has actually *increased* global conflict. In **opposition** to this, we might argue that nuclear weapons have actually acted as a deterrent which has led to a *decrease* in global conflict. They can thus be conceived of as having a broadly positive effect (AO2).

ii)   The second reason also (explicitly) **assumes** that modern technology merely 'pollutes the world'. This, of course, is questionable. In **support** of this claim, we might cite examples – the industrial revolution, global warming etc. – where it is *generally* agreed that such technology *has* had a detrimental affect. In **opposition** to this we might argue that our ability to identify such cases to begin with and, perhaps more importantly, do something about them when they occur, is due to the very technology Jenny seeks to undermine (AO2).

iii) The third reason Jenny offers (modern technology 'made us greedier') is highly contestable. In **defence** of this claim, we might argue that the amount of goods an individual acquires approximates to the amount of wealth he or she collates (this is tenuous). **Alternatively**, we could argue that greed is a biological/psychological rather than materialistic phenomenon and thus claiming that technology produces the desire – rather than the desire the technology – **confuses cause with effect** (AO2).

iv)   It would also be legitimate to argue that Jenny uses the expression 'so-called progress' as a **rhetorical device** and so offers no *legitimate* support for her inference (AO2).

Question 5) refers to the following section of the dialogue:

JENNY: We've become too materialistic, too selfish – we don't even care about our own children, let alone society. We're driven by getting richer, owning more things, but none of that is making us any happier.

NICK: Well if you want to give everything up and go and live in a cave, that's fine. But leave me your iPod before you go.

And requires you to '**comment critically**' on Nick's response to Jenny's reasoning. (*4 marks*)

Commentary

5) Here, you will need to **identify** and **comment on** potential strengths and weaknesses of Nick's reasoning. It could be argued, for example, that his first comment: 'if you want to give everything up and go and live in a cave, that's fine' deliberately distorts/misrepresents Jenny's position in order to make it appear absurd. He is thus guilty of committing the '**straw-man**' fallacy (AO1 and 2). Moreover, it might be said that, in failing to consider viable alternative options to the ones given (i.e. either a materialistic or a cave-dwelling existence but nothing in between) Nick is also guilty of committing the '**false-dilemma**' fallacy (AO1 and 2).

Nick's second comment: 'But leave me your iPod before you go' implies that, because Jenny makes use of the modern technology she so despises, she is being **inconsistent/hypocritical** in her reasoning. If so, this might appear to **weaken** her case (AO1 and 2). But even if her preaching *does* conflict with her practice, this in no way undermines its *general* legitimacy. Here it could be argued that Nick is guilty of committing the '*tu quoque*'/'**you too**' fallacy (see Chapter 11: 'Logical fallacies'). More simply, Jenny's 'wrong' (use of technology) does not make such a practice 'right' (AO1 and 2)!

More general criticisms could focus on the use of **persuasive language** in Nick's response. This could be interpreted **positively** (as an effective use of **humour/rhetoric** to reinforce the point being made) or **negatively** (as a personal 'jibe' made at Jenny's expense) (AO1 and 2). One might also question the legitimacy of moving from a **particular** case (the use of an iPod) to a **general** conclusion (that Jenny is overly materialistic) which many would regard as a '**hasty generalisation**' (AO1 and 2).

Question 6 refers to the final section of the dialogue:

JENNY: So for you quality of life is all about getting richer and living longer.

NICK: At least these are things you can actually measure! Look, my main point is this. Have you ever had an operation? Ever taken antibiotics for a serious infection? If so, you probably wouldn't even be alive if this was a hundred years ago. In fact, you probably wouldn't even have been born – almost certainly one of your parents or grandparents would have died for the same reason, or from some other disease that they can now cure, or vaccinate against. So you've got no right to argue that things are worse than they used to be. The fact that you're alive to have this argument proves that's not the case.

JENNY: You've just proved my point!

(a) Question 6a) focuses on Nick's contribution to the dialogue and asks you to:

(i) **Explain** how the word 'right' (penultimate sentence) might be **ambiguous**. (*1 mark*)

(ii) **Explain** the effect Nick's final sentence has on settling this ambiguity. (*1 mark*)

(iii) **Identify one assumption** Nick needs to presume in order to draw the inference that 'things are [no] worse than they used to be'. (*2 marks*)

(b) Jenny reduces all of Nick's arguments about the improving quality of life to the assertions that:

* we are getting richer
* we are living longer

Question 6b) requires you to **explain** (giving reasons for your answer) whether or not Nick's final argument shows, as Jenny's response implies ('You've just proved my point'), that her analysis is correct. (*5 marks*)

Commentary

6a) Question i) requires you to spot a potential **ambiguity** in Nick's use of language. Here the word 'right' can be understood in one of two ways. Firstly, in a **moral** sense (i.e. she *ought* not/has no *moral* right to argue that 'things are worse than they used to be') and, secondly, as implying that she has no **grounds** or **justification** to argue as she does (i.e. what *reasons* have you got for claiming that …?) (AO1 X 2).

ii) Nick's final sentence: 'The fact that you're alive to have this argument proves that's not the case' indicates that it is the *second* of these interpretations that is correct – it is an attempt to *disprove* her argument rather than show it to be morally *wrong* (AO1).

For more on this, see Ch. 2: 'Ethical discourse' and Ch. 3: 'Value judgements'.

iii) Nick's **assumption** is that Jenny's 'being alive' is a clear indication that things are getting better/not getting worse. Without presupposing this, the inference is invalid (AO1 X 2).

6b) To answer this question you will need to briefly **develop your own argument** either **for** or **against** Jenny's analysis (hence there is 1 mark available for AO3). This will require you to reach a **judgement** (in this case, either Jenny is **right** and Nick's argument does 'prove her point' or she is **wrong** and it doesn't) and provide **grounds** of **support** for it (for example, 'since Jenny claims that all of Nick's arguments can be reduced down to the claims that "we are getting richer", "we are living longer" *and* that Nick's final claim is really just an extension of the second of these points, then Jenny is **right** and Nick's claim really does "prove her point"'). It would also be worth questioning the assumption in Nick's reasoning that people living longer offers an indication that things are getting better. This leaves itself open to the obvious counter-argument that perhaps the world would be a better place with fewer people in it (including Jenny)!

Depending on how you approach a response, there are marks available for all three of the AOs.

You will need to read through Document C ('Clear-Eyed Optimists') before attempting a response to questions 7 and 8.

(a) Question 7a) requires you to explain what the author is implying (see paragraph 6) about the media's attitude to the reporting of good and bad news. (*1 mark*)

(b) Question 7b) refers to a reader's comment about paragraph 6 making an 'unjustified generalisation'. It requires you to **come to a decision**, giving reasons for your answer, as to whether or not you agree with this analysis. (*3 marks*)

Commentary

7a) If you reread paragraph 6, you should be able to **identify** the author's implicit belief that the media favours reporting 'bad' rather than 'good' news (AO1).

7b) Before **commenting on/evaluating** the reader's comment, you will first need to identify the generalisation, implicit in the answer to 7a), that they refer to. This is the (unjustified?) move from a limited amount of cases of the media favouring the reporting of 'bad news' to the general assumption that they always do (AO2 X 1). There are a range of ways in which you could **agree/disagree**

Document C

THE WALL STREET JOURNAL

Clear-Eyed Optimists

The world is getting better, though no one likes to hear it.

BY STEPHEN MOORE, Friday, October, 2007

(1) I'm old enough to recall the days in the late 1960s when people wore those trendy badges that read: "Stop the Planet I Want to Get Off".

(2) The future seemed mighty bleak back then, and you merely had to open the newspapers for the latest story confirming how the human species was speeding down a congested highway to extinction. A group of scientists calling themselves the Club of Rome issued a report called "Limits to Growth." It explained that lifeboat Earth had become so weighed down with humans that we were running out of food, minerals, forests, water, energy and just about everything else that we need for survival. In 1980, US President Jimmy Carter released the "Global 2000 Report," which declared that life on Earth was getting worse in every measurable way.

(3) So imagine how shocked I was to learn officially, that we're not doomed after all. A new United Nations report called "State of the Future" concludes: "People around the world are becoming healthier, wealthier, better educated, more peaceful, more connected, and they are living longer."

(4) Yes, of course, there was the bad news: Global warming is said to be getting worse and income disparities are widening. But the joyous trends in health and wealth documented in the report indicate a gigantic leap forward for humanity.

(5) World-wide illiteracy rates have fallen by half since 1970 and now stand at an all-time low of 18%. More people live in free countries than ever before. The average human being today will live 50% longer in 2025 than one born in 1955. At current rates of growth, "world poverty will be cut in half between 2000 and 2015". The report also notes hopefully that soon laptop computers will cost $100 and almost every schoolchild will be a mouse click away from the Internet.

(6) This is probably the first time you've heard any of this because – while the grim "Global 2000" and "Limits to Growth" reports were deemed worthy of headlines across the country – the media mostly ignored the good news and the upbeat predictions of "State of the Future". However, this is typical of the reaction to just about any good news. When 2006 was declared the hottest year on record, there were thousands of news stories. But last month's revised data, indicating that 1934 was actually warmer, barely warranted a paragraph-long correction in most papers.

(7) So I'm happy to report that the world's six billion people are living longer, healthier and more comfortably than ever before. If only it were easy to fit that on a badge.

Mr Moore is a member of The Wall Street Journal Editorial Board.

Source: adapted from The Wall Street Journal, 5 October 2007 with this assessment. For example, you might **disagree** with the author's claim (AO2 X 1) because two examples do not constitute sufficient evidence for the confidently asserted generalisation he reaches (AO2 X 1). Alternatively, you might **agree** with the author's claim (AO2 X 1) because the two examples of (ignored) 'good news' he chooses (the 'upbeat predictions of the "State of the Future" report and the weather report of 1934 being the 'hottest year on record') constitute particularly *strong* cases (AO1 X 1). You could develop this last point by showing that, in *some* cases, a single example *might* be enough to support a general claim (AO2 X 1).

Question 8 refers to the three individual reports that the article references (the recent UN report; and two older reports – 'Limits to Growth' from the 1960s and 'Global 2000 Report' from the 1980s), and requires you to:
(a) Offer a **comparison** and **contrast** of the author's presentation of these reports by suggesting '**three** ways in which' their 'presentation or treatment of the recent UN report differs from his presentation or treatment of the two older reports'. (*3 marks*)
(b) Come to a **decision**, offering support for your answer, about whether this 'treatment of the different reports is fair or unfair'. It is suggested that a consideration of 'the language used', an analysis of 'any assumptions made' and/or an appraisal of any 'implicit flaws' in the author's reasoning might help you to do this. (*6 marks*)

Commentary

See Ch. 12.

8a) For a reminder of what drawing a **comparison** and **contrast** involves, it would be useful to revisit Chapter 12. Again, there is no determinate set of correct answers here, but 'three ways' might **identify**:

(i)   The author referring to the UN report in a more positive light than the two older reports (AO1).

(ii) The amount of space the author devotes to the treatment of the reports (the UN report is covered in much greater depth and detail) (AO1).

(iii) The author's use of language, when referring to the UN report, is much more favourable/persuasive (AO1).

(iv) The author's reference to evidence and statistics, when presenting the UN report, portrays it as a much more accurate/reliable/factual document than the other two (AO1).

Rereading the document with the above points in mind should help clarify your understanding of these points.

8b) As with 6b), this question will require you to briefly **develop your own argument** (hence there are 2 marks available for AO3). To do this, you will first need to reach a **judgement** – i.e. decide whether the author's treatment of the different reports is either **fair** or **unfair** (given the answer to 8a, it might seem logical to conclude that it is unfair!). The question states that 'you might like to consider the **language** he has used, any important **assumptions** he has made and/or any possible **flaws** in the reasoning'. These are all points that could be referred to in support of your judgement. For example:

LANGUAGE

The author's use of persuasive language (see Chapter 10) throughout the article could be regarded as either **effective** (i.e. legitimate, fair) or **distortive** (i.e. substituting rhetoric for reasoned argument). Examples that might be drawn on in support of your judgement include:

• 'Imagine how shocked I was to learn, officially, that we're not doomed after all.' (paragraph 3)

Here the words 'learn' and 'officially' indicate that the content of the UN report is both factual and from a reliable ('official') source. This could be interpreted **negatively**, i.e. as using **leading language/rhetoric** to make a point, or **positively**, i.e. as countering the already 'extreme' view of the 'Global 2000 Report' which 'declared that life on Earth was getting worse in every measurable way' (paragraph 2).

Other **negative** examples you might have picked up on (see 'Limits to Growth' report, paragraph 2) include the author's reference to 'a group of scientists' (rather than specifying their individual roles/names/areas of expertise etc.) who '[called] themselves' (arguably a put-down/disparaging comment implying that, perhaps others didn't see them in quite the same light as they saw themselves!) 'the Club of Rome' (which makes them sound rather pretentious/self-important/grandiose). For each of the above and similar points, you will attract 1 (AO2) mark for showing why the use of language is fairly/unfairly persuasive.

Assumptions

We have seen that, in our response to 8a), the UN report is presented in a more favourable light than its two predecessors. The first **implicit assumption**, then, is that the UN report offers a more accurate/reliable account. A **negative** interpretation of this point could highlight the absence of justification for drawing such an inference; a **positive** interpretation might regard it as legitimate inasmuch as the UN report is the latest, and hence most up to date (and hence reliable?) of the three. It could also be argued that, because the UN is a much larger/more neutral enterprise than the 'Club of Rome'/US-backed 'Global 2000 Report' then the author's assumption is **legitimate**. Finally, if we look at the end of paragraph 4:

- 'Yes, of course, there was the bad news: Global warming is said to be getting worse and income disparities are widening. But the joyous trends in health and wealth documented in the report indicate a gigantic leap forward for humanity.'

We can see that the implied *significance* (see Chapter 15) of the UN report assumes that the positive trends (in 'health and wealth') overshadow the negative ones (an increase in global warming and income disparity). Were this point not presupposed, the inference that these 'joyous trends … indicate a gigantic leap forward for humanity' could not be drawn. You will attract 1 (AO2) mark for correctly **identifying** an assumption and 1 (AO2) mark for **showing/explaining/suggesting** why it is/isn't warranted.

Flaws

There are a range of potential flaws here. Perhaps the most obvious is the implicit assumption that the ('official') UN report is the most accurate of the three. There is no evidence to support this; it depends upon a **fallacious appeal to authority** (i.e. its accuracy is secured by the authority of its source rather than independent evidential criteria). It might also be argued that the use of such expressions as 'speeding down a congested highway to extinction; 'lifeboat Earth had become so weighed down with humans that we were running out of food, minerals, forests, water, energy and just about everything else' etc. (see paragraph 2) present the opposing view in a deliberately extreme/ absurd/naïve or otherwise unbalanced fashion and so commit the '**straw-man**' or '*ad hominem*' fallacy. It could also be argued that this replaces reason with **rhetoric** and so is an example of the use of '**persuasive language**'. There is 1 (AO2) mark available for each correctly identified fallacy and a second (AO2) mark for explaining *why* it is fallacious. (A combined total of 4 AO2 marks and 2 AO3 marks is available for this question.)

Section B

We have seen the various ways in which an argument can be flawed (see, for example, assumptions, logical fallacies, strengthening and weakening arguments, evaluating claims etc.). We have also looked in some detail at what constitutes a strong argument (see, for example, Chapter 13). It is now time to demonstrate an understanding of these points by incorporating them into your own reasoning. Once again, there is no definitively 'correct' way to go about doing this. What is important is that you meet all the criteria laid out in the specification and that your response follows the structure laid out in the question paper. It would be a good idea to attempt a response to question 9 before reading through the following commentary and 'generic marking guide' and come to a decision about what kind of mark your response would have attracted and why. Here it is important to think about ways in which your reasoning could have been improved (if at all!) and how you might go about doing this.

The advice given in the specification gives a clear explanation of what you will be expected to do for this section of the exam: 'Section B will comprise one or two questions which give candidates the opportunity to present their own reasoning on a subject related to the stimulus materials. No specialist knowledge of the subject matter will be assumed; nor will such knowledge give any advantage to candidates.' You will also be given a clear guide which you can use to structure your response.

Question 9 requires you to 'write a reasoned argument for or against the view that, generally speaking, the quality of life is getting better'. There are 20 AO3 marks available for this question. In doing this, you will be expected to:

- clearly state your conclusion/s
- offer support for the above

- refer to the information presented in Documents A–C when responding to 'any issues or arguments' they present
- explain the criteria you are appealing to in order to judge what constitutes/determines quality of life
- explain *why* you consider these criteria important. (*20 [AO3] marks*)

Conclusion

It is important to remember that there is no 'correct' conclusion here. It would seem, however, that there are three possible options. Either (a) the general quality of life is improving; or (b) it isn't (and is perhaps getting worse); or finally (c) the issue is too broad/complex/subjective to decide. If you argue for option (c) (that there is *insufficient* evidence to come to a decision either way) you will still need to support your reasoning by showing *why* the material presented in the source documents is inconclusive/inadequate, rather than just asserting that it is.

Reasoning and use of documents

Here, your reasoning might focus on:

- Whether or not 'happiness' (Jenny) is a legitimate criterion for determining quality of life (see, for example, Document A) and whether such a criterion is quantitative/measurable.
- The line of reasoning implicit in Nick's response that we should focus only on improvements which *are* quantitative/measurable (see, for example, *The Wall Street Journal*).
- Alternatively, perhaps it could be argued that happiness/unhappiness *is* a quantifiable phenomenon and that the statistics for, for example, the treatment and/or diagnosis of depression (see Document A) offer support for such a judgement (you would need to take care here to show *why* such evidence *can* be regarded as reliable/representative as opposed to just assuming *that* it is).
- A similar, but less forceful/more cautious line of reasoning could be developed which accepts that, whilst happiness might *in principle* be regarded as a quantifiable phenomenon, nevertheless the evidence presented in Documents A and C is insufficient.

- Some of the issues arising in the dialogue, for example materialism, egoism, a decline in society and/or the family unit, scientific advances and/or global issues (either positive or negative), might be raised for discussion in order to support the inference that the quality of life is either declining or improving.

- It would also be legitimate to focus on an issue *not* raised for discussion in the dialogue and/or source booklets, for example the progressive decline in religious belief and value and/or the corresponding augmentation of alienation/loss of purpose which could be seen as a direct result of this decline.

It is important to remember that the above examples do not constitute an 'exhaustive list' of positions. There are other, alternative lines of enquiry that might be pursued with equal force which are not, for practical reasons, addressed here.

Criteria

It is essential that, when developing an argument for determining quality of life, you spell out which criteria you will be using and why. For example, wealth might be regarded as a more important criterion than happiness on account of its being measurable; or that happiness, inasmuch as there are countless examples of individuals who are rich but unhappy; poor but content, might be deemed more important because, without it, it is difficult to see how anything can be of value. It could be argued that both criteria have to be taken into account in order to reach such a decision, or perhaps that neither can be regarded as satisfactory. If you were going to argue for this latter position, you would need to assess both criteria before dismissing them (for example, it might be argued that happiness clearly *is* the most important factor for determining quality of life but because it is qualitative, and thus unquantifiable, it cannot be taken into consideration). You will not be required to employ terms such as qualitative or quantitative (though you certainly wouldn't lose out in doing so) but you *would* need to explain why the measurement of happiness (and other related issues) might be regarded as problematic.

The following generic mark scheme should give you a clear understanding of how your response will be marked.

Generic marking guide, question 9

Descriptor	Award level		
	Good response Communication is clear and appropriate	**Reasonable response** Communication is mostly clear and appropriate	**Limited response** Communication errors may impede understanding
Conclusion A conclusion is clearly stated that is consistent with the reasoning, and directly responds to the question	4	3-2	1
Reasons/Lines of reasoning The above conclusion is well supported with reasons, contributory arguments, examples, clarification of terms, etc.	5-7	3-4	1-2
Use of source documents Candidate has engaged critically with source material	5-6	3-4	1-2
Reference to criteria One or more relevant criteria are deployed	3	2	1

UNIT 2 # INFORMATION, INFERENCE AND EXPLANATION

Chapter 15: Presenting information/evidence

By the end of this chapter you should:

- ✔ Be able to recognise and understand the range of ways in which information can be presented: in tabular form, graphically, verbally etc.
- ✔ Be able to extract, compare and contrast and finally translate relevant information from (and between) each of the above.
- ✔ Understand the various advantages and disadvantages of each approach.
- ✔ Understand the role that criteria such as accuracy, detail, simplicity and selectivity play in determining the above.
- ✔ Understand what is meant by the terms 'motive' and 'agenda'.
- ✔ Understand what is meant by the term 'source'.
- ✔ Understand why a background motive or agenda can affect the credibility of a given source.
- ✔ Understand the further set of criteria that can be used to determine source credibility:
    i.   the primary or secondary status of the source;
    ii. the reputation/reputability of a witness or author;
    iii. the possibility of vested interest on the part of an author (and the extent to which it might influence him or her to say one thing rather than another);

iv. the scope for error, e.g. the physical ability of a person to make a particular observation;
v. the expertise or authority of an author (and whether or not their expertise is relevant to the claim/s being made);
vi. the degree of corroboration provided by other (independent) sources.

PRESENTING INFORMATION

The ability to digest large quantities of information is considerably simplified if it is presented in a systematic fashion. If, for example, you came across the following sequence of numbers:

• 128, 8, 32, 256, 4, 64, 2, 16

the chances are you would think they were chosen at random. For this reason, it would be impossible to infer a number that sequentially followed from the last number in the sequence (16) because the series itself displays no recognisable pattern. If, however, the numbers were to be rearranged, like so:

• 2, 4, 8, 16, 32, 64, 128, 256

It should be easy to see that each successive number merely doubles the number that precedes it. That 512 would be the next number in the sequence should be clear to all. It would, of course, be possible to memorise both sets of numbers, but the difference between merely memorising and *understanding* something is exemplified by the ease with which the second set is grasped. We see *why* rather than memorise *that* the numbers are configured as they are.

So the task of organising information into an intelligible form is clearly an important one. But what form should this take? Well, there are a range of ways in which information can be presented and, depending on context, some of these will be more successful than others. Suppose, for example, that we were presented with a set of figures concerning the life expectancy of humans in the twentieth century. Such information might be presented in three ways:

Tabular form

Human life expectancy in the twentieth century (by decade and sex) in **tabular form**:

	1900	1910	1920	1930	1940	1950	1960	1970	1980	1990
Men	47.9	49.9	55.5	57.7	61.6	65.5	66.8	67.0	70.1	71.8
Women	50.7	53.2	57.4	60.9	65.9	71.0	73.2	74.6	77.6	78.8
Total	49.2	51.5	56.4	59.2	63.6	68.1	69.9	70.8	73.9	75.4

Verbal form

Human life expectancy in the twentieth century (by decade and sex) in **verbal form**:

At the turn of the twentieth century, average human life expectancy was 49.2 years. Men could be expected to live until they were 47.9, whilst women averaged 50.7 years. By the end of the century, this had increased by an average total of 26.2 years. Men could be expected to live until they were 71.8, compared with women who averaged 78.8 – seven years longer than their male counterparts!

Graphical form

Human life expectancy in the twentieth century (by decade and sex) in **graphical form**:

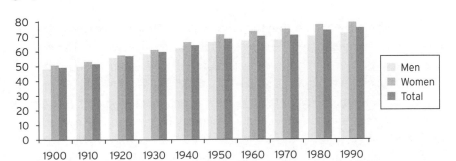

For more on sound (and unsound!) inferences, see Chs 11: ('Overgeneralisation' and 'Cause-correlation fallacy'), 17 and 19.

A range of different chart types can be used to convey the same information – this point is developed in the next chapter.

graphical form
– Presented visually on a graph.

For more on this topic, see Ch. 11: 'Straw man' and 'motive and agenda' in this chapter.

Here the *same* information is translated into different formats, each of which has its own advantages and disadvantages. The first (tabular) format, for example, lays out *all* the relevant information numerically into precise groups and figures. For this reason, it is the most comprehensive form of presentation; certainly more so than its verbal counterpart which merely extracts and summarises the table's most pertinent points. It is, however, rather difficult to digest, given the amount of information provided, and offers us no **graphical** aid to visually clarify and help predict what inferences might be drawn from such data – for example, whether we can expect life-expectancy rates to increase, level off or decrease and at what rate this might occur.

Verbal representations, on the other hand, are clear and concise. For this reason, they are favoured by newspaper reporters and news bulletins where, given obvious time constraints, a brief summary of the key points is needed in order to allow the reader/viewer to form their own opinion. It is easy to see, however, that the lack of data provided by such examples makes the process of drawing reliable inferences rather difficult. Perhaps, more importantly, we have no way of knowing whether the information provided *is* the most relevant without consulting the original table from which it is drawn. For this reason, such summaries are notoriously easy to manipulate and need to be treated with caution.

Graphic representations, on the other hand, offer a visual depiction of the information presented in the original tabular format which marries the accessibility of verbal reports (visual depictions are easier to absorb than numerical ones – they allow us to 'see' any trends or patterns that are present in the data) with the detail of tabular ones. They are not, however, as exact as tabular representations – it would be almost impossible, for example, to distinguish between 49.9 and 50 in any of the above graphs. When greater precision is required, a tabular representation is preferable. For these reasons, each form of presentation suits a particular need. To summarise:

- Data presented in tabular form is comprehensive (i.e. meticulous and precise) but too detailed for the majority of purposes and difficult to absorb and draw inferences from. When detail and precision are required and/or when you wish to compare and contrast specific pieces of information (for example, for research purposes), then the tabular method is preferable. Verbal and graphical information are usually derived from this form of presentation.

- Data presented verbally is brief, concise and accessible, but is not comprehensive and can be easily manipulated. When information needs to be presented briefly and accessibly, as when one outlines key points, then a verbal summary is preferable.

- Data presented in graphical form is accessible and detailed and visible status renders it particularly helpful for drawing inferences and making predictions. However, it lacks the precision of data presented in tabular form. A graph or chart is desirable when a visual stimulus is required to give shape and form to a set of numbers.

Summary questions . . .

1. What are the three main ways of presenting information?
2. What are the advantages and disadvantages of each?

Exercises

1. Read through the following (Yahoo) blog on the immanent axing of the reality TV series *Big Brother* and, taking into the account (a) the number of people that responded and (b) whether they responded negatively or positively, summarise this data in tabular, verbal and graphical form. (Note that the original wording has not been corrected!)

2. Which type of audience do you think might prefer which type of summary? Why?

Big Brother axed!
It has recently been in the news that Channel 4 is to axe the reality TV series, *Big Brother*.

The news comes after ratings for the current run fell to an all-time low, with an average of just two million viewers tuning in to watch the housemates' antics.

A TV commentator has said the reality is that people are bored with it. It appears that even at Channel 4 the vibe among staff is that if you like *Big Brother* you're not cool and if the people commissioning the show don't think it's cool, what hope is there?

How do you feel about Channel 4's decision? Will you miss the show or should it have been axed years ago? Let us know …

From the web:
- *(1)* About time!!
- *(2)* I love Big Brother. It makes our summer with all the characters. Gets better and better
- *(3)* Thank God it's gone. What a nation we must seem to be watching this
- *(4)* Noooo i love the show it always makes me laugh its just a fun thing to watch ill be sad to see it go x
- *(5)* Thank God the show is @#$% and should have ended years ago
- *(6)* Good riddance to bad rubbish, x factor next !
- *(7)* After 10 years? I'll miss it! :-(
- *(8)* Thank GooooooooooooooooooD !!
- *(9)* never liked it, utter garbage, rather watch paint dry

EXTRACTING INFORMATION

> **extracting information** – The process of extracting information requires you to select a specific value/set of values from the range of information presented.

Having looked at the various ways in which data can be presented and how the same information can be translated into different formats, we are now in a position to look at the most basic skill you will be required to use for Unit 2 of the exam: **extracting information**. This is a skill with which you will already be well acquainted – for example, when deciding which university to go for or which career to pursue, and so forth, accurately extracting data forms an essential part of making a correct, or at least well-informed, decision. Comparing league tables, employment prospects or average starting salary and yearly wage increase will be a necessary first step to making your choice.

Even more simply, if you wanted to book a holiday or festival ticket, internet price-comparison sites offer a range of options for doing so. The ability to select the option that best suits your needs, perhaps based on the criteria of price, security, availability etc., requires you to use precisely the same skills that we will be working on here. In its simplest form, extracting information entails selecting a specific value from a range of information. If we refer back to our initial table above:

	1900	1910	1920	1930	1940	1950	1960	1970	1980	1990
Men	47.9	49.9	55.5	57.7	61.6	65.5	66.8	67.0	70.1	71.8
Women	50.7	53.2	57.4	60.9	65.9	71.0	73.2	74.6	77.6	78.8
Total	49.2	51.5	56.4	59.2	63.6	68.1	69.9	70.8	73.9	75.4

the answer to each of the following questions can be found by simply locating the correct cell on the table (note how it would be impossible to do this if we just had a verbal summary and impossible to do so with *precision* if we just had a graph):

1. What was the average life expectancy for men in 1910?

2. What was the average life expectancy for women in 1990?

3. What was the average life expectancy in 1950?

And of course, this doesn't require much in the way of skill!

	1900	1910	1920	1930	1940	1950	1960	1970	1980	1990
Men	47.9	49.9	55.5	57.7	61.6	65.5	66.8	67.0	70.1	71.8
Women	50.7	53.2	57.4	60.9	65.9	71.0	73.2	74.6	77.6	78.8
Total	49.2	51.5	56.4	59.2	63.6	68.1	69.9	70.8	73.9	75.4

But sometimes the information you will need to extract will not be directly present in the data given, but will instead require processing in order to find it:

The following link offers a concise overview of (a) the types of charts on offer and (b) when and where they are best applied: http://en. wikipedia.org/wiki/ Graph_(mathematics). And some basic activities on locating, extracting and translating information (alongside other basic mathematical tutorials) can be found here: www.bbc.co.uk/ scotland/learning/ bitesize/standard/ maths_i/relationships/ data_graphs_rev1. shtml.

1.   At the turn of the century (1900), who had the greater life expectancy, men or women?

2.   By how many years did male life expectancy increase between 1900 and 1950?

3.   By how many years did female life expectancy exceed male life expectancy in 1960?

4.   By how many years did general life expectancy increase in the twentieth century?

Whilst still fairly straightforward, these are slightly trickier than the initial questions and will require you to go beyond the task of merely identifying data explicit in the table. The answer to question 1 can be found by identifying the higher number of the first two cells in column one; question 2 requires you to identify the difference in number between the first cell from column one and the first of column six; question 3, the difference in number between cells one and two from column seven, and finally 4, the increase in number between the third cells in columns one and ten. Try and answer the following, slightly trickier questions yourselves:

Exercises

1.   Was the overall increase in life expectancy in the twentieth century greater for men or for women?

2.   How much greater was it?

3.   Which decade saw the greatest increase in life expectancy for men?

4.   Which decade saw the smallest increase in life expectancy for women?

5.   Which decade saw the greatest *combined* increase in life expectancy?

MOTIVE AND AGENDA

vested interest – If a source has a vested interest, this means it might stand to gain something from distorting the truth of the events it reports on.

Much of this book has focused on the nature of evidence and how it can be extracted, presented, analysed and subsequently assessed. We now turn our attention to a different, but related topic – that of **credibility**. Here our concerns lie, not with the evidence itself (although clearly this will be important), but rather with the status of its author and whether or not such a source can be trusted. Where a source is untrustworthy (for whatever reason), it is likely, though not certain, that the evidence which it presents us will be contaminated. Facts, particularly those which are statistical in nature, can be very compelling indeed but are also often very **selective** (i.e. used for the purposes of distorting rather than getting at the truth). The Victorian Prime Minister Benjamin Disraeli, summing up precisely this point, is reported to have stated: 'There are three types of lies – lies, damned lies and statistics.' This was mirrored in a quote from the comedian Vic Reeves: '88.2% of statistics are made up on the spot'! In general terms, a source (and here the term is used fairly loosely to refer to any type of physical record or document and/or its author) can be called into question if it can be shown to have a background **motive or agenda**. By this we mean that, if it is in any way one-sided, selective, exaggerated and/or biased, or can be shown to have been put forward with a **vested interest** (these terms will be explored in greater detail shortly), then we have solid grounds for rejecting it. However, a word of warning before continuing! In our earlier chapter on logical fallacies we looked at an invalid form of reasoning called the *ad hominem* attack – a fallacy which disposed of an argument by attacking the character of its author rather than the argument itself. This move, if you remember, was said to be invalid because character and argument ought always to be kept separate (and with good reason). Here, it would seem, we are at odds with our earlier principle. The point to bear in mind though, also applicable to the principle of charity, is that, unless we are duly careful and attentive when approaching the claims of others, we are in danger of leaving ourselves open to all sorts of fallacious or distorted reasoning. It is certainly true that bad characters can present good arguments, and no less true (alas!) that good characters can present bad ones. But the key here lies with our ability to judge when this is so. This is the essence of thinking critically. Unfortunately, no hard and fast rules can be given for doing this, for as with riding a bike, judgement can only be developed over time.

SOURCES

The degree of trust we should invest in a **source** should directly correlate with its level of credibility. This is the key to fair appraisal. But how do we decide

---

credibility – Approximates to trustworthiness. To gauge the reliability of a source, a set of **credibility criteria** needs to be applied to it.

selective – An author or a source is said to be selective if the evidence they select is chosen to support their own purposes.

motive or agenda – If a source has a background motive or agenda, we have good (though not conclusive!) reason to believe that the information it presents us with will be either biased, one-sided, selective, exaggerated or put forward with a vested interest.

The principle of charity was touched upon in Ch. 4.

source – Refers to any type of physical record or document and/or its author.

corroboration – Refers to other sources that agree with the one in hand.

reputable – This term is interchangeable with reliable, trustworthy etc.

ability to see – The expression refers to how well a source can be expected to observe/judge a course of events. Whether they offer a primary (eyewitness) or secondary account; or their judgement could have been affected by (i.e.) loss of memory, inebriation, poor eyesight, shock, positioning, age etc.

vested interest – If a source has a vested interest, this means it might stand to gain something from distorting the truth of the events it reports on.

neutrality – Here equates with a lack of bias – i.e. a source is said to be **neutral** if it presents both sides of the account; **biased** if it presents only one.

upon this level? In essence, we do so via asking (and responding to) the right sorts of question. These include:

- Is the source **corroborated**? Are there other sources which agree with the one in hand?
- Does it stem from a **reputable** (reliable) source?
- Was this source a witness to the reported events or is the evidence purely anecdotal – i.e. reported second-hand (the difference between a primary and secondary account)? If they were there as a witness, could their **ability to see** have been hampered in any way by factors that could cloud or otherwise affect their judgement (loss of memory, inebriation, poor eyesight, shock, age etc.)?
- Does the source have a **vested interest** to distort the truth (i.e. do they stand to gain anything by doing so)? Do they have a vested interest to be truthful?
- Does the source have any relevant **expertise** (i.e. one that relates to the evidence being presented)?
- Is the source **neutral** (i.e. does it present both sides of the argument) or could it be guilty of bias – for example, could the evidence have been interpreted in some way that is less than objective (i.e. one-sided)? Does it employ any emotive language in order to get its points across?

In reality, of course, not all of these questions will need to be addressed. Nor, as far as the exam is concerned, will there be time enough to do so. For this reason, you will need to judge for yourself which are the most relevant or appropriate for a particular source, and of course this will vary from context to context. What is important is that you recognise which criteria positively affect, and which negatively affect, the credibility of a source and thus the evidence they present. Corroboration, for example, is a positive credibility criterion. The greater the amount of agreement between sources or evidence, the greater the likelihood that that evidence will be true (although, of course, this will not always be the case). The same can be said of evidence put forward by reputable sources – i.e. ones with a reputation to uphold. Such sources might include teachers, lawyers, police officers, broadsheet newspapers, news corporations or, more generally, those that can be *relied* upon to tell the truth. An ability to see/understand/interpret/judge etc. will also lend weight to evidence. In particular, a primary report – i.e. one given by somebody who was there at the time, can be regarded as more credible than a secondary one since it offers a first-hand account of the issue on which it is reporting. Where a source has a vested interest to report the truth (for example, a reputable newspaper or news broadcaster) or a relevant expertise in the field that is being reported on, we have strong grounds for believing it. And finally, a neutral account (i.e. one that gives details of both sides of a debate and does so in neutral, i.e. not emotively charged, terms) can be regarded as more credible than one which is slanted or biased (i.e. one-sided or emotively charged). Turning this on its head, where a source is not corroborated; lacks a solid reputation; has no clear ability to see/understand/interpret/judge the issue it reports on; has an apparent vested interest in (i.e. stands to gain from) distorting the truth of events; lacks relevant expertise and/or offers a one-sided account, then any one of these points will affect its credibility. Applying them to an example will help clarify each of these points, but before doing so, a final word of advice. You may have noticed that the first letter from each of these criteria: **C**orroboration; **R**eputation; **A**bility to observe/judge; **V**ested interest; **E**xpertise and **N**eutrality (or lack of it) spells out the word **craven**. This mnemonic is often employed by critical thinkers as a memory aid for dealing with each (there is no 'correct' order in which to do this).

The following table offers a comprehensive method for mapping out these criteria against the individual sources they can be applied to, though of course in an exam your response should be laid out briefly in prose:

Corroboration	Reputation	Ability to observe/ judge etc.	Vested interest	Expertise	Neutrality
Source x					
Source y					
Source z					

Bearing this in mind, read through the document below which explains the curious events that took place at Roswell New Mexico, the alleged location of an alien landing in 1947 and the subject of much controversy and conspiracy theory ever since:

Roswell, weather balloon or UFO?

On July 8, 1947, the Roswell Army Air Field (RAAF) issued a press release stating that personnel from the field's 509th Bomb Group had recovered

> Corroboration, reputation, ability to see and neutrality are **positive** credibility criteria – they lend weight to the testimony of the evidence put forward; lack of corroboration and reputation, inability to see (or a clouded judgement), vested interest to distort the truth and bias are **negative** credibility criteria – they detract from/call into question the weight of the evidence put forward. These are points that need to be factored in when considering whether or not a source can be regarded as credible.

> The word **CRAVEN** is a helpful mnemonic for remembering each of the credibility criteria.

a crashed 'flying disc' from a ranch near Roswell. Later the same day, the Commanding General of the Eighth Air Force stated that, in fact, a weather balloon had been recovered by RAAF personnel, rather than a 'flying saucer'. Then, in 1978, Jesse Marcel who was involved with the original recovery of the debris in 1947, expressed his belief that the military had covered up the recovery of an alien spacecraft. Additional witnesses and reports emerged over the following years. They added significant new details, including claims of a huge military operation dedicated to recovering alien craft and aliens themselves. In 1989, former mortician Glenn Dennis put forth a detailed personal account, wherein he claimed that alien autopsies were carried out at the Roswell base. In response, the General Accounting Office launched an inquiry and directed the Office of the Secretary of the Air Force to conduct an internal investigation. Subsequent congressional inquiries were summarised in two reports. The first, released in 1995, concluded that the reported recovered material in 1947 was likely debris from a secret government program called Project Mogul, which involved high altitude balloons meant to detect sound waves generated by Soviet atomic bomb tests and ballistic missiles. The second report, released in 1997, concluded that reports of recovered alien bodies were likely a combination of innocently transformed memories of military accidents involving injured or killed personnel, innocently transformed memories of the recovery of anthropomorphic dummies in military programs like Project High Dive conducted in the 1950s and hoaxes perpetrated by various witnesses and UFO proponents. (Adapted from Wikipedia)

Question: How credible do you find the above document's account of the events that happened at Roswell?

Exercise

1.   Before reading on, and selecting the most relevant of the credibility criteria outlined above, see if you can offer a brief response to this question. Remember, it relates to the document as a whole (including its author), rather than the individual sources or evidence it presents us with.

Because there is only one document to be considered, questions concerning corroboration need not concern us here. If there were further documents relating to the same issue, or if we were considering the specific sources presented within the text itself, then of course it would. The above question, however, focuses on the *nature* of the document, rather than the sources contained within it. The first question that concerns us then is: 'What kind of a document is it'? And here we can start with reputation. The article itself is taken from Wikipedia, an online encyclopaedia, which many (now!) regard as a *fairly* reliable source of information. I say fairly because this point is not without controversy and a case could be made either way. Certainly this source has become more reliable over the years (articles are constantly being checked and revised). In terms of ability to see/judge/interpret, the author is obviously offering a secondary account (although it contains first-hand reports), but given that the incident took place over half a century ago, this point has limited significance. It could also be argued that, given Wikipedia has a (growing!) reputation to maintain, the document has a vested interest to portray the truth. They certainly do not stand to gain anything and arguably stand to lose (in terms of a damaged reputation) through *not* doing so. The author of the source is unidentified. However, the encyclopaedia is produced and maintained by individuals with a relevant knowledge base, so perhaps it would be comparatively safe to assume a relevant expertise. Nevertheless, their anonymity, coupled with the fairly high incidence of mistakes uncovered in this online encyclopaedia, means that we should not be *overly* confident about this. Finally, given that the document is couched in fairly neutral terms (there is limited, if any, employment of persuasive/emotive language) and also that it lays out both sides of the debate (here an overview is given rather than an argument put forward) then it can be regarded as being neutral. All in all, then, it can be regarded as being fairly credible.

Let us now turn our attention to the credibility of the individual *sources* cited in the document. Focusing on one particular source will help show you how this is done:

Question: How credible a source do you find the Commanding General of the Eighth Air Force?

2. Before reading on, and selecting the most relevant of the credibility criteria outlined above, see if you can offer a brief response to this question. Remember, it relates to a specific source quoted in the document rather than the document itself.

Corroboration and conflict

Let us start with the evidence he submits and look for corroborating sources:

> [The CGEAF] stated that, in fact, a weather balloon had been recovered by RAAF personnel, rather than a 'flying saucer.'

This account is supported by at least one further source:

> the General Accounting Office launched an inquiry and directed <u>the Office of the Secretary of the Air Force</u> to conduct an internal investigation.

Which concludes that:

> the reported recovered material in 1947 was likely debris from a secret government program called Project Mogul, which involved high altitude balloons meant to detect sound waves generated by Soviet atomic bomb tests and ballistic missiles.

There are, however, several accounts that conflict with this initial statement:

1. The Roswell Army Air Field (RAAF) issued a press release stating that personnel from the field's 509th Bomb Group had recovered a crashed 'flying disc'.

2. Major Jesse Marcel expressed his belief that the military had covered up the recovery of an alien spacecraft.

3. Former mortician Glenn Dennis put forth a detailed personal account, wherein he claimed that alien autopsies were carried out at the Roswell base.

4. Additional witnesses and reports emerged over the following years. They added significant new details, including claims of a huge military operation dedicated to recovering alien craft and aliens themselves

And before we can decide upon the extent to which these weaken the evidence given by our original source (and to what extent), we first need to decide upon their individual level of credibility. The RAAF, Major Jesse Marcel and former mortician Glenn Dennis, for example, can all be regarded as having a reputation to uphold, relevant expertise and (at least a potential to) observe/judge events from a primary perspective. But do they have a vested interest, natural bias etc. and if so, why? We might also question the significance of expressions such as 'a crashed flying disk' (source 1); 'expressed his *belief*' (source 2) and '*personal account*' (source 3). The first of these is at best vague, whilst the second and third express judgements of a subjective nature. The information provided about the 'additional witnesses and reports' is also rather unclear. Who were these witnesses? What kind of reports are we talking about? What is meant by the expression 'significant new details'? Just how plausible is the claim that there was a 'huge military operation dedicated to recovering alien craft and aliens themselves' unless supplemented with detailed evidential support? Each of these points, which of course need developing, call into question the reliability of such sources. Counter to this, we might also focus on the *positive* credibility of the corroborating source. Whilst the 'Office of the Secretary of the Air Force' may well have a vested interest to distort the truth – perhaps so as to cover up material of a sensitive nature – nevertheless, their reputation, ability to observe/interpret the facts and obvious relevant expertise lend considerable weight to their claims and these points should not be overlooked.

Reputation, ability to observe and expertise

The commanding general, given the nature of his job and the level of responsibility it entails, can also be regarded as having a fairly strong reputation to uphold. This strengthens the credibility of his account because one would expect someone in such a position to be fairly trustworthy. Although not explicit in the text, it is also probably safe to assume that he was there at the time the events took place and, moreover, observed the evidence itself:

> Later the same day, the Commanding General of the Eighth Air Force stated that, in fact, a weather balloon had been recovered by RAAF personnel.

This offers a first-hand account of the events, and so reinforces the plausibility of his claim. For the same reason, it would be fairly safe to assume that his ability to recall the day's events would be fairly strong. It is also safe to assume he has relevant expertise in the field he is reporting on. His job, the fact that he was selected to offer the official verdict etc., is a clear indication of this.

For more on hypothetical claims, see the Glossary and Ch. 4: 'The principle of charity'.

Hypothetical reasoning (in the form of claims/ arguments etc.) can be used to effectively assess the credibility of a source without having to reach a conclusive judgement as to its status. E.g., instead of asserting that: 'source x has a natural bias/vested interest (etc.) so the evidence they present us with cannot be trusted', it would be better to assert that: '*if we were to assume* that source x had a natural bias/vested interest etc., then it would follow that the evidence they presented could not be trusted'. This will ensure that you do not overcommit yourself when assessing source credibility and give your reasoning a sense of objectivity that it would otherwise lack.

Vested interest and neutrality

The most obvious problem with this source, as should be clear, is whether or not it can be regarded as having a vested interest. Of course this would not be a problem if we knew that the claim were true (vested interest or not, fact remains fact), but it is precisely this point that is in question. In the absence of proof, we settle for plausibility (or 'likelihood' of truth), and this is arrived at, at least in part, by judging source credibility. If the Commanding General did have a vested interest to distort the truth, for example to counter potentially damaging reports of a military cover-up or simply to put forward an account that agreed with 'the official doctrine' put out by the military, then we might have reservations about trusting his claim. That is not to say that, if a vested interest *was* present, then this claim should be dismissed, but rather that we should treat it with caution. Expressed as a hypothetical claim, we might say that: '*if* the Commanding General of the Eighth Air Force *did* have a vested interest to distort the truth, perhaps on account of …, *then* this would give us good reason to dispute the truth of his claim'.

Because the reference to the source is brief, there is not enough information to go on to decide whether a bias is present. It might be argued that his claim:

> In fact, a weather balloon had been recovered by RAAF personnel, rather than a 'flying saucer.'

is expressed in neutral terms, or alternatively that, because he would have a duty to side with the army, then any account he might have gone on to offer would almost certainly be one-sided. But here, because there is not enough evidence to go on, it would be unsafe to deliver such a verdict. Note, however, that the 'scare quotes' around 'flying saucer' suggest that he pronounced the words with a sceptical tone, which casts doubt on the **neutrality** of his account.

---

3.   Bearing in mind the points we have just looked at, try and summarise, in a brief paragraph, the credibility of the above source. You may find framing your answer as follows: 'On the one hand, this source can be regarded as fairly credible because … But on the other …' helps you to do this.

Remember, you do not need to decide whether the account given is (or isn't) accurate, but rather whether or not a case can be made for regarding it as credible.

Considering evidence

The final thing we need to look at here is **evidence** itself. Going back to the example of the claim that:

> A weather balloon had been recovered by RAAF personnel, rather than a 'flying saucer.'

there are various points that we need to consider before deciding on the credibility of this evidence. Firstly, of course, we need to think about whether or not a piece of evidence is accurate. This is not always such an easy task however. Of course if the claim above could be confirmed beyond reasonable doubt, then the evidence provided would be conclusive. In the majority of cases, however, this cannot be done. Where there is doubt, we need to think about how **credible** the evidence is. This we do, as should by now be clear, by examining the reliability of its source or author and/or whether or not it is corroborated by evidence put forward by other sources. The issue of **selectivity** is also an important one here – in particular as regards whether or not an author might have selected a particular piece of evidence to suit their own purpose.

Secondly, we need to consider how **relevant** it is. If a piece of evidence, for whatever reason, fails to relate to the matter being discussed, then the question of how accurate or credible it is will be irrelevant and the information should be discarded. For example, the following claim:

> There have been no conclusively confirmed UFO sightings since records began. (Sceptical Report)

might appear superficially relevant (it might be used to bolster a disbelief in such objects). However, this would only be the case if we *assume* that this particular claim is sufficient to demonstrate that no UFOs actually exist. As it stands, however, this would be an illegitimate consequence to draw. The evidence also has no real bearing on the specific events that occurred in Roswell. Contrast the above example with the following one:

> It has been revealed that the Commanding General of the Eighth Air Force has three previous convictions for conspiring to pervert the course of justice concerning matters of national security. (Source: author's own)

neutrality – Here equates with a lack of bias – i.e. a source is said to be **neutral** if it presents both sides of the account; **biased** if it presents only one.

evidence – Simply refers to material of a factual nature which is appealed to in support of a claim.

credibility – Approximates to trustworthiness. To gauge the reliability of a source, we need to apply a set of **credibility criteria** to it.

selective – An author or a source is said to be selective if the evidence they select is chosen to support their own purposes.

For more on this topic, see Ch. 11: 'Argument from ignorance' (*argumentum ad ignorantiam*).

Expressions such as 'selective', 'significant', 'credible' etc. are semi-technical terms which may well be used to phrase exam questions. It is important you understand their function.

significance – The significance of a piece of evidence can be assessed by considering the effect it would have, if true, on the issue in hand.

For obvious reasons (in particular, reputation credibility), this evidence *would* be relevant to the case in hand and would thus negatively affect, although not conclusively disprove, the general's explanation. It is possible that, on this occasion, he may be telling the truth.

Finally we need to consider the **significance** of the evidence – what it *shows*. To do this we need to ask what effect, if the claim were true, would it have on the issue being discussed? To use an example, if the Commanding General's statement, and hence the weather balloon hypothesis, *were* true, the significance of this would be that it disproves the claims that the debris discovered was from a UFO or flying saucer. We need to be careful, however, that when considering the significance of evidence we do not overstate our inference. For example, it would be unsafe to conclude from the RAAF press release that:

> personnel from the field's 509th Bomb Group had recovered a crashed 'flying disc' from a ranch near Roswell

or Major Jesse Marcel's belief that:

> The military had covered up the recovery of an alien spacecraft

or mortician Glenn Dennis' claim that:

> Alien autopsies were carried out at the Roswell base

were all *deliberately* fraudulent as this assumption would rule out any alternative explanations for their evidence. This point should be clear when we look at the information provided in the second official report:

> Reports of recovered alien bodies were likely a combination of innocently transformed memories of military accidents involving injured or killed personnel, innocently transformed memories of the recovery of anthropomorphic dummies in military programs like Project High Dive conducted in the 1950s and hoaxes perpetrated by various witnesses and UFO proponents.

Before continuing, it is worth remembering that each of the above points is also applicable to evidence of a more statistical nature which we shall be dealing with in the remainder of this chapter.

Summary questions . . .

1. What is meant by the term 'source'?
2. What is meant by the term 'credibility'?
3. What factors can affect source credibility? Which of these are negative and which positive?
4. Explain the role that accuracy, credibility, relevance and significance play in judging the effectiveness of evidence.
5. What is meant by the terms 'motive' and 'agenda'?
6. What is a source? What different types of sources might you expect to come across?
7. How might a background agenda or motive affect source credibility?
8. What are the different credibility criteria? How do they help us to judge source credibility?
9. Which of these criteria can be regarded as positive, and which negative?

END OF CHAPTER ACTIVITY

1. Fill in the credibility table on the next page for the individual sources identified in the above document. Make sure you start with the most relevant (it will not be necessary to fill in every space).
2. Thinking about positive and negative criteria, which source do you believe gives: (a) the most reliable account? (b) the least reliable account? Explain your answers.
3. Bearing in mind (a) the nature of the document and (b) the nature of the individual sources, come to a reasoned judgement about whether the events at Roswell were the result of a weather balloon or a flying saucer. Remember, there is no necessarily 'correct' answer here; what is important is that you give reasons to support your judgement.
4. Stretching activity: It is further reported that:

   Significant numbers of UFO researchers discount the probability that the incident had anything to do with aliens.

   Bearing in mind the precision of the language used here and the type of evidence given, explain the accuracy, credibility, relevance and significance of the above claim.

	Corroboration (flying saucer or weather balloon)	Reputation	Ability to observe/ judge etc.	Vested interest	Expertise	Neutrality
(1) The Roswell Army Air Field (RAAF)						
(2) The Commanding General of the Eighth Air Force						
(3) Major Jesse Marcel						
(4) 'Additional witnesses and reports'						
(5) Glenn Dennis						
(6) Office of the Secretary of the Air Force internal investigation						

SUMMARY CHECKLIST

Points you need to remember:

✔ Some of the ways in which information can be presented, such as in tabular form, verbally and graphically.

✔ How to extract and translate data from and between each of the above forms.

✔ The basic advantages and disadvantages of each method and some of the criteria (detail, simplicity etc.) which help us to determine these.

✔ What is meant by the terms 'motive' and 'agenda'.

✔ What is meant by the term 'source'.

✔ Why a background motive or agenda can affect the credibility of a given source.

✔ The further set of criteria that can be used to determine source credibility:
  i.   the primary or secondary status of the source;
  ii. the reputation/reputability of a witness or author;
  iii. the possibility of vested interest on the part of an author (and the extent to which it might influence him or her to say one thing rather than another);
  iv. the scope for error, e.g. the physical ability of a person to make a particular observation;
  v.   the expertise or authority of an author (and whether or not their expertise is relevant to the claim/s being made);
  vi. the degree of corroboration provided by other (independent) sources.

The OCR website, although a different syllabus to the AQA, has links to several past papers dealing with credibility. These can be accessed via the following link: www.ocr.org.uk/qualifications/type/gce/hss/critical_thinking/documents/index.aspx. Further information and advice can be found at: www.criticalthinking.org.uk/unit1/.

16

UNIT 2 INFORMATION, INFERENCE AND EXPLANATION

Chapter 16: Numerical and statistical reasoning

LEARNING OBJECTIVES

By the end of this chapter you should:

✔ Be able to apply basic methods of numerical and statistical reasoning to a given body of evidence or data.
✔ Understand both what is meant by and how to apply terms such as 'percentage', 'average' ('mean' and 'median') and 'simple probability' to the above information.
✔ Be able to read and interpret commonly used graphs and charts such as bar charts, pie charts, line and scattergraphs, flow charts, tree diagrams and Venn and Carroll diagrams.

Much of the Unit 2 exam requires you to apply basic mathematical and statistical reasoning in order to support any inferences, judgements, predictions, generalisations and/or causal claims that you may wish to draw. You might argue, for example, based on the life-expectancy figures outlined in our initial table (p. 171), that women live longer than men; that life-expectancy rates will continue to increase; that the increase in life-expectancy rates is due to better health care, nutrition etc., and to do this, you will need to show *how* a given body of evidence supports such inferences. Much of this we have already covered in the first section of this book, but we return to it here in a mathematical format. Nevertheless, the skills involved are the same. A final word of warning before continuing, if you are a non-mathematician, this unit may make your brain hurt, but persevere. You may find out that you are better at maths than you thought!

Rereading Chs 1 and 3 will help refresh your memory of these.

MATHEMATICAL KNOWLEDGE

The material used thus far, in this unit of the book, has been rather dry. This has been necessary in order to give you a basic understanding of the skills on which we will be working. To spice things up a little (remember, it is the skill, rather than content, that is important here!), let us imagine a scenario where, in the distant future (say the year 3010!), cats have evolved to the extent that some of them have developed a basic capacity for speech. Let us also imagine that you have transported yourself forward in time in order to study these 'talking cats'. There is only one island which is inhabited by such animals, Baal, and a set of 'raw' data has been compiled by a team of visiting zoologists who have a keen interest in feline abnormality. It runs as follows:

Baal

	3001	3002	3003	3004	3005	3006	3007	3008	3009	3010
Talking cats	100	200	300	500	1,000	2,000	4,000	8,000	16,000	32,000
Non-talking cats	14,900	10,000	7,500	6,000	4,500	3,500	2,500	1,500	1,000	500
Total number of cats	15,000	10,200	7,800	6,500	5,500	5,500	6,500	9,500	17,000	32,500

The human inhabitants of the island ('Baalanders'), worried about this sudden 'talking-cat' influx, are considering a cull in order to protect the native non-speaking cat population which they believe to be under threat of extinction as a result of interbreeding with their more vocal relatives. The zoologists, rightly appalled at such an idea, are anxious to avert such an outcome. In order to come to a reasoned decision about what should and should not be done, certain questions need addressing:

1. What was the initial percentage of talking cats?

2. What is the current percentage of talking cats?

3. What is the overall percentage increase in the talking-cat population?

Unfortunately the data provided, in its raw form, is rather unhelpful, failing to provide us with the information that we need to answer such questions. To do so, it needs processing. But how do we go about doing this?

Percentages and ratios

For more of this, see Chs 17, 18 and 19.

percentage – Simply means a part out of a hundred. When dealing with two figures, if you divide the smaller number by the larger one then multiply by 100, this will show you the percentage it represents.

As with visual graphs, seeing numbers in **percentage** form considerably simplifies the process of digesting information, comparing and contrasting data, recognising patterns and correlations, and subsequently making predictions. If, for example, you scored 47 out of 100 in one exam and 58 out of 120 in another, it would be difficult to judge in which exam you performed better, until you converted the result into a percentage. A simple way of calculating this figure is to divide the smaller figure by the larger one (which represents 100%) and then multiply by 100:

Exam 1: (47 / 100) x 100 = 47 (%)

Exam 2: (58 / 120) x 100 = 48.3 (%)

And you have your answer. In the case of the talking-cat question, if we were trying to figure out the initial percentage of talking cats then the equation we would be dealing with would be:

1. (100 / 15,000) x 100 = 0.67 (%)

From here, it is easy to work out that the percentage of non-talking cats would be 99.33% (100 – 0.67). If we were trying to figure out the *current* percentage of talking cats, then the equation would be:

2. (32,000 / 32,500) x 100 = 98.46 (%)

Finally, to work out the overall percentage of increase in the talking-cat population, we need to start with our initial figure, 100, and calculate the % increase from 100 to 32,000. To do this we first need to work out the initial difference between 100 and 32,000 (i.e. 32,000 – 100) which is 31,900 – this being the *raw* increase in number of the talking-cat population. Then we divide this difference by the original (31,900 / 100) which is 319. Finally, as with our previous equation, we multiply this number by 100 which yields an overall increase rate of 31,900%! The equation looks like this:

3.   (32,000 – 100) / 100 x 100 = 31,900 (%)

It is also sometimes helpful to state values such as these in **ratio** form (where a relationship between two separate quantities, for example water and cordial, is expressed in number: 4:1 – four parts to one). Let us say, for the purpose of simplicity, that for every 100 cats, 70 (%) can talk whilst 30 (%) cannot. Here, the ratio of talking to non-talking cats would be 7:3 (ratios are expressed as two numbers separated by a colon: 'x:y'). The ratio of talking cats to the overall cat population would be 7:10 (for every 10 cats, 7 of them will be talkers – expressed as a fraction, 7/10ths of cats). Bearing the above points in mind, see if you can answer the following questions:

Exercises

1.   In 3001, what was the percentage of cats that couldn't talk?

2.   In 3007, what was the percentage of cats that *could* talk?

3.   What is the overall percentage decrease in the non-talking-cat population?

4.   If 75% of cats could talk (and 25% couldn't) how would this be expressed as a ratio?

5.   How would the ratio 1:2 be expressed as a percentage?

Averages

Having gathered the relevant information, let us say that the islanders of Baal, being an inquisitive race, wish to know more. Most importantly, they wish to know the **average** yearly rate of increase in the talking-cat population believing this will help them predict the rate at which this species might reasonably be expected to continue reproducing. There would be three ways of calculating such an increase (the **mean**, **median** and **mode**), only two of which need concern us here. The first of these is the *mean* average, which is calculated by

---

ratio – Expresses a relationship between two separate quantities. I.e. if a glass of cordial requires 4 parts water to 1 part cordial, the ratio can be expressed as 4:1.

averages – To calculate the **mean** average, add all the values in a set and then divide this new number by the original amount of values. The **median** average can be found by listing all the numbers in a set from small to large. The median value will be the middle number in this sequence. The **mode** average is simply the value that occurs most frequently in a set of numbers.

mean average – To calculate the mean average, add all the values in a set and then divide this new number by the original amount of values.

median average – The median average can be found by listing all the numbers in a set from small to large. The median value will be the middle number in this sequence.

mode average – The mode average is simply the value that occurs most often in a set of data.

adding up all the values in a set, and then dividing this new number by the original number of values. The second is the *median* average, which is achieved by listing the values in order (small to large), and then identifying the middle value in this sequence. Each method suits a specific purpose.

If we wished to calculate, for example, what an average salary was for a specific company, then before we decided which method to use, we would first need to know about the range of salaries paid out. Let us say there are ten employees, nine of whom earn £25,000 a year and one, the director, who earns £150,000. Appealing to the mean would be rather unhelpful here as it would generate an average income of £37,500 per person:

* (9 x 25,000) + (1 x 150,000) /10 = 37,500

a figure clearly unrepresentative of the majority of employees. Using the median, however, we can see that a much fairer calculation can be arrived at:

* 25k, 25k, 25k, 25k, 25k, 25k, 25k, 25k, 25k, 150k

The midpoint here would be £25,000 – values 5 and 6 (if these are different, then the median will be the midpoint *between* the two values) and this *would* be a reasonable representation of the general level of pay. If we were to change the example, however, and say that two of the employees were on £5,000; two on £6,000; two on £25,000; one on £70,000; one on £100,000, and the final two on £250,000, here the median would still generate an average wage value of £25,000:

* 5k, 5k, 6k, 6k, 25k, 25k, 70k, 100k, 250k, 250k

which would clearly be disproportionate as it represents the wage value of only two employees and bears no relation whatsoever to those of the other eight.

Applying this to the situation that confronts the islanders of Baal, in order to calculate the mean and median yearly rate of increase of the talking-cat population, we first need to extract the raw figures of this increase – i.e. by how much the cat population has increased each year.

	3001	3002	3003	3004	3005	3006	3007	3008	3009	3010
Talking cats	100	200	300	500	1,000	2,000	4,000	8,000	16,000	32,000
Yearly increase	n/a	100	100	200	500	1,000	2,000	4,000	8,000	16,000

And once we have this, calculating the mean average increase is straightforward:

- (100 + 100 + 200 + 500 + 1,000 + 2,000 + 4,000 + 8,000 + 16,000) / 9 = 3,544

And so too the median:

- 100, 100, 200, 500, **1,000,** 2,000, 4,000, 8,000, 16,000

Exercises

1. Which, if either, average do you believe best serves the islanders of Baal?

2. Why is this so?

3. Can you think of a better method for predicting the future population growth of talking cats?

You have probably noted that, whilst offering a partially adequate account of how much the cat population has increased *up until now* (and here, for obvious reasons, it would seem that the mean average is more suitable than the median) neither of the above methods is particularly useful for determining by how much we can expect this trend to continue. This is because the increase appears to be exponential (i.e. extremely rapid rather than constant). You might have suggested, for example, that a more helpful way of doing this would be to plot the figures on a line or bar graph, or generate a set of percentage figures that would help us see an underlying pattern, and you would be right:

Identifying trends and judging what can and cannot safely be inferred from a given body of evidence are issues taken up in Chs 3 and 19.

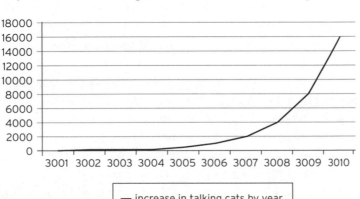

— increase in talking cats by year

Here, if the current trend were to continue, we would expect the yearly increase to double, assuming there to be no other factors such as lack of resources, feline cull etc. that might limit this growth.

Exercises

1. Calculate the average yearly *mean* decrease of the non-talking-cat population.

2. Calculate the median yearly decrease.

3. Which of these do you think offers a more accurate picture? Why?

Probability

The islanders of Baal, still concerned by the rate at which the talking-cat population is expanding, have decided, against the wishes of the zoologists, to cull a significant proportion of these in order to stem this increase. The cats, however, hearing of this plan, have other ideas. One of the brightest of these puts forward a suggestion. If all (talking) cats remain silent, he argues, it will be impossible for the islanders to tell apart talking cats from their mute relatives and, this being so, the Baalanders, who are known for their great love of this native creature, will be forced to call off their campaign. Realising this duplicitous action, the Baalanders have to make a choice. They reason that, since the vast majority of felines will be talking cats, if they cull a sizeable percentage of the overall cat population, say, 20,000, then the chances are that only a few non-talkers will be destroyed and this is perhaps a price worth paying. Nevertheless, they would like to know what, if they were to select a single cat entirely at random, the chances or **probability** would be of its being a native non-talker.

probability – A measurement of how likely it is that an event will happen. If you toss a coin, the probability rate of it turning up heads is ✛ (one in two).

    To draw an analogy here, if one were to select an individual card from a deck, assuming it to be a standard fifty-two card pack (Jokers removed), the chances of selecting, say, the 7♣ would be 1/52. Thus the probability of selecting any particular card at random would be 1/52 (or, for every fifty-two attempts, one should be successful). The probability of selecting any spade would be 1/4, since there are only four suits in a pack. The chance of picking either a red or a black card would be 1/2, and the chances of picking out a numbered or head card (including aces), for similar reasons, would be 36/52 and 16/52 respectively. It is also possible to work out the probability of picking out a succession of cards. The chances of picking out two red cards in a row (assuming one places the first card back in the pack after selecting!), for example, would be 1/2 x 1/2 (1/4); the chances of picking out a red card, then a club would be 1/2 x 1/4 (1/8) and so on. Equations such as these are particularly helpful when it comes to risk calculation – as we see with the situation that confronts the islanders of Baal, not to mention their cats!

Exercises

1. What would be the probability of selecting either the 7♣ or the J♥ randomly from a pack of cards?

2. What would be the probability of picking out two head cards successively (assuming you replaced your first card back in the pack)?

3. Choose two types of card that would offer combined odds of 39/52 of coming up (there are many correct answers here). Explain your answer.

Applying the above reasoning to the Baalanders case, if there were an equal proportion of talking and non-talking cats (50:50), then the probability of selecting either cat at random would be 1/2. Given that the ratio is 32,000:500, however, the equation is slightly trickier. See if you can work it out!

Since the overall cat population is 32,500 and the number of talking cats 32,000, the probability would be 32,000/32,500. But this is rather a large number to handle! We could break it down further: 32,000/32,500 = 16,000/16,250 = 8,000/8,125 etc., but in this case, it might be easier to convert such a value to a percentage. Going back to our earlier method of doing this, we would be left with the following equation: (32,000 / 32,500) x 100 = 98.46. The probability of selecting a talking cat at random, then, would be 98.46%. Fortunately, there is a clause written into the Baalanders' constitution which states that, for any activity which might endanger a native feline, unless this has a greater than 99% safety rate, it must not be pursued. So, for now at least, the cats are safe!

For a range of resources and activities on percentage, ratio and proportion see: http://www.themathpage.com/arith/ratio-and-proportion_1.htm. For a range of resources and activities on calculating averages see: www.primaryresources.co.uk/maths/mathsF1e.htm#mean. For a range of resources and activities on simple probability see: //www.aaamath.com/sta-prob-simple.htm.

Summary questions . . .

1. What do the concepts percentage, ratio, average and probability mean?
2. How do we go about determining each of the above? (Offer a brief explanation for each.)

Exercises

1. Calculate the probability of randomly selecting a non-talking cat.

2. Convert this value to a percentage.

COMMON GRAPHS AND CHARTS

We have already looked at some basic examples of commonly used graphs and charts and how and why these might be used. We now need to explore the theme in greater detail.

Some important concepts

Let us return again to our original data of the feline population of Baal:

	3001	3002	3003	3004	3005	3006	3007	3008	3009	3010
Talking cats	100	200	300	500	1,000	2,000	4,000	8,000	16,000	32,000
Non-talking cats	14,900	10,000	7,500	6,000	4,500	3,500	2,500	1,500	1,000	500
Total number of cats	15,000	10,200	7,800	6,500	5,500	5,500	6,500	9,500	17,000	32,500

range – A range in data simply means the quantitative difference between the highest and lowest number in a set.

Introducing some semi-technical language here, of the kind you might expect to find in an exam, we might say that the above data (relating to *talking cats*) has a **range** of 31,900. Range – broadly speaking the difference between the highest and lowest number in a set – is calculated by subtracting the latter from the former (i.e. 32,000 – 100). For the same reason, the range of data for non-talking cats is 14,400 (14,900 – 500) and for the total number of cats 17,500.

Another important concept which (ironically!) often crops up in data analysis is **frequency**. 'Frequency' relates to the rate at which a particular value occurs in any given set. The number 5,500, for example, in the data compiled for the total number of cats, has a frequency value of 2 (it occurs twice); the value 32,500, on the other hand, only occurs once, so it has a frequency rate of 1. In the above table, the data which expresses the yearly increase in the talking-cat population is laid out **cumulatively**. In a 'cumulative' set of data, each successive number includes (i.e. 'adds on') the number that precedes it. If this data were presented so as to include only the specific yearly increases, like so:

> **frequency** – Means the rate at which (i.e. the amount of times) a particular value occurs in any given set.

> **cumulative** – A cumulative set of data adds each number successively to the number which precedes it.

	3001	3002	3003	3004	3005	3006	3007	3008	3009	3010
Yearly increase of talking cats	n/a	100	100	200	500	1,000	2,000	4,000	8,000	16,000

Then this would be **non-cumulative**. Each value is given independently of its predecessor.

Finally, the values (**variables**) of any given set of data can be regarded as **discrete** or **continuous**. A 'discrete' variable is one that takes on only certain values. For example, the above data is restricted to whole (cardinal) numbers. It would not be possible to include half a cat; at least not in any sense that might interest us here! Continuous variables, in contrast, take on *any* value. If we were compiling data on *weight*, rather than *amount*, this would *not* be restricted to whole numbers alone since a cat's mass can be continuous (2.4; 2.5; 2.6 kg etc.). It is worth taking some time to digest these terms before continuing.

> **discrete variable** – A discrete variable will only take on whole values (e.g. 1, 2, 3 etc.).

> **continuous variable** – This variable takes on *any* value (for example, 1.1, 1.2, 1.3 etc.)

Exercises

1. Calculate the value of the range of the total number of cats in the above table.

2. Calculate the frequency of each value in this set.

3. Express each individual value non-cumulatively (i.e. as a separate, rather than combined, increase).

4. Give two examples of a discrete and two examples of a continuous variable. Explain your answer.

Bar charts

bar chart – Presents **data** visually in either a vertical or a horizontal column.

As we have seen, **bar charts** present data in the form of either vertical or horizontal columns. The x (horizontal) axis of the chart represents the type of data we are dealing with and the y (vertical) axis assigns a value (number/amount) to it. Translating the information from the above grid generates the following graph:

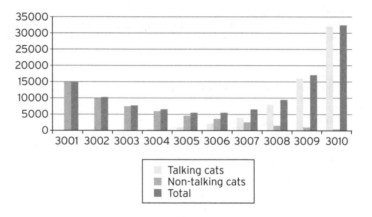

Bar charts offer an effective method for comparing two or more sets of data, especially when these have been compiled over a given period of time (a weakness, as we shall see, of pie charts). As previously noted, they generate a visual depiction which can reveal patterns and trends in numerical data, which other charts, particularly those in tabular form, may well keep concealed.

Pie charts

pie chart – Presents data visually in 'sectors' or 'slices'.

Pie charts are divided into sectors ('slices'), each of which represents a specific quantity of data or 'slice of the pie'. For this reason, they are particularly useful for comparing a range of amounts or a specific amount with a total one (ratio and proportion). This is especially true when these are expressed as a percentage (360° = 100%).

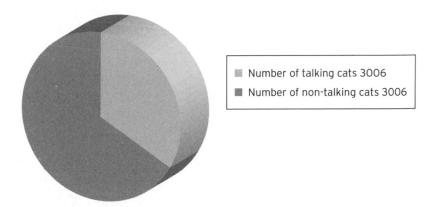

- Number of talking cats 3006
- Number of non-talking cats 3006

Whilst simplicity renders such charts visually attractive, their inability to incorporate a range of data (here it has only been possible to present a particular piece of data from a specific year) means they are unpopular with those wishing to present their findings in a more comprehensive or scientific fashion. When a more complex representation of data is required, we need to look elsewhere.

Line graphs

As with bar graphs, **line graphs** offer an effective way of visually depicting a relationship between a set of two or more variables (for example, amount and type) and this relationship is reflected in the comparative steepness (or gentleness) of the lines' gradients:

line graph – A line graph, unsurprisingly, presents data from one or more variables in a linear fashion.

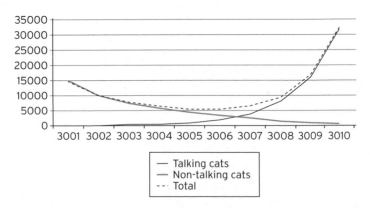

- Talking cats
- Non-talking cats
- -- Total

The range of variables that can be accommodated for in a line graph is clearly an advantage that this type of chart has over others, but when the data you are dealing with does not display any trend or pattern (for example, if it deals with proportionate amounts, rather than an increase or decrease over time) then here you would be better off using a pie chart.

Scattergraphs

scattergraph – A scattergraph plots dots or crosses against the x and y axes of a chart.

As with line graphs, **scattergraphs** can be used to depict, where one exists, a proportionate relationship between two or more sets of data. Such graphs do so by plotting dots (or crosses) against the x and y axes of a chart. They are particularly useful for comparing quantities of information where timescale is not a relevant factor. For this reason they would not, however, offer a suitable arrangement for laying out our above data on cats. Where a positive trend (i.e. a direct relationship between x and y) can be identified, the pattern will look something like this:

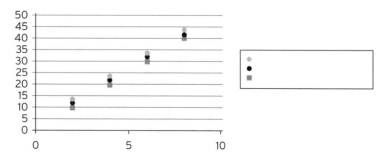

Where a negative trend (i.e. when there is an inverse relationship between x and y) can be identified, the pattern will look something like this:

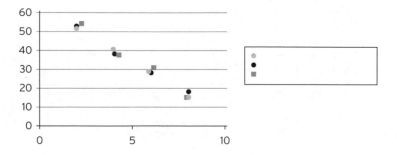

Where no trend is present, the pattern of dots will appear fairly random:

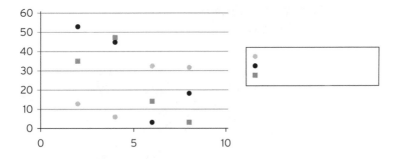

Summary questions . . .

1. Briefly describe each of the following types of chart: bar chart; pie chart,
    line graph and scattergraph.
2. Which type of chart suits which type of data?

> ### Exercises
>
> 1. Compile (or invent) a similar set of data to the one given above. Try
>   and translate this into each of the four chart types listed above (you
>   might find doing this on a computer simplifies the process). Which did
>   you find to be the most successful? Why? Which did you find to be the
>   least successful? Why?
>
> 2. Giving a justification for your answer, give your own example of a set
>   of data that would be well suited for each of the four types of chart we
>   have just looked at (one for each).

For some excellent activities on creating and interpreting graphs and charts see: www. primaryresources. co.uk/maths/mathsF1d. htm#pie.

Flow charts and tree diagrams

Further graphs/charts you might expect to come across include:

Flow charts

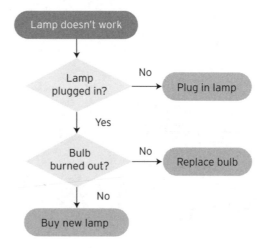

(Wikipedia)

flow chart – Lays out
the steps of a process
in order of the priority
in which they are to be
carried out.

In a **flow chart** the steps of a process (sometimes referred to as an 'algorithm')
are laid out in order of the priority in which they are to be carried out. A good
way of understanding this is to think about trying different keys in a lock, in
turn, in order to establish which the correct one is. The diagram gives us a flow
chart for a non-functioning lamp.

Tree diagrams

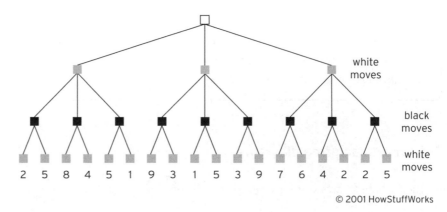

© 2001 HowStuffWorks

A **tree diagram** systematically lays out all the possible outcomes of a given process. The above diagram describes the first three available possible combinations of moves for a computer chess program.

> **tree diagrams**
> – These systematically map out all the possible outcomes of a given process.

Exercises

1. Create a flow chart giving instructions for making a cup of tea (remember it is possible to have tea with or without milk and sugar).

2. Create a tree diagram showing the range of possible outcomes for rolling a die three times. How many are there?

Venn and Carroll diagrams

Finally we come to **Venn and Carroll diagrams**, both of which offer an effective, if not dissimilar, method for categorising information. Suppose we were to say of the cats of Baal that they fall into the category of being either tabby or non-tabby, then we have a set of four possibilities into which each of the entire cat population must fall. These are:

> **Venn and Carroll diagrams** – These diagrams visually group numbers or objects into groups of x (having a certain property) or non-x (lacking it).

1. Non-tabby, can't talk

2. Non-tabby, can talk

3. Tabby, can't talk

4. Tabby, can talk

Each of these combinations can be presented in the following ways, where the overall population (universal set) is represented by the rectangle/square, and the different subsets (being tabby, non-tabby, talking or not talking) by the spaces enclosed within this area. Note how Venn diagrams are helpful in being able to depict where these qualities can overlap.

Venn diagram

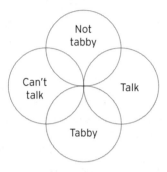

Carroll diagram

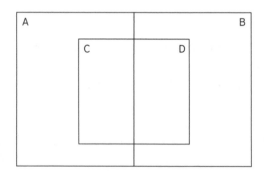

A – Tabby, talk
B – Not tabby, talk
C – Tabby, can't talk
D – Not tabby, can't talk

Here, each numbered space corresponds to the type of variable we are dealing with (this can be made clearer by inserting the amount/type etc. of entity adjacent to each number). More complex data can be accommodated for by more complex diagrams:

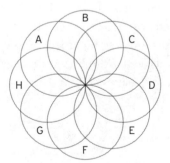

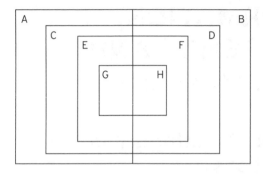
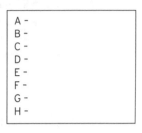

Note, however, that beyond a range of eight variables such diagrams become too complicated for practical purposes.

Summary questions . . .

1. What are Venn and Carroll diagrams?
2. Why are they useful?

END OF CHAPTER ACTIVITY

Choose your own set of variables of the form: not-x (for example, not tabby) and not-y (non-talker); x but not-y; y but not-x; x and y, and create your own Venn and Carroll diagrams for each.

SUMMARY CHECKLIST

Points you need to remember:

✔ How to apply basic methods of numerical reasoning to a given body of evidence or data.

✔ What is meant by, and how to apply, concepts such as percentage, average (mean and median) and probability.

✔ How to read and interpret commonly used graphs such as bar charts; pie charts; line and scattergraphs; flow charts; tree diagrams and Venn and Carroll diagrams.

The following links contain a range of resources offering detailed explanations of both Venn and Carroll diagrams coupled with a range of activities that you can use to develop your understanding of how they function: www. primaryresources. co.uk/maths/mathsF1b. htm#carroll; www.sjsu. edu/depts/itl/graphics/ venn/venn.html.

17

INFORMATION, INFERENCE AND EXPLANATION

Chapter 17: Patterns and correlations

correlation - this occurs when two or more events are regularly observed to occur in close proximity (i.e. at the same time or in direct succession) to one another. Whilst correlation may indicate a causal relationship, the two terms should not be confused (see **cause-correlation fallacy**).

LEARNING OBJECTIVES

By the end of this chapter you should:

✔ Understand what the term 'correlation' means.
✔ Further understand the difference between cause and correlation.
✔ Understand the different types of correlation and be able to apply this information to evidence of a factual nature.

For a detailed explanation of the difference between causation and correlation, see Chs 3 and 18 'Causal explanations'. For an explanation of how the two terms are often fallaciously conflated, see Ch. 11: 'Cause-correlation fallacy'.

That the data above shows a direct inverse **correlation** between the increase in talking cats and decrease in non-talking ones is, or at least might be, significant. That this increase corresponds with the amount of money on offer in the game show *Who Wants to be a Millionaire* is not. The first exhibits a pattern which, at least in principle, might be causally explained. The second can only be regarded as coincidental. Patterns and correlations may well offer an indication of some causal relationship common to two sets of variables, but this point should never be taken for granted (see for example Chapters 11, 'Cause-correlation fallacy' and 18). Nevertheless, the ability to observe such patterns precedes the act of judging their significance – an issue we will return to in the next two chapters. Such observations can be worded along the following lines: 'according to the figures, cases of … have fallen off steadily in line with the increasing incidence of …', or conversely, 'according to the figures, cases of

… have risen directly in line with the decreasing incidence of …' etc. Some examples will help us here.

Drugs and crime

New heroin addicts and recorded crime in England and Wales (Index 1980=100)

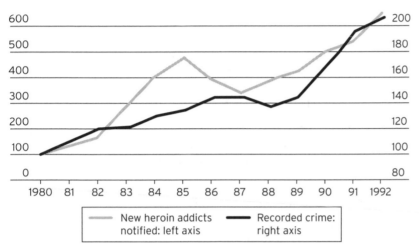

Source: Home Office

For exam purposes, in order to show that a pattern/correlation is significant (i.e. might be causally explained), you should phrase your answer 'according to the figures, cases of … have *fallen off* steadily in line with the increasing incidence of …' or 'according to the figures, cases of … have *risen directly* in line with the decreasing incidence of …'

In the 'Drugs and crime' line graph, a fairly clear pattern can be observed to exist between the rise in heroin addiction and recorded crime. However, that is not to say, at least not without further investigation, that the former *causes* the latter, although obviously this might offer a fairly plausible explanation. Rather, all we see at this stage is that the increase in rate of addiction coincides with that of crime. Such an observation may well go on to support an inference (that there *is* a direct causal relation; that some third factor, for example poverty, is responsible for both rises etc.), but at the time it is made it is just an observation, nothing more. This type of correlation is said to be *positive*; it indicates that an increase in one variable coincides with that of another. Correlations can also be *negative*, where an increase in one variable coincides with a *decrease* in another, as shown in the 'Top 40' graph.

For more on 'plausible explanations', see Ch. 18.

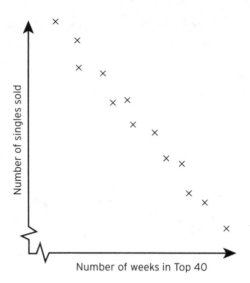

And of course there will be times when no correlation can be observed at all. Compare, for example, the following figures for the comparative international suicide rates of men and women:

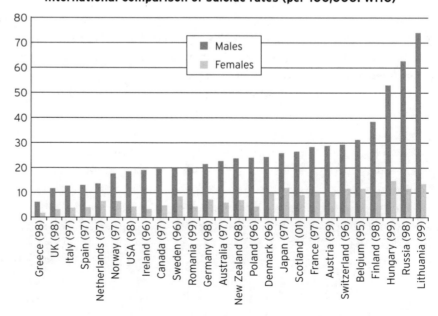

International comparison of suicide rates (per 100,000: WHO)

Summary questions . . .

1. What is meant by the term 'correlation'? How does this differ from a causal explanation?
2. What are the different types of correlation that can be observed?

END OF CHAPTER ACTIVITY

1. Explain whether or not the following diagrams show evidence of correlation.
2. If they do, is it positive or negative?
3. Using internet facilities, see if you can discover your own examples of negative and positive correlation. Plot your findings onto a line graph or bar chart.

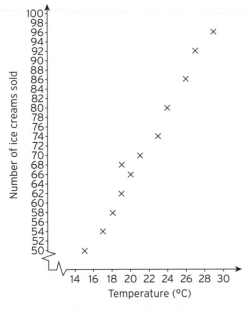

(a) Ice creams sold and temperature

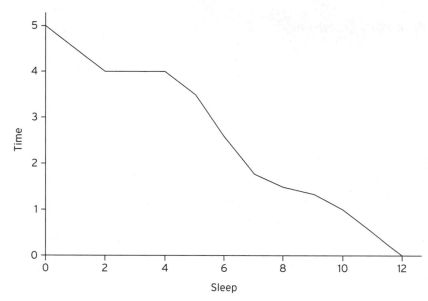

(b) The relationship between sleep (in hours) and time taken to complete a questionnaire (in seconds)

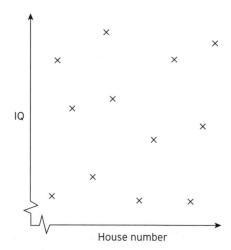

(c) IQ and house number

SUMMARY CHECKLIST

Points you need to remember:

✔ What is meant by the term 'correlation' and how this differs from a causal explanation.

✔ The different types of correlation: positive and negative and what each implies.

The following website has a range of explanations for the different types of correlation that may be observed. There is also a section which covers the distinction between causation and correlation: www.uwsp.edu/geo/faculty/ozsvath/lectures/Cause_and_Effect.htm.

18

INFORMATION, INFERENCE AND EXPLANATION

Chapter 18: Plausible explanations

LEARNING OBJECTIVES

By the end of this chapter you should:

✔ Be able to recognise *when* an explanation is needed and *why*.
✔ Be able to distinguish between plausible and implausible explanations.
✔ Be able to offer your own plausible explanations, particularly in response to unusual findings or evidence.
✔ Be able to distinguish between a plausible explanation and a causal one.

Weeping Madonna of Syracuse Sicily, 1953

The [Madonna] was purchased as a wedding gift for Antonina and Angelo Iannuso, who were married March 21, 1953. They admitted that they were tepid and neglectful Christians, yet they hung the image with some devotion on the wall behind their bed.

Angelo was a laborer who had taken his bride to live in the home of his brother on Via Degli Orti. When his wife discovered that she was pregnant, her condition was accompanied by toxemia that expressed itself in convulsions that at times brought on temporary blindness. At three in the morning on Saturday, August 29, 1953, Antonina suffered a seizure that left her blind. At about 8:30, her sight was restored. In Antonina's own words:

I opened my eyes and stared at the image of the Madonna above the bedhead. To my great amazement I saw that the effigy was weeping. I called my sister-in-law Grazie and my aunt, Antonina Sgarlata, who came to my side, showing them the tears. At first they thought it was a hallucination due to my illness, but when I insisted, they went close up to the plaque and could well see that tears were really falling from the eyes of the Madonna, and that some tears ran down her cheeks onto the bedhead. Taken by fright they took it out the front door, calling the neighbors, and they too confirmed the phenomenon. (www.visionsofjesuschrist.com)

When we come across evidence of an unusual nature, such as the above, we feel obliged to offer an explanation for our findings – or at least in principle, when a convincing one is not forthcoming, accept that one should nevertheless be provided. Contrast the view that the Madonna's tears are miraculous:

The Blessed Mother's tears are part of her signs. Her tears testify to the fact that there is a Mother in the Church and in the world . . . These tears are also tears of prayers. They are the tears of the Mother's prayers, which give strength to all other prayers and are offered up as an entreaty for all those who are preoccupied with numerous other interests and, thus, are refusing to lend their ears to the calls from God, and are not praying. (John Paul II, 1994)

with that of chemistry researcher Dr Luigi Garlaschelli:

The secret ... is to use a hollow statue made of thin plaster. If it is coated with an impermeable glazing and water poured into the hollow centre from a tiny hole in the head, the statue behaves quite normally.

The plaster absorbs the liquid but the glazing prevents it from pouring out. But if barely perceptible scratches are made in the glazing over the eyes, droplets of water appear as if by divine intervention – rather than by capillary attraction, the movement of water through sponge-like material. ('Science debunks miracle', *The Independent*)

Why do we find ourselves naturally sympathising with the latter, when neither response has effectively been proved (the effigy itself lies safely secured behind a glass panel)? The answer here is, of course, simple. In the absence of proof,

plausibility – Approximates to trustworthiness. A **plausible** explanation is one that, in the absence of proof, it would nevertheless still be *reasonable* to accept.

For more on circularity, see Ch. 11: 'Begging the question/circularity'.

we settle for **plausibility**. But what is meant by *plausible*? Responses to this question tend to be question-begging. We might, for example, say that a plausible explanation isn't too 'far fetched' or 'fanciful' or that it offers a 'tenable' hypothesis. But here we are in danger of circularity – for what we are really saying boils down to: 'a plausible explanation is one that is plausible!' However, in daily life, we use the term for just those occasions where we are convinced of something (e.g. an alibi or an excuse) despite there being insufficient evidence for it to count as a proof. We nonetheless accept it until a rival explanation comes along to equal or upstage it. Look at the following example from the philosopher Bertrand Russell:

> There is no logical impossibility in the supposition that the whole of life is a dream, in which we ourselves create all the objects that come before us. But although this is not logically impossible, there is no reason whatever to suppose that it is true; and it is, in fact, a less simple hypothesis, viewed as a means of accounting for the facts of our own life, than the common-sense hypothesis that there really are objects independent of us, whose action on us causes our sensations.

Believe it or not, philosophers, in their quest for certainty, played around with the idea that the world which surrounds us might be the product of some vivid dream or complex virtual reality machine. Whilst such a hypothesis cannot be falsified – it remains at least a *possibility* that we are currently asleep and simply dreaming that we are reading a book on critical thinking – the alternative story, that objects, rather than dreams or virtual reality machines, cause our experiences of them, in virtue of its simplicity and obviousness seems far more credible.

Whilst plausible explanations cannot be regarded as true or false, they can nevertheless be regarded as strong or weak. A competing hypothesis that explains the same set of data with the same degree of force will always, to an extent, weaken the original. So how do we judge the relative merits of such explanations? Looking at a further example will help clarify this point:

Ghost 'caught' on Packhorse Bridge

Does a photograph prove that ghosts really exist?

Ghost hunters from Cheshire Paranormal Society took a photo of a ghostly figure, standing on the Packhorse Bridge at Caergwrle, near Wrexham. At the time members had reported feeling uneasy and other paranormal activity was also recorded, such as so-called orbs of light.

Locals believe that the bridge is haunted by the ghosts of a young girl, two women and a certain Squire Yonge who lived in the area 300 years ago. The sighting of ghosts on the bridge is also thought to relate to a former burial ground in the area to which the bridge gave access.

Melanie from Scarborough

Looks like a ghost to me. Very rare indeed – a little blurred, but definitely a ghost standing there. Don't know what the other blurry light is though. It has to be a mystery. I'm looking forward to buying myself a camera so I can go out and investigate all these spooky places for myself here in Scarborough!

Stuart

I'm a professional photographer and have just analysed this picture in Photoshoot. It's definitely moisture on the lens being lit up by the street lamp behind. That would also explain the other light on the left. Given that tens of millions of photographs are taken every year, it is not surprising that every once in a while one turns up that looks like a ghostly apparition. What nonsense. I've had photos which I've taken myself where similar results have occurred as a result of moisture on the lens and I'm not the only one. The only thing which is slightly unusual about this is that the moisture looks like a person. So what!

The phantom menace

Stuart could not be more wrong if he tried! The colour of the light is a dead giveaway – if it was the street lamp reflected in the moisture, it would be orange-coloured. Clearly the flash had been left on and it's accidentally captured a falling snowflake or raindrop.

Here we have three rival hypotheses all attempting to explain the same phenomenon(!). So which do we run with? The first, as should be clear, doesn't sound very plausible at all. The second, on the other hand, does. Its author has relevant expertise:

For more on relevant expertise, see Ch. 15 'Motive and agenda' and 'Sources'.

I'm a professional photographer.

has devoted time into researching the matter:

and have just analysed this picture in Photoshoot. It's definitely moisture on the lens being lit up by the street lamp behind. That would also explain the other light on the left.

and backs his explanation up with further evidence:

Given that tens of millions of photographs are taken every year, it is not surprising that every once in a while one turns up that looks like a ghostly apparition.

And taking each of these points into account, the explanation begins to look very plausible indeed. It is, however, weakened by the final comment which expresses reservations about 'moisture on the lens' accounting for the ghostly apparition:

if it was the street lamp reflected in the moisture, it would be orange coloured.

The alternative explanation offered, however:

it's accidentally captured a falling snowflake or raindrop.

cannot be regarded as particularly strong. It is speculative, opinionated and lacks any evidential support to give it credence. For this reason, it would seem that the second of the three offers the strongest/most plausible explanation.

Exercises

1. Offer both a plausible and an implausible explanation (or explanations) for each of the following pieces of evidence. Explain your answer:
   - In terms of GCSE exam results, girls significantly outperform boys.
   - The number of television sets in American homes increased around 10,000% between 1947 and 1952.
   - The average person who stops smoking requires one hour less sleep a night.
   - German Shepherds bite humans more than any other breed of dog.

2. Suggest a plausible explanation which might explain the trend in data presented in the following chart:

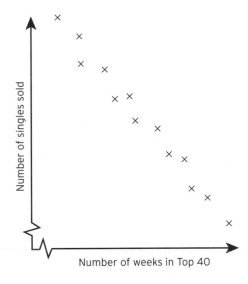

The following website contains an interesting plausible explanation of the events surrounding the terrorist attacks of 9/11: http://bushstole04.com/911/911_plausible.htm.

CAUSAL EXPLANATIONS

Because an analysis of causal explanations has already been given, there is only one question which we will be addressing here, namely: 'What distinguishes a causal explanation from a plausible one?' Let us suppose, for a moment, that our 'ghost' photo was submitted to rigorous scientific testing which confirmed the second explanation above, that 'moisture on the lens' rather than a ghostly apparition was the actual cause of the ghostly image. Furthermore, let us suppose that the original photographers were finally forced to admit that their photo was a hoax. What difference would this make? Well, first and foremost, it would rule out the other alternative explanation for this event. A causal explanation, if true, must be regarded as the *actual* and thus *only* explanation. Plausible explanations, on the other hand, for lack of confirmation, can only ever be regarded as possible or probable. Whilst plausible explanations may well be causal *in kind* (for example, it would be plausible to suggest that a current increase in drug addiction is responsible for – i.e. *caused* – a current rise in crime rates – see the graph on p. 209), unless we can conclusively

The issue of causal explanations has already been dealt with in Ch. 3. The issue of how such claims can be fallacious has been dealt with in Ch. 11 – see 'Cause-correlation fallacy'.

establish this then we are not entitled to assume its truth. In the case of the drug/crime statistics, for example, no matter how plausible the connection between the two, it would seem likely that there will still be many addicts who do not turn to a life of crime, and many criminals who are not addicts. This point is of particular importance if we wish to avoid committing the cause-correlation fallacy.

The following example, which gives an account of a recent Turkish plane crash, should further clarify these points:

> Yesilyurt, Turkey – An Atlasjet plane crashed on a mountain shortly before it was due to land in southwest Turkey early Friday, killing all 57 people on board, including a 6-week-old girl. The cause of the crash was not immediately known. (Fox News)

Here, there could be a range of plausible hypotheses which could explain such a tragedy, the most common of which would include pilot error, terrorism, faulty equipment, violation of FAA regulations, structural and design problems, service negligence, air traffic control error, maintenance or repair error and fuelling problems.

But the essence of coming to a decision as to the *actual*, rather than just probable, cause of the crash (which here would be deeply inappropriate) requires that we decide upon which of these is correct. To do this, one needs to rule out any viable alternatives:

> Doganer [the airline's chief executive] said the cause was unknown, but ruled out technical failure or maintenance problems and said the weather and visibility were good.
>
> Ali Ariduru, head of Turkey's civil aviation authority, said there were no indications that terrorism was the cause.

And eventually this process allows us to root out the real cause which seems to have been that the pilot became disoriented while preparing to land.

Summary questions . . .

1. What is a plausible explanation?
2. How does a plausible explanation differ from a causal one?

END OF CHAPTER ACTIVITY

1. See if you can identify a range of (at least three) plausible explanations for the data collated in the following graph:

Fatalities in relation to climbers reaching the summit of Everest

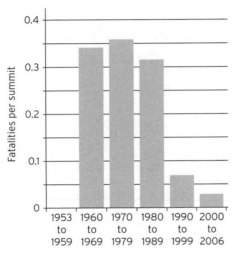

(AQA Specimen Assessment Materials)

2. Which do you think might offer a causal explanation for this data? Give reasons for your answer.
3. Offer a causal explanation for each of the following points:
    (a) The stimulating effect of coffee.
    (b) Polar bears' white fur.
    (c) Melting ice-caps.

SUMMARY CHECKLIST

Points you need to remember:

✔ When a plausible explanation is needed and why.

✔ The difference between plausible and implausible explanations.

✔ What would constitute a plausible explanation, particularly for findings of an unusual nature.

✔ The difference between a plausible explanation and a causal one.

> For a range of explanations, examples and activities on causal explanations, see: http://philosophy.hku.hk/think/sci/basic.php.

19

INFORMATION, INFERENCE AND EXPLANATION

Chapter 19: Drawing safe inferences

Read through the following article and think about how the term 'unsafe' functions:

Conviction for robbery ruled unsafe

A man jailed for 14 years for armed robbery had his conviction overturned by the Court of Appeal as a result of criminal charges brought against Scotland Yard detectives.

George Ellis, 38, from east London, had claimed during his trial that a Flying Squad officer planted evidence against him. The court heard yesterday that 25 members of the same squad, who cannot be named for legal reasons, had been charged or suspended or would have been suspended if they had not already retired. None of those charged had yet been tried. After an appeal hearing in London yesterday, Lord Justice Rose, sitting with Mr Justice Maurice Kay and Sir Patrick Russell, ruled that his conviction was unsafe.

Mr Ellis was convicted at Woolwich Crown Court in September 1997. He was sentenced for robbery, unlawful wounding and having an imitation firearm with intent arising out of a 37,000 pounds raid on a Thomas Cook bureau de change in Chingford, Essex, in June 1996.

Lord Justice Rose, giving the court's decision yesterday, said at Mr Ellis's trial there was DNA evidence in relation to saliva said to have been found in two masks – evidence Mr Ellis claimed was planted. The judge said the Flying Squad officer who 'alone had taken the saliva samples from the masks' was arrested and charged last summer with offences involving dishonesty. 'He is ... suspended from duty and committal proceedings are expected to take place shortly against him.'

Lord Justice Rose, who was also ruling on the case of one of Mr Ellis's co-accused, Anthony Zomparelli, said: 'In relation to these 25 officers, the Crown takes the attitude that it is right not to invite the court to rely on any evidence which any one of those 25 officers might have given in relation to the trial of these appellants when considering the safety of their convictions.'

In the case of Mr Ellis, the Crown took the view that the most damning evidence was the DNA in relation to the saliva – a big issue at trial was the suggestion that this had been planted – and in the light of subsequent events, it could not seek to uphold the conviction as being safe.

John Kelsey Fry, counsel for the prosecution, said the Crown did not intend to rely on the evidence of those officers where their evidence was in issue at trial.

The three judges also allowed the appeal of Zomparelli and ordered a re-trial in his case. He is in custody. (*The Independent*)

Here, the initial conviction was based around DNA evidence, in the form of saliva, found on the two masks presumably used in the robbery. At the time, this was regarded as a fairly safe inference to draw. What later made it unsafe was the subsequent revelation that: 'the Flying Squad officer who "alone had taken the saliva samples from the masks" was arrested and charged last summer with offences involving dishonesty'. Thus, the initial grounds of support upon which the original inference was based (and thus the inference itself) could no longer be regarded as acceptable. Of course, this does not mean that the original inference was *wrong* – even if the evidence was, as George Ellis claimed, 'planted' – it could still, nonetheless, be true that he was guilty of the crime. What it does mean is that the degree of support offered in defence of such an inference was inadequate, rendering the conviction unsafe. Note, however, that the terms 'unsafe' and 'inaccurate' retain very different meanings which we should take care not to conflate. The way in which the terms '**safe**' (or 'adequate', 'acceptable' etc.) and 'unsafe' ('inadequate', 'unacceptable' etc.) function here mirrors the way in which they are used in critical thinking and we need to make sure that, when drawing inferences based on evidential criteria, we do not overstate the strength of our conclusions, nor misjudge what can, and subsequently cannot, be safely inferred from the grounds given. Let's apply these points to another, hypothetical example:

> **safe inference** – An inference is **safe** if (a) its strength is not overstated and (b) it reasonably follows from the premises provided. An **unsafe** inference fails to meet either one or both of these criteria. For these reasons, the terms 'safe' and 'unsafe' function as they would when delivering a verdict in a court of law.

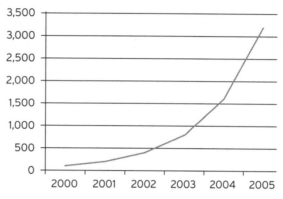

Figures for recorded knife crime in London (2000–5)

What can be inferred from the above data? Well, the most obvious inference to draw would be that knife crime is on the increase. Superficially, of course, this looks like a fairly reliable conclusion. But note how the inference specifies 'knife crime' rather than '*recorded* knife crime'. There is an important difference. If the latter rather than the former of these inferences had been stated then the inference, assuming the figures were correct, would be sound. But conflating the word *actual* with *recorded* would be inappropriate here. Firstly, it may well have been the case that police were cracking down hard on this type of crime during the period in which the data was collated. If this were true, then an alternative and equally plausible inference could be drawn: that the *amount* of knife crime remained constant whilst the *rate of detection* increased. This would also be consistent with the above set of figures but would challenge the reliability of our original inference.

Thus, when judging what can and cannot safely be inferred from a given body of evidence we need to take care not to include any unwarranted assumptions in our reasoning. A second way in which the original inference, and indeed inference in general, can be called into question is if the claim being made is guilty of overgeneralisation. Even if it could be proved that knife crime in London were on the increase, this would not confirm the general inference that 'knife crime is increasing'. This is because the sample of data may well be *unrepresentative*. If, for example, we took a broader view and found that knife crime figures were decreasing in the majority of other places around the country, then such an inference would be invalid. To summarise: as long as an inference: (a) is supported by evidential criteria, (b) considers and evaluates any alternative, plausible counter-examples, (c) does not depend upon any illegitimate assumptions and (d) is not guilty of overgeneralisation, then it can be regarded as acceptable. This is particularly so if further evidence can be supplied which supports it. These points apply equally to the analysis and evaluation of the reasoning of others as they do to your own.

For more on this issue, see Ch: 11 'Overgeneralisation'.

Summary questions . . .

1. What is meant by the term 'unsafe' inference? How do we judge whether or not an inference is unsafe?
2. What is meant by the term 'safe' inference? How do we judge whether or not an inference is reliable?

END OF CHAPTER ACTIVITY

1. Come to a decision about whether or not the following inferences are reliable. Give reasons for each answer:
    (a) The mananger of Barchester United categorically denied that his own players had started the brawl. 'They are decent lads,' he said, 'and were only acting in self-defence. We have many eyewitness reports from local people which confirm this beyond the shadow of a doubt.'
    (b) Look at those kids from the housing estate graffitying those walls. That's all the kids from that estate ever do – born troublemakers, the lot of them.
    (c) My train has been late every morning this week. It must be because they just can't get drivers that are reliable.
    (d) It's chucking it down with rain outside. If I don't take an umbrella with me, I'm going to get wet.

2. Draw both a reliable and an unreliable inference for the following, previously looked-at set of data. Give reasons for your answer:

Drugs and crime

New heroin addicts and recorded crime in England and Wales (Index 1980=100)

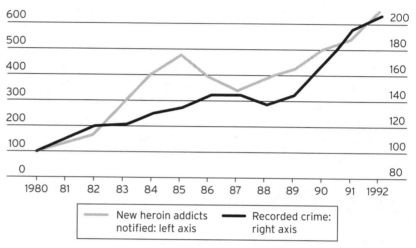

Source: Home Office

The following link contains an excellent worksheet on the process of drawing reliable inferences: www.canterbury.ac.uk/ education/quality-in-study-support/docs/ DrawingConclusions Guide.pdf.

SUMMARY CHECKLIST

Points you need to remember:

✔ What is meant by the term 'safe' or 'reliable' inference.

✔ What is meant by the term 'unsafe' or 'unreliable' inference.

✔ How to identify and explain when examples of each of the above occur in reasoning.

INFORMATION, INFERENCE AND EXPLANATION

20

Chapter 20: Unit 2 exam guide

The Unit 2 section of the exam will require you to apply your skills of analysis and evaluation to texts presenting information and data in a wide variety of formats. You will be expected to be able to critically respond to such sources, draw reliable inferences from the information provided and also construct a reasoned argument of your own. A summary of these skills runs as follows:

Students should:

- appreciate the various ways in which information or evidence can be presented;
- follow and apply basic methods of numerical and statistical reasoning;
- recognise significant patterns and correlations;
- offer plausible explanations;
- judge what can (and cannot) be safely inferred from a given body of information/evidence;
- use information and data provided to draw conclusions of their own; and construct reasoned arguments to support or justify them.

A breakdown of each can be found in their correspondent chapters.

For a detailed breakdown of the Unit 2 exam, the scheme of assessment and links to past papers and specimen assessment material see: http://store.aqa.org.uk/qual/gce/pdf/AQA-2770-W-SP-10.pdf.

UNIT 2 ASSESSMENT

In the specification, the method of assessment for Unit 2 is laid out as follows:

Candidates will be assessed by means of a written paper lasting 1½ hours. The exam will be based on a set of source documents presenting information, either on a single topic or on two closely related topics. Between them the documents will present data in a range of forms: verbal, numerical, graphical. The question paper will consist of two sections, A and B.

Section A will contain a number of questions requiring short written answers. Candidates will engage in: extracting and interpreting information, assessing claims and conclusions, drawing inferences and offering explanations.

Section B will present candidates with a short statement or proposal related to the examination topic(s), which they will be invited to argue for or against.

Both sections of the paper will require candidates to draw on skills from Unit 1 as well as Unit 2.

We will deal with each of these sections in turn.

Section A

For a detailed explanation of each of the assessment objectives (AOs) see: http://store. aqa.org.uk/qual/gce/ pdf/AQA-2770-W- SP-10.pdf.

The first set of questions will relate to Documents A–D and will mainly draw on your skills of analysis (AO1) and evaluation (AO2). It would be a good idea to try and answer these questions on your own before reading through the subsequent commentary (which has been informed by the mark scheme). Rereading the earlier section on 'The examination' (see Introduction) will help you to do this.

As with the first exam chapter, expressions in **bold** below either indicate command words relating to these assessment objectives or refer to material covered in previous chapters. There are 40 marks available for this section.

Document A

Illegal music downloads hit all-time high

Illegal music downloads have soared to an all-time high, with more people than ever filling up their computer hard drives with MP3 booty according to the Digital Music Survey 2007 study.

The survey found that 43% of UK consumers admitted to downloading music without paying for it, adding up to a hefty hike from 36% in 2006.

The study also found that the growth of social networking websites such as *MySpace* and *BeBo* is helping to 'democratise' the music industry, with more people discovering top tunes online instead of though the radio or music TV.

Of the 1,700 UK consumers surveyed (aged 13–60), 86% said that they had used a social networking site this year, up from 74% in 2006, with 40% of social network users having music embedded in their personal profiles. This figure rises to 65% among teenagers.

Source: adapted from http://digital-lifestyles.info, 30 July 2007

You will need to read Document A before answering questions 1 and 2.

Question 1 requires you to 'assess the level of support given' for each of the following claims. You will need to offer reasons in support of your answer.

(a) 7% more music was downloaded in 2007 than in 2006. (*3 marks*)
(b) The increase in the number of consumers illegally downloading music is almost certainly due to an even larger increase in the numbers of people using social networking websites. (*3 marks*)
(c) If the 2007 survey was representative, at least one in every two teenage consumers had a profile on the internet that contained some music. (*3 marks*)

Commentary

For each of these questions (a–c) you will attract 1 (AO1) mark for **identifying** whether or not the claim is supported and 2 (AO2) marks for **justifying** your response. For example:

(a) Claim a (see paragraph 2) is **inadequately supported** (1 X AO1) because the data refers to the amount of *people* downloading music rather than the amount of music downloaded (1 X AO2). It is possible that the first 36% of people downloaded more music than the additional 7% (1 X AO2). The document also specifies UK figures whilst the claim itself appears to be general (1 X AO2). It could also be pointed out that the figures refer to those people who *admitted* downloading music – this might not correspond with the *actual* amount of people doing so (1 X AO2).

(b) It could be argued that claim b (see paragraphs 3 and 4) is **supported** (1 X AO1) because there is a **correlation** to be drawn between the rise in use of social networking sites (12%) and illegal downloading (7%) (1 X AO2). Alternatively it could be argued that the claim is **not well supported** (1 X AO1) because correlation does not imply cause.

There is no **evidence** to show that a rise in one activity causes a rise in the other (1 X AO2). It is possible that the rise in illegal downloading is responsible for the increasing use of social networking sites or that both events have a further unrelated cause (1 X AO2). Either way, the claim 'is almost certainly due to' is too strongly expressed given the amount of support offered (1X AO2).

(c) It could be argued that claim c is **supported** (1 X AO1) because 65% of 86% (see paragraph 4) = 56%, which is more than half and hence *at least* one

For more on this issue, see Ch. 11: 'Cause-correlation fallacy'.

For more on this issue, see Chs 3 and 18 'Causal explanations'.

in every two (1 X AO2). Alternatively it could be argued that the claim is **not well supported** because we do not know the overall **proportion** of teenagers that use such sites (1 X AO2) nor how many of the 86% of consumers polled were in fact teenagers (1 X AO2).

Question 2 requires you to assess the extent to which the claim 'the growth of social networking websites is helping to "democratise"* the music industry' (Digital Music Survey) is justified. (*2 marks*)

    (*democratise means to 'pass power over to the people')

Commentary

2) Once again, there is 1 (AO1) mark available for reaching a **judgement** and 1 (AO2) mark available for **justifying** your response. For example:
Such a claim **is justified** (1 X AO1) because, when it comes to television and radio, the selection of music played/types of programmes broadcast are controlled/chosen by a select few, whereas with the internet, *anyone* can upload music and/or choose *what* to listen to and *when* to listen to it (1 X AO2). It could also be argued that the statistics show that more and more people are discovering (and downloading) music online, and this makes the industry more democratic (1 X AO1).
OR
Such a claim **is not justified** (1 X AO1) because people who illegally download music do not do so to make the industry more democratic, but rather to get something for free/act illegally (1 X AO2).
OR
A **middle ground** response could be offered which combines the above points (1 X AO1). No doubt some people's concerns lie with getting something for nothing but this will not be the case across the board. Even those whose intentions are not honourable are, nevertheless, in making music more accessible to the masses, helping to democratise the industry (1 X AO2).

    NB These are sample responses. There may well be others of equal merit or plausibility.

Document B

Online music & the UK record industry

The BPI is the trade association for the UK record industry. It represents over 300 record companies in the UK. The bulk of these are small independent music companies, but the BPI also represents the four biggest multinational players, the so-called 'majors': Universal, SonyBMG, EMI and Warner.

Frequently Asked Questions (FAQs)

1. What is filesharing?

Filesharing is the activity of trading digital files with other users over the internet. Users trade files by downloading (to obtain them) and uploading (to distribute them).

2. Why is filesharing illegal?

British record companies invest tens of millions of pounds annually in new artists, and recoup that by having the exclusive rights to copy, distribute and make available their recordings. Without copyright, labels would have no financial incentive to invest in new music and Britain would not have its world-beating music business.

3. Does filesharing damage music sales?

Aside from the fact that filesharing infringes and undermines the rights of the creators and investors in music, it's enormously damaging to music sales. While there is evidence that a small percentage of filesharers do download illegally to 'try before they buy' this is more than outweighed by the much larger number who download illegally instead of buying music. If record companies are unable to derive income from music sales, that means less money to invest in new music. This is not only bad news for record companies but also for musicians, who rely on that investment, and for customers, who want to keep on listening to new British music.

4. I paid £10 for my CD, why am I not allowed to copy it and share it with my friends?

When you buy a CD, you buy a personal copy of the music, you do not buy the right to copy or distribute it. Copying a CD and giving the copy to a friend is an infringement of copyright and is illegal. Uploading music to the internet is an infringement on a much larger scale, as filesharers effectively give away perfect copies of someone else's work to millions of people for free.

5. What proportion of downloads in the UK are made illegally?

It's very difficult to determine what proportion of downloads are illegal. A study in March 2004 suggested that as many as 7.4 million people in the UK have downloaded music illegally at one point, but many legal services have launched since then and awareness around illegal filesharing has increased. We estimate that around 8 million people are on filesharing networks at any one time.

6. Pop stars and record companies are rich; surely it won't matter if I download their song for free?

Everyone knows that it's not legal to steal from someone just because they're perceived to be rich, but this misses the point. The real impact is felt by the record company which invested in the artists concerned and have to recoup on that investment to invest in new music. In other words, it's the new artists that are looking for record contracts that will suffer most, not established artists. Besides, it's illegal and it's wrong; people have a right to be paid for their work.

Source: adapted from British Phonographic Industry, Illegal Filesharing Factsheet, May 2006.

You will need to read through Document B before answering questions 3–5.

Question 3 points out that 'the answer to FAQ3 can be understood as two connected arguments, one following from the other'.

(a) Question 3a) requires you to **identify** their two conclusions. (*2 marks*)

(b) Question 3b) requires you to **identify** and then **assess** two possible **assumptions** that are implicit in the second of these. (*4 marks*)

Commentary

For a recap on identifying conclusions (the point an argument is attempting to get us to accept) revisit Chs 1 and 14. Remember, the easiest way of doing this is to think about what the argument is trying to persuade you of.

3a) The two **conclusions** are that (i) filesharing is 'enormously damaging to music sales' (1 X AO1) and (ii) that this is 'not only bad news for record companies but also for musicians ... and for customers' (1 X AO1). These are the points the arguments are trying to get us to accept.

b) The two most obvious **assumptions** are that (i) musicians are dependent upon the investment made by record companies for their income (1 X AO1) and (ii) that without this investment, new music would not become available (1 X AO1). Without assuming these points, the above inferences (see 3a) cannot be drawn. It might also be argued that the author **assumes** that record companies would have invested the money lost (through illegal downloading) in new music, rather than, say, advertising or pre-existing acts (1 X AO1).

Each of these assumptions is questionable (1 X AO2) not least of all because they assume that it is the record companies alone that are responsible for protecting the rights of musicians and consumers (1 X AO2). There is no reason to suppose, for example, that musicians cannot generate an income and/or new music independently of them (1 X AO2).

Question 4 requires you to **identify** 'which of the answers to the FAQs most strongly rely on principle'. You will then need to identify the principle in question. (*2 marks*)

Commentary

4) The answer is paragraph 6, last sentence (1 X AO1), and the **principle** is that 'people have a right to be paid for their work' (1 X AO1).

For a recap on 'statements of principle', see Ch. 3.

Question 5 requires you to 'critically assess the explanation given in response to FAQ4'. You will then need to explain whether or not it answers the question. (*3 marks*)

Commentary

5) If we go back to the explanation (of why it is illegal to copy and share the contents of a [legally bought] CD) itself:

> When you buy a CD, you buy a personal copy of the music; you do not buy the right to copy or distribute it. Copying a CD and giving the copy to a friend is an infringement of copyright and is illegal. Uploading music to the internet is an infringement on a much larger scale, as filesharers effectively give away perfect copies of someone else's work to millions of people for free.

For a recap on explanations, revisit Ch. 1, and for some thoughts on how they can be assessed, see Ch. 18.

It could be argued that such an explanation is **satisfactory** because it clearly explains why such an act (i.e. copying and sharing) is illegal: i.e. that buying a CD does not give you the right to share/distribute its content – a 'personal copy' means just that.

Alternatively it could be argued that the explanation is **not satisfactory** because it merely states *that* such an activity is illegal without explaining *why* (this could be regarded as **circular/question-begging**, i.e. you're not allowed to do it because it's illegal!).

For similar reasons, it could be argued that such an explanation is completely **inadequate** because, whilst it explains that the act of sharing/distributing is *illegal*, it doesn't explain why it is *immoral*, i.e. why the act of filesharing is ethically unacceptable.

For more on this issue, see Ch. 2.

It might also be noted that the final sentence: 'Uploading music to the internet is an infringement on a much larger scale, as filesharers effectively give away perfect copies of someone else's work to millions of people for free' is an example of a **slippery-slope**-type fallacy. It also adds nothing to the content of the explanation which is supposed to clarify the legality of sharing material *between friends*. It is thus of questionable relevance.

Depending on how the question is answered, there are 2 marks available for AO1 and 1 mark available for AO2.

Document C

Piracy is not all that bad for musicians

Most artists actually profit from unauthorized sharing of files. A study in Denmark, which analysed the change in royalties* paid to musicians in the first half of the decade, showed that 75% of all artists benefit rather than losing out. This is contrary to the claims made by the major record companies.

Figure (i): Changes to artists' income from royalties

There are less albums sold in total compared to some of the years when album sales were booming – as shown in Figure (ii). However, it is hard to attribute this decline in sales to piracy (alone).

One of the things we can be pretty sure of is that the music industry is starting to

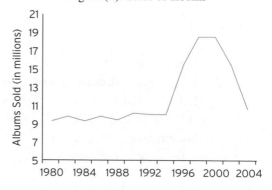

Figure (ii): Sales of albums

lose control over their customers. A great deal of their income was generated by overly promoted albums and artists. It is those artists and albums that suffer the most from piracy. It gets harder and harder for the music industry to market artists to the top position of the charts now the customers have all kinds of alternative ways to discover new music.

To conclude we could say that music is more alive and healthy than ever before. Piracy, far from inhibiting music, is a tool for artists to build a fanbase, and the times when the music industry could dictate what we were listening to are over.

Source: Ernesto at *TorrentFreak*.com

*Royalties = money paid to artists for each sale of their work

You will need to read through Document C before answering questions 6–9.

Question 6) requires you to state what is odd about the information presented in both the texts and graphs in Document C. You will then need to suggest a **plausible explanation** for this anomaly. (*3 marks*)

Commentary

6) The initially surprising fact is that, whilst we have seen a rapid decline in album sales in recent years (see figures i and ii) more artists (75%) have *benefited* from unauthorised filesharing than have lost out (surprising because one would have expected the converse to be true) (1 X AO1).

There are a range of **plausible explanations** for this trend, perhaps the most obvious being that more bands are gaining greater exposure, or conversely/negatively, that fewer bands were gaining widespread exposure before filesharing became prolific (1 X AO2). This could have led to an increase in album sales for less well-known bands and hence would only have had a detrimental effect on those bands who were already in the limelight/didn't require further exposure (1 X AO2). It could also be argued that album sales have increased *in spite of* unauthorised filesharing because more bands are touring/performing live (and hence gaining greater exposure) in order to stave off the negative effects that this practice has had (1 X AO2).

It has been estimated that a Danish musician earning 200 000 DKK in royalty fees in 2001 would have seen their income fall below 165 000 DKK by the end of 2005.

For a recap on analysing data and offering plausible explanations, see Chs 15 and 18.

Question 7) requires you to **identify** (a) the evidence in Document C which supports the above estimate and (b) **one** dubious **assumption** the evidence relies on (even if the evidence itself is trustworthy). (*3 marks*)

Commentary

7) The **evidence** is located in the bar graph (Figure i) and shows us that artists earning more than 150,000 Krone have seen an average drop (see Chapter 16) in income of around 18% (36,000 Krone). To remind yourselves of how to go about finding this information, see Chapter 15 ('Extracting information') (1 X AO1).

One questionable **assumption** (once again, see Chapter 5) that this estimate depends on is that this (18%) fall will be distributed evenly over the whole category (1 X AO2). This is questionable because the likelihood is that those at the top end of the scale (perhaps those earning over a million Krone) will be more greatly affected than those towards the bottom end (150,000) (1 X AO2).

In 2001, fewer than a quarter of Danish musicians were receiving more than 150 000 krone.

Question 8) requires you to explain, giving a reason for your answer, whether this statement is supported by the data in paragraph 1 and Figure i of Document C. (*2 marks*)

It is supported (1 X AO2). We know this because if, as the paragraph clearly states, 75% of musicians were better off (i.e. 3/4) then 25% (1/4) must have been worse off (see Chapters 15: 'Extracting information' and 16) (1 X AO2). This information is also reflected in the bar graph.

(a) Question 9a) requires you to **outline** Ernesto's **explanation** for the claim that 'the music industry is starting to lose control' and can no longer dictate what we listen to. (*2 marks*)
(b) Question 9b) requires you to **identify** an **assumption** he has to make in order to draw the conclusion that: 'music is more alive and healthy than ever before' and explain whether or not this assumption is justified. (*3 marks*)

Commentary

9a) Ernesto's **explanation** for the music industry losing control (see paragraph 3) is that 'customers have all kinds of alternative ways to discover new music' (1 X AO1), so 'it gets harder and harder for the music industry to market artists to the top position of the charts' as they used to (1 X AO1).

9b) Ernesto's inference that 'music is more alive and healthy than ever before' depends upon a range of **assumptions** (see Chapter 5), the most obvious being that the music industry's loss of control is good for the life and health of music – or conversely, that the industry's prior control was bad for it (1 X AO2). There are a range of points that could be used to challenge the legitimacy of this belief. It might, for example, be argued that the music industry was responsible for the maintaining of standards (1 X AO2) or that there is no reason to suppose the bands that have been discovered now are any better (and plausibly worse) than those previously promoted (1 X AO2). Either way, the assumption is questionable.

You will need to read Document D before answering questions 10 and 11

Question 10) requires you to 'assess whether each of the following claims can be reliably concluded from the data in **Document D** – the table and the bar chart'.

(a) If the trend in the American music market (shown in the bar chart) remains unchanged, revenue from digital sales will overtake revenue from physical sales by 2011. (*2 marks*)

(b) According to the latest US figures (2007) the increasing value of digital sales has more than made up for the declining value of physical sales. (*2 marks*)

Commentary

10a) Claim a) *does* draw a **reliable** inference (1 X AO2). We can see this if we extrapolate the evidence presented in the bar chart. This shows us that digital sales have been rising by 7% a year from 2004, whilst physical sales have been *decreasing* by 7%. This means the gap between both types of sale is closing by 14% a year. If this trend continues, then the next four years will see a 56% further fall (4 X 14% = 56%) and because the difference in sales in 2007 was only 54%, we can expect the revenue from digital sales to overtake revenue from physical sales by the year 2011.

For a recap on how to draw a reliable inference from a given body of information/ evidence, see Ch. 19.

Document D: Music sales in the United States: 1997–2007

	1997	1998	1999	2000	2001	2002	2003	2004	2005	% change 2004–05	2006	% change 2005–06	2007	% change 2006–07
Physical[1]														
Million units	1063.4	1123.9	1160.6	1079.2	968.5	859.7	798.4	814.1	748.7	-8.0%	628.2	-13.4%	543.9	-16.1%
Value ($ million)	12236.8	13711.2	14584.7	14323.7	13740.9	12614.2	11854.4	12154.7	11195.0	-7.9%	9868.6	-11.8%	7985.8	-19.1%
Digital[2]														
Million units	–	–	–	–	–	–	–	143.9	553.1	284.4%	940.3	70.0%	1229.4	30.7%
Value ($million)	–	–	–	–	–	–	–	190.3	1101.9	479.0%	1889.6	71.5%	2384.2	26.2%

1. 'Physical' means CDs, records, cassettes, etc. sold in shops or by mail order.
2. 'Digital' means tracks or albums downloaded legally and paid for.

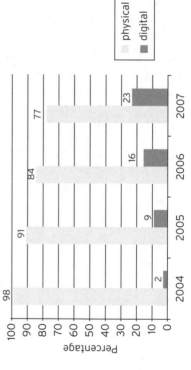

Percentage of revenue from music sales

Source: Data from RIAA (Recording Industry Association of America)

10b) The inference presented in claim b, on the other hand, is **unreliable/false** (1 X AO2). This is because the sum value, i.e. the total value of both physical and digital sales, has been steadily falling; hence the increase in digital sales has not made up for the decline in value of physical sales (1 X AO2).

> The record companies can't complain that piracy is theft. For years they've been ripping off the customers, and the musicians. Piracy is just giving the music industry a taste of their own medicine.

Question 11) requires you to explain a 'flaw or weakness' in the above reasoning. (*2 marks*)

Commentary

11) The general **flaw** in this argument is that, even if the record companies have been 'ripping off the customers' for years, this doesn't imply that piracy is not theft (2 X AO2). You might also have identified this as an example of the ***tu quoque*/'you too' fallacy** (1 X AO2) since two wrongs do not make a right (1 X AO2); or alternatively as an example of the ***ad hominem* fallacy** (1 X AO2) for attacking the record companies themselves rather than any argument they present (1 X AO2).

> The issue of flaws has been discussed in detail in Ch. 11.

Section B

Question 12) requires you to develop a 'reasoned case' either in favour of, or against, the following claim:

> Unauthorised sharing of music is a serious offence with nothing but harmful consequences, and should be dealt with as severely as other forms of theft.

In order to do this you will need to:

- develop a coherent argument, clearly stating any conclusions you may wish to draw

- refer to evidence presented in the source documents (you may also wish to draw on your own relevant background knowledge and experience here)
- identify any principles that may be appealed to in support of your reasoning
- think about and respond to any possible counter-arguments that may be used in opposition to your reasoning. (*30 marks*)

Commentary

Rereading Ch. 13 will help remind you of what a response to this type of question requires. You might also find that revisiting Ch. 14 helps sharpen your understanding of the types of response that the examiners will be looking for.

12) Once again, it is important to remember that there is no 'correct' response to this question. What is important is that you argue your case clearly and concisely and stick closely to the structure laid out in the question paper. Remember, there are 30 marks available for this question (out of a possible 70 for the whole of Unit 2!) – 26 for **developing your own argument** (AO3) and 4 for **selecting/analysing** relevant material from the source documents to support your claims (AO2). It would be a good idea to attempt a response to question 12 before reading through the following mark scheme and 'generic marking guide' and coming to a decision about what kind of mark your response would have attracted and why.

Conclusion

A conclusion could either affirm, reject or modify all, most, or part of the above claim. If you wish to argue a 'middle-ground (i.e. 'sitting on the fence') position it is important that you consider the issues surrounding each side of the debate before reaching such a judgement.

Support for the claim could draw on:

- the economic impact that filesharing has had on the music industry
- the economic impact that filesharing has had on the artists
- the moral principle that filesharing is just another form of theft …
- … and that if dealt with accordingly, this would act as a deterrent for future would-be filesharers
- the sheer scale of filesharing that goes on due to the internet.

Challenges to the claim could draw on:

- the fact that the music industry no longer has a monopoly on music (Ernesto). NB you would need to show *why* this could be regarded as positive
- the fact that filesharing has encouraged a more competitive pricing of albums and singles
- the fact that, given the nature and scale of the activity, filesharing would be almost impossible to police
- the fact that filesharing encourages people to listen to bands that might otherwise not have gained widespread exposure
- the moral principle of 'scapegoatism' – that it is unfair to punish the few for the actions of the many and that the stigmatisation of filesharers has actively encouraged this approach
- the fact that music should be free or paid for in the form of voluntary donations.

A 'balanced' account might draw on relevant material from each of the above sections.

This is not an exhaustive list. There may well be other lines of enquiry which offer similar grounds of support to the ones above. What you will need to remember is that, whichever angle you take, in order to score highly each of your points will need to be developed and/or illustrated using sub-arguments, explanations and justifications where appropriate. You should also refer to evidence presented in the source booklet in support of your claims. Your response will be marked in line with the generic marking grid below.

Generic mark-grid for Section B:

Criteria	Award level		
	Good response Criterion thoroughly met, with insightful comments where needed and communication that is clear and appropriate	**Reasonable response** Criterion partially met with communication that is generally clear and appropriate	**Basic response** Limited achievement of criterion with communication which may impede understanding
Conclusion A conclusion is clearly stated that is consistent with the reasoning, and directly responds to the question	4	2-3	1
Reasoning The above conclusion is well supported with reasons, contributory arguments, examples, clarification of terms, etc.	9-12	5-8	1-4
Use of information Relevant references are made both to the documents and/or to other relevant information or experience	5-6	3-4	1-2
Reference to principle One or more general principles are introduced relevant to the arguments	4	2-3	1
Counter-argument Challenges and objections are anticipated and answered effectively	4	2-3	1

GLOSSARY

ability to see – The expression refers to how well a source can be expected to observe/judge a course of events. Whether they offer a primary (eyewitness) or secondary account; whether their judgement could have been affected by such factors as loss of memory, inebriation, poor eyesight, positioning, shock, age etc.

ad hoc – An argument or claim is said to be *ad hoc* (literally: 'for this [specific and limited task]') if it serves the sole purpose of rescuing a theory or hypothesis from refutation.

ad hominem – The *ad hominem* fallacy attacks the arguer rather than the argument they present.

additional evidence – This is material of a factual nature which can be brought in to strengthen, weaken, confirm or refute an argument, hypothesis or explanation.

aesthetic discourse – An aesthetic discourse contemplates questions of value – for example, those focusing on the 'beauty' or 'artistic merit' of a particular artwork or object.

allegation – A claim made to accuse somebody of something, the truth of which has yet to be established.

ambiguous – A word or expression is ambiguous if it has more than one meaning.

analogy – An analogy draws a comparison to help clarify/simplify a difficult concept or idea. It works along the principle that, if two things are similar in certain key respects, then they are probably similar in other respects as well. If the items of comparison are not suitably similar, then any reasoning which employs them in argument will be guilty of committing the **weak analogy fallacy**.

area of discourse – The area of discourse to which an argument or debate belongs indicates the type of reasoning that it employs – for example, moral, legal, scientific etc.

argument – A **persuasive** piece of reasoning formed of **reasons** (premises) and a **conclusion**.

argument from ignorance – This works on the premise that a claim can be regarded as true if not proven false, and false if not proven true.

assumption – An (often unstated) part of an argument which is needed for the conclusion to be drawn. Many assumptions are **legitimate** (i.e. acceptable and unproblematic). When an argument depends upon an **illegitimate** (i.e. unacceptable) assumption, we have good reason for rejecting its inference.

averages – To calculate the **mean** average, you will need to add up all the values in a set and then divide this new number by the original amount of values. The **median** average can be found by listing all the numbers in a set from small to large. The median value will be the middle number in this sequence. The **mode** average is simply the value that occurs most frequently in a set of numbers.

bar chart – Presents **data** visually in either a vertical or a horizontal column.

causal explanation – Explains an event or action in terms of the prior event which brought it about. Scientific discourses frequently make use of this type of claim. A **causal explanation** differs from a **plausible** one because it provides an *actual*, rather than just *probable* explanation for why a particular event has occurred.

cause-correlation fallacy – This occurs when a causal connection is illegitimately inferred (see 'Causal explanations', Chapter 3) between two events because either both events occur together, or one event regularly proceeds the other.

claims – Claims form the basis of all reasoning. They assert or deny that something is the case. There are many different types of claim and each needs to be analysed and evaluated on its own terms.

comparative evaluation – This evaluation employs value judgements in order to draw a comparison.

comparison and **contrast** – Drawing a comparison and contrast requires us to consider the relevant similarities and differences between two (or more) objects of comparison.

conclusion – The conclusion of an argument is the point an argument is trying to get us to accept.

confusing necessary and sufficient conditions – The fallacy of confusing necessary and sufficient conditions comes about when either a **necessary** condition is seen as **sufficient** or a sufficient condition seen as necessary.

continuous variable – This variable takes on *any* value (for example, 1.1, 1.2, 1.3 etc.)

correlation – this occurs when two or more events are regularly observed to occur in close proximity (i.e. at the same time or in direct succession) to one another. Whilst correlation may indicate a causal relationship, the two terms should not be confused (see **cause-correlation fallacy**).

corroboration – Refers to other sources that agree with the one in hand.

counter-argument – A counter-argument is put forward to challenge the premises or conclusion of an argument.

counter-examples – Used to challenge a general claim or argument. They can also be considered and then responded to in order to strengthen one's own reasoning.

credibility – Approximates to trustworthiness. To gauge the reliability of a source, we need to apply a set of **credibility criteria** to it.

credibility of evidence – This can be assessed by appealing to the credibility of the source that puts it forward.

critical questioning – Used to challenge or reveal flaws or weaknesses in an opponent's reasoning.

cumulative – A cumulative set of data adds each number successively to the number which precedes it.

deductive argument – An argument where the truth of the premises absolutely guarantees the truth of the conclusion.

definition – A definition offers a clarification or explanation of what a concept, term or expression *means*.

discrete variable – A discrete variable will only take on whole values (e.g. 1, 2, 3 etc.).

doublespeak – This occurs when a naturally positive or negative term is expressed in cognitively neutral terms. This is often done so as to present a negative issue, event or trait in an acceptable light.

embedded argument – A report or summary of an argument rather than the argument itself.

emotional appeal – An emotional appeal, unsurprisingly, appeals to the emotions rather than reason as a means to influence belief. The most common of these include appeals to fear, pity, spite, vanity, prejudice and loyalty (in fact there are probably as many of these as there are human emotions!).

emotive – A word or expression is said to have an emotive content if it is emotionally charged (i.e. its expression has either positive or negative connotations). An emotive content is typically contrasted with a **neutral** or **cognitive** one which captures an expression's *actual* meaning.

ethical discourse – An ethical discourse carries with it implications for how we ought to behave.

expertise – This term is interchangeable with relevant skill/knowledge relating to the evidence that is being presented.

explanations – These explain *why*, but do not persuade *that* something is the case. They are superficially similar to arguments but have no persuasive function.

extract – An **embedded argument** needs to be extracted before it can be treated as an argument in its own right.

extracting information – The process of extracting information requires you to select a specific value/set of values from the range of information presented.

evidence – Simply refers to material of a factual nature which is appealed to in support of a claim.

fallacious appeals – Fallacious appeals (illegitimately) appeal to emotions, common practices, illegitimate authorities etc. in the place of (legitimate) reasons, sources and evidence in order to convince us that something is the case.

fallacy of equivocation – This occurs when an ambiguous word or expression (i.e. one with more than one meaning) is used in order to deliberately mislead.

false dilemma/dichotomy – This fallacy (sometimes referred to as the fallacy of **restricting the options**) presents us with two options, one of which isn't really an option at all, so we are forced to consent to the second.

flawed argument – An argument is said to be flawed if, for whatever reason, its conclusion doesn't follow from the premises given.

flow chart – Lays out the steps of a process in order of the priority in which they are to be carried out.

frequency – Means the rate at which (i.e. the amount of times) a particular value occurs in any given set.

graphical form – Presented visually on a graph.

hypothesis – A claim put forward for testing which attempts to explain why something has occurred/occurs. Once a hypothesis is accepted/confirmed, it will then be regarded as a theory or explanation.

hypothetical claim – This takes the form of an if … then … statement. Hypothetical claims are a useful tool because they allow us to consider the consequences of an argument without having to establish the truth of its premises. For example, we can understand the content and implications of the claim that 'if God exists then he must be white', without having to prove God's existence.

inference – An inference is the move from the **premises** to the **conclusion** of an argument.

intermediate conclusion – The conclusion of a sub-argument which goes on to offer support for the main conclusion – the ultimate point the argument is trying to get us to accept. For this reason, an intermediate conclusion functions both as a conclusion (for a sub-argument) and as a premise (for the main argument).

line graph – A line graph, unsurprisingly, presents data from one or more variables in a linear fashion.

logical fallacy – A general term which refers to a set of common errors in reasoning. If a piece of reasoning is said to be **fallacious** (i.e. if it commits a logical fallacy), we have solid grounds for rejecting it.

mean average – To calculate the mean average, you will need to add up all the values in a set and then divide this new number by the original amount of values.

median average – The median average can be found by listing all the numbers in a set from small to large. The median value will be the middle number in this sequence.

misdirected appeal – Misdirected appeal petitions the support of an authority or source whose expertise is not relevant to the claim being made. Three of the most common of these are the **appeal to authority** (where the authority has expertise, but not in the relevant field of enquiry); the **appeal to popular opinion** (where, if a significant number of people can be shown to believe or do x, then x is regarded as justified/correct/true), and the **appeal to precedent**

(where, because a precedent [standard] has been set in a previous case, then so too it can be applied to *all* cases of a similar nature).

mode average – The mode average is simply the value that occurs most frequently in a set of data.

motive or agenda – If a source has a background motive or agenda, we have good (though not conclusive!) reason to believe that the information it presents us with will be either biased, one-sided, selective, exaggerated or put forward with a vested interest.

necessary condition – If x is a necessary condition of y, then if x is lacking, y won't come about.

neutrality – Here equates with a lack of bias – i.e. a source is said to be **neutral** if it presents both sides of the account; **biased** if it presents only one.

overgeneralisation – The fallacy of overgeneralisation (sometimes referred to as '**hasty generalisation**') occurs when a small number of observed cases are appealed to in order to support a general claim or inference.

percentage – Simply means a part out of a hundred. When dealing with two figures, if you divide the smaller number by the larger one then multiply by 100, this will show you the percentage it represents.

persuasive language – Used either in place of or in supplement to argument in order to convince somebody of something.

pie chart – Presents data visually in 'sectors' or 'slices'.

plausibility – Approximates to trustworthiness. A **plausible** explanation is one that, in the absence of proof, it would nevertheless still be *reasonable* to accept.

prediction – A claim made about the future based upon something else being true in the present or past.

principle of charity – The principle of charity dictates that, when an argument admits of more than one interpretation, we should always choose the more charitable/persuasive one.

probability – A measurement of how likely it is that an event will happen. If you toss a coin, the probability rate of it turning up heads is ½ (one in two).

question-begging – An argument or claim is said to be question-begging or **circular** if it depends upon the very thing it is trying to prove in order to prove it.

range – A range in data simply means the quantitative difference between the highest and lowest number in a set.

ratio – Expresses a relationship between two separate quantities. If, for example, a glass of cordial requires 4 parts water to 1 part cordial, the ratio can be expressed as 4:1.

reason – A reason (sometimes referred to as a **premise**) provides grounds for why we should accept (be persuaded of) the conclusion of an argument.

reasoning indicators – Expressions such as 'if', 'since', 'because', 'however', 'therefore' etc. which allow us to (a) identify when reasoned argument is taking place and (b) recognise what type of reasoning is being used.

recommendation – A recommendation advocates a particular course of action.

reductio ad absurdum – Literally, 'reduction to absurdity', is a form of argument which disproves a proposition by showing it to have absurd or ridiculous consequences.

refutation – To **refute** an argument by proving it wrong (using reasons and evidence).

reputable – This term is interchangeable with reliable, trustworthy etc.

resolution – Resolution occurs when two conflicting viewpoints come to a mutual agreement.

rhetoric – An umbrella term which refers to the use of persuasive language, rather than reason, as grounds for persuasion.

safe inference – An inference is **safe** if (a) its strength is not overstated and (b) it reasonably follows from the premises provided. An **unsafe** inference fails to meet either one or both of these criteria. For these reasons, the terms 'safe' and 'unsafe' function as they would when delivering a verdict in a court of law.

scattergraph – A scattergraph plots dots or crosses against the x and y axes of a chart.

scientific discourse – This supports a theory, hypothesis or causal explanation. It appeals to evidence and data of a factual nature and tends to move from singular observations to general hypotheses/explanations. Unlike ethical and aesthetic discourses, its subject matter is factual rather than value-based.

selective – An author or a source is said to be selective if the evidence they select is chosen to support their own purposes.